Toni Morrison's *Beloved*

A Reader's Companion

for
my parents

Toni Morrison's *Beloved*

A Reader's Companion

edited by

AYESHA IRFAN

Asia Book Club

Series in Contemporary Classics

General Editor: Dr. R. K. Dhawan

Published by
ASIA BOOK CLUB
New Delhi 110 058
Ph. 5500091

Jacket Design: Kam Studio
Cover Photo: Courtesy, The American Center

Printed at Chaman Offset Press, New Delhi 110 002

Contents

<u>Toni Morrison's *Beloved*</u>
<u>An Introduction</u>

by

Ayesha Irfan

Toni Morrison: Life and Works 9

Toni Morrison's *Beloved*: A Critical Commentary 14

Black Feminist Criticism and *Beloved* 47

Beloved: A Feminist Perspective 51

Self-Discovery and the Role of History and Community 56

Narrative Technique in *Beloved* 62

<u>Critical Perspectives</u>

Emergence of African American Literature
and Toni Morrison
K. Sumana
72

Black Women Novelists:
Development, Flowering and
Fruition of a Tradition
Bharati A. Parikh
117

Contribution of
African-American Women Writers in the
Cause of Women with Special Reference to
Toni Morrison and Alice Walker
R. Gandhi Subramaniam
131

Re-Organizing the Lives of Women:
Toni Morrison's Beloved and
Alice Walker's The Color Purple
Madhumalati Adhikari
143

Black Magic:
The Works of Toni Morrison
Asha S. Kanwar
151

The Female Protagonist's Search for Wholeness
and Toni Morrison's Discourse in *Beloved*
Madhumalati Adhikari
156

"This is Where I am": Topos as Trophe for
Self and Society in *Beloved*
Urbashi Barat
168

Memory, Creativity and Writing:
Semiotic Discourse in *Beloved*
Jayita Sengupta
185

A Study of *Beloved* as a
Neo-Slave Narrative
Madhu Mehrotra
195

Delineating the Apparition:
The Mystery Streak in *Beloved*
Monika Gupta
204

Memory, Text and Subtext in *Beloved*
Satish C. Aikant
213

Collective Class Struggle
against Capitalism in *Beloved*
K. Sumana
237

The Saga of Black Suffering:
A Study of *Beloved*
Ashok Mahashabde
244

Voice-less Discourse:
Silence as Strategy in Toni Morrison's *Beloved*
Meenakshi Paul
253

Convergence of History
and Feminism in *Beloved*
Usha Puri
269

Motherhood in *Beloved*
Bharati A. Parikh
283

The Saga of Black Courage
in *Beloved*
Pashupati Jha and T. Ravichandran
293

Contributors

Madhumalati Adhikari	R.D. University Jabalpur
Satish C. Aikant	H.N.B. University Srinagar-Garhwal
Urbashi Barat	R.D. University Jabalpur
Monika Gupta	H.N.B. University Srinagar-Garhwal
Ayesha Irfan	Dyal Singh (E) College University of Delhi
Pashupati Jha	Indian Institute of Technology Roorkee
Asha S. Kanwar	IGNOU New Delhi
Ashok Mahashabde	Govt. Arts and Comm. College Indore, M.P.
Madhu Mehrotra	Lucknow University Lucknow
Bharati A. Parikh	M.S. University Baroda
Meenakshi Paul	H.P. University Shimla
T. Ravichandran	Indian Institute of Technology Roorkee
Jayita Sengupta	South Calcutta Girls' College Calcutta
R. Gandhi Subramaniam	Govt. Arts College Tiruppur
K. Sumana	Canberra Australia

Toni Morrison's *Beloved*
An Introduction

AYESHA IRFAN

Toni Morrison: Life and Works

Toni Morrison achieved the impossible by becoming the first African-American to win the Nobel Prize in literature in 1993. She has added substantially to the body of African-American literature through both her fiction and critical essays. Her critical essays add immensely to the canon of African-American aesthetics. They enlarge on the theme of African-American woman novelist's role. They give a clear understanding of black life, society and culture.

Morrison, a woman of immense talent, comes from a family of industrious and hard working black people, who fought racial oppression and an inferior socio-economic status. Her maternal grandparents left Alabama and travelled to Ohio in search of better educational opportunities for their children. Her father, a Georgian by birth, also fled the state's hostile racial climate and settled in Ohio. Morrison, the second of four children, was named Chloe Anthony Wafford. She grew up in Lorain, Ohio, during the great depression. Her childhood world was not dominated by black responses to white oppression. In Lorain where everyone was poor, there was not much of segregation on class basis and overt racial hostility was not prevalent.

Her recollections of the richness of black lore, music, myths and the cultural rituals of family and community are memorable. Her grandfather played the violin and her mother sang in the choir. Storytelling, especially of ghost stories, was a shared activity for men and women in her family. As a teenager, Morrison read the European literary masters, English, Russian and French.

Morrison excelled in her studies, she received an undergraduate degree in English from Howard university, where she changed her name to Toni. She did her masters from Cornell University. Her M.A. thesis was on Faulkner and Virginia Woolf. Her first teaching appointment was at Texas Southern University. From there, she returned to Howard as an instructor of English. She married Harold Morrison, a Jamaican architect, and had two sons. They divorced in 1964 and Morrison became a senior editor at Random House, a major publishing company. Here she devoted her time to writing and her first novel *The Bluest Eye* appeared in 1970. Her subsequent novels are *Sula* (1974), *Song of Solomon* (1977) which won "The National Book" critics award, *Tar Baby* (1981), *Beloved* (1987) which won the prestigious Pulitzer, *Jazz* (1991) and *Paradise* (1998).

Her works deal with major contemporary social issues like racism, class exploitation and sexism. It is best to sum up the worth of Morrison's works in her own words. She writes:

> If anything I do, in the way of writing novels (or whatever I write), isn't about the village or the community or about you, then it is not about anything. I am not interested in indulging myself in some private, closed exercise of my imagination that fulfills only the obligation of my personal dreams—which is to say yes, the work must be political. . . . It seems to me that the best art is political and you ought to make it unquestionably political and irrevocably beautiful at the same time.

Morrison through her novels presents the non-linear African-American socio-historical reality, fragmented by a historical past of disconnection and ruptures. Her works offer a fresh perspective on black life, their history and genealogy. The major focus of her works is apartheid, slavery and racism, and their psychological and social effects on the blacks over the ages. Not only restricting themselves to the effects of these practices, writers like Toni Morrison have traced the historical development of these ideologies. Morrison's novels show the victimization of black people within the context of a racist social order. The social history found in her novels is the history of daily inescapable assault by a world which denies minimum dignity to the Blacks.

The overriding theme of her novels is the sense of identity of a black person trying to recover his history and culture, which had so far been suppressed due to white narcissism. The questions, which come to one's mind on reading her novels, are: What is history without representation? What is the identity of the person for whom reading and writing were prohibited? The reality of dehumanization of black people is one for which there are no adequate words.

Henry Louis Gates, Jr. points out the crucial role that blacks so far believed that the creation of art would bear upon their dubious political status. According to him, "it is not surprising that first predictions of renaissance of black literature and art, made by William Stanley Braithwaite in 1901, precisely overlap, W.E.B DuBois's efforts to form an organization lobbying for Black rights. He writes: "What is upsetting this country is a sense of its own identity. If for example one managed to change the curriculum in all the schools so that Negroes learn more about themselves and their real contribution to this entire culture, you would be liberating not only the Negroes, you'd be liberating the white people who know nothing about their own ancestry." Viewed in the light of this statement, one feels that Morrison's contribution to literature and to humanity itself is immense. She has highlighted some of the major problems of society like the issues of racism, subjugation of women, the destruction of cultural identity of the African-Americans which needs to be dealt with.

Toni Morrison says in one of her interviews, "I don't want to bow out with easy answers to complex questions. It is the complexity of how people behave under white duress that is of interest to me." What she means to say is that it is the complexity of how people behave under the pressure of white hegemony that is of interest to her. Toni Morrison has produced some of the intense studies in the strains that a madness inducing white society puts on its black members in America.

Pecola goes mad, Cholly rapes his daughter, Guitar joins a band of racial avengers, Joe kills his beloved, Sethe kills her daughter. All these characters represent the mad, anarchic and destructive tendencies afflicted by the psychological wounds caused by racial discrimination.

Morrison's *Beloved* draws our attention to the psychological turmoil experienced by Sethe in the context of slavery. All the history that the readers have learnt about slavery is stretched out on a giant canvas, the separation of women and children from men, the treatment of slaves, both male and female, children and adults, as beasts of burden, the sexual exploitation of African women by white men. Beloved herself is a spiritual manifestation of history. She is the embodiment of sixty millions or more dead and enslaved Africans, who has returned to reclaim her space and haunts us throughout the narrative with her enigmatic appearance. However, as Amy Denver, the white girl, says: "anything dead coming back to life hurts." There is no denying of the pain involved in the act of self-revelation. But the process of self-discovery and rememory form an important part of Toni Morrison's narration. For her, coming to grips with our past is the best way to have control over our future. In fact, this quest for identity is true for the entire African-American literature of the twentieth century.

In *Song of Solomon*, Milkman undertakes a long journey from city to the countryside in the quest of his identity. After tracing his roots in Detroit, where he was familiar with Pilate's version of the Solomon song, he goes to Pennsylvania where his father grew up and then to Shalimar, Virginia, where his grandfather was born and children still sang of Solomon. Milkman deciphers the twin text of history (hidden in the song) and genealogy. The novel evokes the history of black immigration and chain of economic expropriation from hinterland to village, from village to metropolis. The end point of milkman's journey is the starting point of black races' history in America, the confrontation with the reality of slavery coming at the end of the novel marks the end to Milkman's penetration into the historical process.

Morrison in each of her novels highlights the effects of cultural subjugation of blacks in a racist society. Through her novels, she presents the distorted emotions produced by living in a world where white standards and values are presented to blacks as uniquely important and, at the same time, impossible for them to achieve. In *The Bluest Eye*, black girlhood assumes tragic propensities, when it borrows identity models from the mandates of white culture. We see how Pecola is forced to long for blue eyes like those of the white children, so that she would be loved and accepted by both blacks and whites.

Further, Morrison's status as a black woman writer cannot be neglected. There is an acute lack of historical accounts of black women as autonomous and determining participants during the period of slavery, emancipation and reconstruction. In *Beloved*, by drawing attention to the circumstances under which Sethe makes her escape, Morrison gives women's experience of slavery a voice and most importantly a language. Sethe here is an active historical agent as opposed to a passive victim or absence. Morrison is the second American woman and first African-American to achieve the status of distinction in the mainstream of American literary tradition. The works of this versatile writer portrays black women who have nothing to fall back on, not maleness, not whiteness, not ladyhood, in their struggle to discover the authentic black female self.

In Sethe, Nel, Pecola and Hagar, Morrison highlights the misery of black women who are victims of both sexist and racist oppression. To what extent women can go in order to help their family is evident in Eva's sacrifice of her leg (town gossip says that she deliberately stuck it under the train so that she could sue the railroad). Morrison's most articulate statement in regard to female oppression appears in *Sula* when Nel and Sula first meet: "Because each had discovered years before they were neither white nor male, and that all freedom and triumph was forbidden to them, they had set about creating something else to be." Within this statement are found both the dilemma of the novel and the solution to the dilemma. African women are oppressed, and to escape their oppression, they must become self-propagators.

Jadine in *Tar Baby* is a picture of liberated African-American woman. She refuses to choose between the apparent opposites offered her—"blackening up or universaling out," that is, she refuses to internalize an external image—either black or white—as a definition of self. "I belong to myself" (54) Jadine tells Son and she becomes most outraged at him in their initial encounter when he tries to impose a dualistic definition on her.

Morrison's *Jazz* is a novel set in Harlem in 1926. While black writers have used musicians and music as theme and metaphor for their writing, none have attempted to draw upon Jazz as the structuring principle for an entire novel, until Morrison's *Jazz*. *Jazz* is Morrison's disturbing psychological study of a childless African-American couple desperately seeking to come to terms with their frustrations and aspirations. Their fragmented directionless lives propel them towards grotesque and absurd. The story essentially focuses on Violet who slashes the face of dead Dorcas, her husband's girlfriend, whom he had shot dead to preserve the feeling of narcotized bliss, which he knows is temporary, for Dorcas is young, ambitious and attractive.

Morrison's latest novel *Paradise* opens starkly—"they shoot the white girl first"—and then the novel coils back and forth through a century of imagined history to explain who "they" are and why, on a dewy Oklahoma morning in 1976, they felt compelled to storm a decaying mansion and wreak violence on the handful of women living in it.

Toni Morrison's *Beloved:* A Critical Commentary

Note: *The novel is divided into 28 unmarked chapters of unequal length. For the convenience of students, I have numbered the chapters.*

Section One

Chapter 1

Beloved opens within the historical present of 1873, in the house of a former slave Sethe and her daughter. Their "grey and white house on Bluestone Road" is described as "spiteful" and "full of a baby venom." This has led Sethe's son to flee long ago and has made "victims" of those left behind. There is a ghost in the house, it is a ghost that shatters mirrors, and puts its "tiny handprints in the cake." (It is she who has driven Howard and Buglar from home). Those who remain wage "a perfunctory battle against the outrageous behavior of the place." And yet they tolerate its presence in the hope that "an exchange of views or something [would] help." For past twelve years "no visitors of any sort and certainly no friends" have entered the house on Bluestone Road. The ghost here is a primary source of repression and repulsion, of fear and flight of victims and death.

Fragments emerge just enough to expose their repression. The presence of "the dead one"—of a child who as Sethe tells Denver "wasn't even two years old when she died"—presents itself as a reminder to Sethe that, as Baby Suggs knows, "death is anything but forgetfulness,"[1] it is an imprint upon the soul, and in *Beloved*, the ghost remains at the centre of life and memory. But Sethe "count[s] on the stillness of her own soul in order to forget the other one, the soul of her baby girl." (5) And thus she actively denies life and memory in the hope that the ghost of her past life will not intrude. Sethe's serious work in life is "beating back the past." (173)

Sethe and Denver try to end the persecution by calling forth the ghost that tried them so, but it does not come. This is perhaps because the baby was too small when it was killed, too little to understand anything. She recalls that she had traded ten minutes of sexual pleasure in order to inscribe "Beloved" on the headstone of the grave while the engraver's son had watched with disgust.

Sethe suggested to Baby Suggs that they should move away from the house which harbours a baby ghost. Baby Suggs' response is that "not a house in the country ain't packed to its rafters with some dead Negro's grief." (4) Baby Suggs feels that Sethe is lucky to have her three children with her, and only one "raising hell from the other side. "Be thankful," she tells Sethe, "I had eight. Every one of them gone away from me. Four taken, four chased, and all. I expect worrying somebody's house into evil." (5)

Sethe's consciousness expands further back to the Sweet Home plantation, "rolling, rolling, rolling out before her eyes,"

(6) welling up into a hopeful living memory. Soon Paul D, one of the men from the old plantation, stands before her in the present. Sethe was only thirteen when she had taken Baby Suggs' place on the Sweet Home. Out of Paul A, Paul D, Paul F, Halle and Sixo, Sethe had chosen Halle. Mrs. Garner, after the death of her husband, had sold the plantation to Mr. Garner's brother to pay debts. The cruelty of the new master had compelled the slaves to flee Sweet Home.

Sethe invites Paul D to the house. As soon as he enters 124, Bluestone, his only response is: "what kind of evil you got in here?" When Paul D enters the house, it exudes a sadness "so thoroughly he want[s] to cry" but he does not. Sethe, Denver and Paul D are enveloped in this sadness. "My daughter," Sethe says "the one I send ahead with boys" (10) is the sadness that gives the home its character. It supplies them with the living history, personal, private, ignored and shameful.

A tale is told, and a narrative journey starts. Sethe narrates to Paul D how she had made an escape; there is the memory of a white girl who helped Sethe escape, the memory of white boys who suck milk from her breasts, the memory of "schoolteacher" who with cowhide strap carves out the tree on Sethe's back which, as she says, "grows there still." (17) Paul D embraces the tree on Sethe's back, her visible reminder of an intolerable past. "Aw, Lord girl. And he would tolerate no peace until he had touched every ridge and leaf of it, with his mouth, none of which Sethe could feel because her back skin had been dead for years." (18) As they both embrace, he offers Sethe the chance to live in this world, the world of love and remembrance, the world of hope and some kind of tomorrow.

One of the most powerful grotesque images in the novel is the deforming tree-shaped scar which Sethe bears on her back and reveals to the former slave, Paul D, soon after his arrival at 124. It is a clear example of the qualities of physical deformity and degradation. As the physical inscription of a brutal humiliation and beating by the slave master, schoolteacher, the scar recalls the horrors of the historical past. This deadening scar tissue on Sethe's back is also emblematic of her repressed feelings or blocked memory related to this experience. Taking away of her milk has affected her more profoundly than the physical beating that followed. As she recalls: "the picture of men coming to nurse her was as lifeless as the nerves on her back, where the skin buckled like a washboard." (6) Susan Cory comments: "the scar then becomes a bodily sign of Sethe's estrangement from her imagination and her innermost life. Like the dead nerves which alienate her from bodily sensation, the "lifeless" picture represents blocked memory and also emotions that separate her from a full subjective identity."

Chapter 2

Lying besides Sethe, Paul D recalls how he had cherished her memories for past twenty years. He remembers that Sixo was only one of the Sweet Home men not paralyzed by a yearning for Sethe because of the woman he was seeing. He walked seventeen hours on Saturday night and walked back the same distance to be in time for work on a Monday morning.

This is followed by an insight into Baby Suggs' life. "In all of Baby's life as well as Sethe's own, men and women were moved around like checkers." (23) Baby Suggs recalls how "anybody Baby Suggs knew, let alone loved, who hadn't run off or been hanged, got rented out, loaned out, bought up, brought back, stored up, mortgaged, won, stolen or seized." So, Baby's eight children had six fathers. What she called the nastiness of life was "the shock she received upon learning that nobody stopped playing checkers just because the pieces included her children." (23) She managed to keep her son Halle, the longest, i.e., twenty years. The two girls were sold off as infants before either of them had their adult teeth. She did not even get a chance to wave her children goodbye. In order to keep her third child, she sold herself to her boss, only to find herself pregnant by the man who promised not to and did. Sethe, felt Baby Suggs, had the amazing luck of six whole years of marriage to only one man who had fathered every one of her children—a blessing Sethe was reckless enough to take for granted.

Lying with Paul D, Sethe is reminded of Halle, who was more like a brother than a husband. His way of caring suggested family relationship, "rather than a man laying claim." For years they saw each other in full daylight only on Sundays. Rest of the time, they spoke or touched only in darkness. She recalls when Halle had asked her to be his wife, she had consented happily. When she informed Mrs. Garner about her and Halle's desire to get married, she had laughed at the idea of a slave marriage. Chapter two ends with Paul D's and Sethe's embrace.

Baby Suggs' and Sethe's example is just one that demonstrates the ruthlessness of the institution of slavery. Slavery represented a perfect mechanism through which personal space was controlled and drained of all emotional investment and meaning. Human beings were treated only as commodities, their bodies sold to the highest bidder. A slave's life was stripped of all individuality and robbed of all possessions. Mothers, fathers, sons and daughters were separated ruthlessly by the slave owners.

Chapter 3

Denver's favourite spot of hiding was in the woods, between the field and the stream. Here five boxwood bushes, planted in a ring, had started stretching towards each other and looked like a room. Once while in the boxwood, it started snowing and Denver started towards home. Denver regarded the house more like a person than a structure. A dim glow came from Baby Suggs' room. When Denver looked in, she saw her mother on her knees in prayer, which was not unusual. What was unusual was the white dress that knelt besides her mother and had its sleeve around her mother's waist. The dress and her mother together looked like two grown-up women.

The snow that day reminded Denver of the story of her own birth she loved so much. Denver remembers her mother's story of escape from Sweet Home. Sethe's feet were swollen from the long walk she had undertaken. The baby in her womb, like a little antelope, rammed her with horns. Sethe was concerned for the life of "her children's mother," her daughter she knew would be starving for food she carried. After her husband had disappeared, after her milk had been stolen, her back pulped and her children orphaned, she felt she was to have no easeful death. At this point of time, a while girl came to her help.

Amy Denver, the white girl, was "the saggiest looking white trash" Sethe had come across. She was hungry and hunting for food to eat. She was on her way to Boston, looking for finest velvet. She was escaping her owners, for whom her mother had worked, who is dead now. Amy asks Sethe her name and Sethe, for the fear of getting discovered, says "Lu." Since Sethe cannot walk, Amy helps her to crawl to a lean-on close by. The lean-on was full of leaves which Amy pushed into a pile for Sethe to lie on. Then what she did was magic—she lifted Sethe's feet and massaged her legs, until she cried salt tears. And Amy had said: "Anything dead coming back to life hurts." (35) A truth for all times, Denver thought.

She wonders if the white dress holding its arms around her mother's waist was in pain or if the baby ghost had plans. Then she describes to Sethe the dress that was leaning besides her while she was praying. Denver feels that probably the baby ghost had plans.

Sethe had given little thought to the white dress until Paul D came. The morning after first night with Paul D, Sethe smiled thinking what the word "plans" could mean. It was a luxury she had not afforded for past eighteen years. The only set of plans she had made was of getting away from 'sweet Home,' which went wrong so completely that she had never dared to make more. And the morning she woke up next to Paul D, this word of her daughter came to her mind and she wondered if it "would be all right to go ahead and feel? Go ahead and count on something?"

On Paul D's arrival, she suddenly notices how devoid of colour the house looked. In the keeping room, where Sethe went to "talk think," it was clear why Baby Suggs had so starved for colour. There wasn't any except for the two orange squares in a quilt. The walls of the room were slate coloured, the floor earth-brown, the wooden dresses the colour of itself, the curtains white. In that sober field, the two patches of orange looked wild—like life in the raw.

The house 124 Denver regarded "as a person rather than a structure." A person that "wept, sighed, trembled and fell into fits." For Sethe "124 was so full of strong feelings perhaps she was oblivious to the loss of anything at all." There was a time she remembers she had scanned the field every morning and evening for her boys when every face on the road looked like Howard and Buglar. There was no room in the house for anything or anybody until Paul D came. He worked hard to shift the things to their places.

It was after Paul D's arrival that Sethe had noticed that the room was devoid of any colour. He was responsible for that: "Emotions sped to the surface in his company." (39) And he sang while he mended things. Paul D has a feeling that Denver does not entertain his company. But for Sethe, Denver was a charmed child from the beginning. She explains to Paul D that when she was sure she was not going to make it, this girl had pulled a white girl from the hill. And Sethe had to go to jail, after schoolteacher found her out. She survived in the jail where rats bit everything except her. Paul D wanted to know more about the jail but defers it.

Chapter 4

Denver is jealous of the presence of Paul D in the house. He had taken away her only company—her mother. The third day, Denver questioned Paul D directly as to how long he intended to stay. Sethe scolds Denver for being rude to Paul D. When Paul D in Denver's absence shows resentment to her question, Sethe's response is: "Excuse me, but I can't hear a word against Denver." And Paul D thinks that it was risky for a used to be slave woman to love anything so much, "especially if it was her children she had settled on to love."

What Paul D meant could best be illustrated through the example of Baby Suggs. All her children had been sold away from her. Halle, whom she had managed to retain the longest, was also missing or dead. The right thing, according to Paul D, was to love just a "little bit . . . so that when they broke its back or showed it in a crocker sack, maybe, you'd have a little love left over for the next one." (45)

Paul D takes Sethe and Denver on a carnival in the town. Sethe is dressed in her best attire. Paul D was in the happiest mood. He was wishing good day to everyone within twenty feet, making fun of the weather, yelling back at crows. Paul D brought everything Denver asked for. He teased Sethe into tents she was reluctant to enter and stuck pieces of candy she didn't want between her lips. Sethe notices that, as they walked, their shadows were holding hands, even though they were not holding hands. While they walked back home, their shadows still held hands. This chapter ends on a harmonious note, with the baby ghost driven away by Paul D's presence and a promise of new beginning for Sethe, Paul D and Denver.

Chapter 5

A fully dressed woman walked out of water. She sat down resting her head against the tree trunk. While she lay dozing, her breath sounded as if she was suffering from asthma. It took her the whole of next morning to lift herself from the ground and make her way through the woods, and then exhausted she sat down on the first handy place, a stump not far away from the steps of 124.

On their way home from the carnival, this woman was the first thing that Paul D, Denver and Sethe noticed as they rounded the curve on the road. This stranger is invited inside the house by Paul D and Denver. She is extremely thirsty and drinks four glasses of water that Denver offers her. She is dressed in good clothes and a rich woman's hat. Her skin, Denver notices, is flawless, except for three vertical scratches on her forehead so fine and thin that they look like baby hair.

Paul D asks her name and she answers in a voice that is barely audible 'Beloved.' When Paul D asks if it was her last name, she says, "no," and she spells it for him. They do not press this young woman immediately with questions as to where and how she came from. What occupied them at this moment was what she needed, although each harboured a set of questions. Paul D wondered at the newness of her shoes. Sethe was deeply touched by her name, the remembrance of the glittering headstone made her feel especially kind towards her.

She collapsed in Baby Suggs' bed, with her breath sounding like steam engine. She slept continuously for four days, waking up only for water. Finally, after the fourth day, her eyes flew wide open and she looked at Denver for the first time with no trace of sleep in her eyes. It seemed that fever had caused her memory to fail. She did not have any idea of what she was doing in that part of the country or where she had come from. There didn't seem any place for her to go. Sethe had no objection against her staying with them because she could see that Denver had taken a liking for Beloved. She felt that Beloved would be a good companion to Denver who was so lonesome.

Paul D is surprised at Sethe's readiness to take the girl in the house. What surprises him even more is that even though she "Acts sick, sounds sick, but she don't look sick: good skin, bright eyes and strong as a bull." (56) He even saw Beloved picking up a heavy rocking chair single-handedly.

A number of questions arise in the mind of the readers about this mysterious girl, walking out of water. For Marc C. Conner, Beloved is the physical embodiment of Sethe's murdered daughter, as well as those thousands who died during the "Middle Passage": "Beloved resembles one of the African River goddess who easily crosses boundaries between the living and the dead. She represents the eruption of the uncanny, the anti-rational, or the mythic into the realm of normal existence, an event that may unlock previously locked emotions and open the mind to a wider experience of life."[2]

Chapter 6

Beloved is intensely devoted to Sethe. Her affection is such that could spring only from a long familiarity. She rose early in the morning before Sethe left for work. She was on the window when Sethe returned from work in the afternoon. Then she moved to the porch, its steps, the path, the road, till finally surrendering to the habit. Beloved began inching down Bluestone Road further and further, each day to meet Sethe and walk her back to 124. Sethe is flattered by Beloved's devotion.

On one occasion when Sethe sat down to rest while cooking, she fell asleep, and Beloved woke her up. The longing she saw in Beloved's eyes was "Bottomless," "loaded with desire." She then asks Sethe about the diamonds she had worn in her ears. Sethe replied that she had no diamonds, she only had crystal ear-bobs presented to her by Mrs. Garner.

Sethe discovers the profound satisfaction Beloved derives from story-telling. It amazes Sethe (as much as it pleases Beloved) because earlier every mention of her past life had hurt her. Everything in it was painful or lost, and she and Baby Suggs had agreed without saying that it was unspeakable. To Denver's enquiries, Sethe gave short replies or rambling incomplete reveries. Even with Paul D, with whom she had shared some of her past, that hurt was always there. But talking to Beloved about the events of her past was always a pleasure. Perhaps this was because of Beloved's distance from the events or her thirst of knowing the events.

The crystal earrings, Sethe recalls, were Mrs. Garner's present to her on her wedding to Halle. Mrs. Garner was amused by Sethe's request that her marriage should be dignified by a wedding ceremony. She had probably guessed how bad Sethe had felt to know that there would be no ceremony.

The next question that Sethe encounters from Beloved, while she sits down to comb Denver's hair, is whether Sethe's mother never fixed up Sethe's hair. Sethe is surprised at this inquiry about her past. She answers that she cannot recall since she had seen her mother only a few times. She barley remembers her mother who, she recalls, was pointed out to her by the eight-year-old child who watched over the young ones—pointed out as the one among the many backs turned away from her, stooping on a watery field. She remembers her mother simply as an image who worked in the field day and night.

Sethe has another quite specific memory of this obscure mother, their only interaction following the two weeks the nameless Ma'am was allowed to nurse her. She remembers that Ma'am picked her up and carried her behind the smokehouse. There, she opened the front of her dress and pointed to a mark on her rib. It was a circle, she recalls, with a cross burnt right in the skin. Pointing to the mark, she had said, "this is your Ma'am, this, . . . I am the only one who has got this mark the rest are dead. If something happens and you can't tell me by my face, you can tell me by this mark."[2] It scared Sethe, and all Sethe could think of saying was "Ma'am . . . but how will you know me? . . . Mark me too." Her mother slapped her face in response. Sethe couldn't understand this until she had a mark of her own.

Sethe's mother was hanged—in what circumstances, she did not know. But a woman Nan, who knew her mother, helped her locate her mother's body through the mark. Nan had told Sethe that her mother and Nan were together from the sea. Both were taken up many times by the crew. All other children born to her were thrown away by her into the sea, except Sethe, whom she had given the name of a black man she loved. The talk of the diamond earrings and Sethe's mother suggests a shared memory. Denver is now sure that Beloved is a reincarnation of her sister. This rememory of her past life unsettles Sethe: "She was remembering something she had forgotten she knew. Something privately shameful that had seeped into a slit in her mind right behind the slap on her face and the circled cross." (61) At the same time we know that Sethe liked telling those stories to Beloved. Beloved thus triggers the process of remembering and in fact teaches that these stories are lifegiving and cannot be ignored.

This novel is important because it is a slave narrative, from a woman and emphasizing what slavery meant to a woman. It shows how slavery impaired the most important aspect of a woman's life, the mother and child bonding. Sethe chooses death for her baby, rather than slavery. Baby Suggs grieves inconsolably when her children are sold. Sethe sees her own mother, a woman who was brought from Africa on a slave ship, only a few months before the woman is killed. Denver loves her mother but also fears her because she is a murderer. These and other incidents illustrate the destruction of family ties brought about by slavery.

Chapter 7

Beloved was glowing, she looked "gilded and shining" and Paul D didn't like it. Five weeks had passed and they didn't know anything more about her than they first knew when they found her on the slump. It was while they sat down for dinner and he could see pet like adoration in Beloved's eyes for Sethe that he asks her for the first time if she had a brother or sister. Beloved answers: "I don't have nobody?" He further inquires if someone had brought her there. She simply answers, "I walked here, a long, long, long, long way. Nobody bring me. Nobody helped me." (65) He asks her how she had new shoes when she came, how come her shoes didn't show that she had walked a long way. The only explanation that she gives is that she carried her shoes because the strings didn't fix.

Beloved, Paul D feels, was different from all the Negroes Paul D had met. During, before and after the war, he had seen Negroes so stunned and hungry or tired or bereft, it was a wonder they recalled or said anything. People like him, who had hidden in caves, fought owls for food, stole from pigs, slept in the trees in the day and walked by night. He had always been on a move. Only once it had been possible for him to stay in a spot with a woman or a family.

Beloved was different from all the slaves Paul D had known. Moreover, she had appeared at a time when he had started settling down with Sethe like a family. He didn't want her in the house, but he knew Sethe wouldn't allow him to throw a helpless girl out in a territory infected with the Klan. Sethe defends keeping Beloved, saying that she is a good company to Denver. Their conversation shifts to Halle who, Sethe feels, has mistreated her by deserting her and her children.

Paul D knew that something had hurt Halle badly, and made him lose his mind. He was otherwise a strong man and those years of extra work had never touched him. When Sethe cried over her stolen milk, Paul D had guessed that Halle was probably hiding in the barn while it happened and was helpless to stop it. Sethe asks him how he knew this. Paul D answered that something had happened which had broken Halle. Last time he saw Halle, he was near the churn, with butter smeared on his face. The milk schoolteacher and his nephews had stolen was probably on his mind.

Chapter 8

Beloved and Denver are alone. Beloved is dancing and invites Denver to dance with her. When they sit down tired from dancing, Denver asks her why she called herself Beloved. Beloved's response is: "In the dark my name is Beloved." Denver further inquires "What it was like over there where you were before?" "Dark," Beloved answers and curls up in order to demonstrate her position. She says: "it was hot in there with no room to move." When Denver inquires if she saw anybody, Beloved answers, "A lot of people is down there, some is dead," whose identities she did not know. From that darkness, she got to the bridge. She waited for two days before she came to see Sethe. Denver felt a little hurt that she was not the main reason for Beloved's return. Beloved complains "that she [Sethe] left me behind, by myself." Denver is now sure that it was her baby sister who has come in the shape of a young woman. Denver asks Beloved to conceal her identity from others and Beloved does not like it. Denver now narrates the story of her birth to Beloved who is hungry for stories.

Denver tells her about Amy Denver, the white girl, who helped Sethe in bringing Denver to this world. She had rubbed Sethe's feet back to life. It hurt but it made her think that she could make it over to where grandma Baby Suggs and her children were.

In narrating the tale of Sethe's escape, Denver feels what Sethe must have felt while escaping from Sweet Home. Her mother, she realizes for the first time, was only nineteen years old, just a year older than herself while she was making the escape, all alone and pregnant. She is not afraid of darkness, but afraid that some tracker might hunt her. Denver was seeing it all and feeling it through Beloved. The back of her body was on fire because of beatings, her feet seemed to be on fire because of constant running. When Amy saw the back of Sethe's body, she was struck dumb. The whip marks on her body looked like a "chokecherry tree." There was a trunk spit wide open full of a sap, and there were parting branches.

Amy sang songs which her mother had taught her. She massaged Sethe's legs. She tore down two pieces from Sethe's shawl, filled them with leaves, and tied them on her feet to comfort her. With the help of Amy, she had given birth to a daughter in the boat. At twilight, Amy took leave of Sethe, saying she did not want to be caught with a runaway. She asks Sethe to tell the baby when she grew up that it was Amy Denver of Boston who had helped her to bring the baby into the world.

This is the first time that the ghost child actually reveals her identity to Denver. Her crouching in the dark, with no room to move, and dead people lying over her, recalls the experiences of "middle passage." Morrison explains this in one of her interviews:

> So when they say "what was it like over there?" they may mean—they do mean—"what was it like being dead?" She tells them what it was like being where she was on that ship as a child. Both things are possible, and there is evidence in the text that both things could be approached, because the language of both experiences—death and Middle Passage—is the same.[3]

The tale, narrated above by Denver, of Sethe's escape, her birth and the aftermath are told by or remembered through the consciousness of various characters—Denver, Sethe, Stamp Paid and Beloved. The assumption is that a story will be repeated and will change with every telling. This implies the multiplicity of perspectives and historical positions

Maggie Sale points out that the process of "creating oral history out of memories depends upon the interaction between the perspectives and needs of tellers and listeners. . . . The boundaries of the text challenge notions of objectivity in creation of history. Who is saying (or writing) what to whom, and how they're saying (or writing) it, is of most importance to the meaning of what gets said (written). Not only does Beloved foreground its own construction as history and fiction, but it asserts that all historical narratives participate in a similar fictionalizing that reveals as much about the writer (teller) as it recovers of the past."[4]

Chapter 9

This chapter begins with Sethe's reverie. She thinks about her life with Baby Suggs, the only woman she had been close to. Before Paul D came and sat down on the porch, it was Baby Suggs' words that had kept Sethe going. She wished for Baby Suggs' fingers moulding her nape saying, "'Lay em down, Sethe. Sword and shield. . . . Don't study war no more. Lay all that mess down. Sword and shield.' And under the pressing fingers and the quiet instructive voice, she would." (86)

Nine years without the fingers or the voice of Baby Suggs was too much. She decided to go to the clearing where Baby Suggs had preached her gospel and danced in sunlight. 124 had been a cheerful, buzzing house where Baby Suggs loved, cautioned, fed, chastised and soothed, before it became a plaything of spirits. It was in front of 124 that Sethe climbed off a wagons, with the newborn tied to her chest and felt for the first time the wide arms of her mother-in-law. Slave life had "busted her back, legs, and head, eyes, hands, kidneys, womb and tongue." (87) Baby had nothing left to make her living except her heart which she put to work at once. She slowly became an unchurched preacher who visited pulpits and opened her heart to people who could use it.

Baby Suggs preached her gospel in a clearing, cut deep into the woods. After praying silently, she asked the children to come towards her and asked them to laugh so that their mothers could see them. Then she asked the men to dance and women to give vent to their sorrows by crying. It started with children laughing, men dancing and women crying, and then it got mixed up. Women stopped crying and danced, men sat down and cried, children danced until exhausted, and each lay about the clearing gasping for breath.

She did not tell them to clean up their lives nor to go and sin no more. She did not tell them they were blessed of the earth, its inheriting meek, or its glorybound pure. She told them that the only grace they could have was the grace they could imagine. She preached them to love their flesh "love it hard." She asks them to love all that the whites hate in them, their skin, their eyes, their hands. She asked them to love their neck and hold it up, because their masters did not like their necks unnoosed or straight. And more than anything else she asks them to love their heart.

124 now only put up with the venom of the baby ghost. There were no lamps all night long, or neighbours dropping by. Baby Suggs had come to believe that whatever she had preached was a lie. There was no grace, imaginary or real. Her faith, love and imagination and her big old heart had begun to collapse after her daughter-in-law had arrived. Baby Suggs attributed all her miseries to the white folks. Sethe recalls the day she had arrived on Bluestone Road with the help of Stamp Paid and Ella. Baby Suggs took care of her here, she bathed her body and gave her a newly stitched dress to wear.

Sethe goes to the clearing where Suggs had preached her gospel with Denver and Beloved. In the clearing, she locates Baby's old preaching rock and rests her head upon it. She calls for Baby in her mind and longs to feel her finger on her neck, and they were there. She bows her head and tries to relax. Slowly, the fingers that touched the back of her neck became stronger and bolder and she felt she was being literally strangled. Denver rushes to her help and finds bruises on her neck. Beloved was now stroking her skin. She bends down and kisses Sethe. Sethe grabbed Beloved by her hair and separated herself, because the girl's breath was exactly like new milk. Sethe was sure of one thing that grandma Baby had not choked her, it was probably the baby ghost who had done it. And the hands that stroked her (Beloved) later were exactly like those of the baby ghost. But she does not give a further thought to this. On her mind now was a wish to launch a newer and stronger life with Paul D.

On returning home, Sethe saw Paul D in the kitchen tub and he held her in his arms. They did not hear when Beloved came through the door. Seeing them together, Beloved felt like crying, an anger she always felt when Sethe did or thought anything that excluded her. She turns away and rushes to the woods till she is joined by Denver who accuses her of trying to strangle Sethe.

This is followed by Denver's reveries. Denver's desire for company of children had brought her to Lady Jones's school. She had peeped inside several times before she was invited to attend school. Her brothers, Sethe and Baby were proud of her attending school. She enjoyed her lessons till Nelson Lord—a boy as smart as she—put an end to them. He had said "Didn't your mother get locked away for murder? Wasn't you in there with her when she went?" (104) She was too scared to ask anyone Nelson Lord's questions. Even when she did, she got no reply. Later, when Baby Suggs died, announcing that there was no bad luck in the world but white people, and Howard and Buglar ran away, she did not agree with Sethe that they left because of the ghost. Denver feels that she would prefer a venomous ghost of her sister to Paul D's presence. She treasured Beloved's company and did not wish to lose it.

In this chapter, the baby ghost makes its first attempt to revenge its murder by Sethe. Sethe's and Denver's consciousness expands and answers various questions that had arisen in the mind of readers. It reveals why the neighbours kept away from 124 or why Baby Suggs had stopped preaching the gospel and resigned her life in pondering over colour.

Chapter 10

Paul D recalls the time he had spent as a convict, tied to the walls of the cage. There were forty-five others who were linked to each other through coffles and to the walls of the cage. He was sent here after trying to kill Brandywine, the man schoolteacher had sold him to. Brandywine had led him to Virginia from Kentucky along with ten others.

Paul D recalls how the forty-six men chained to each other had made an escape from the prison with Hi Man leading them.

All forty-six of them ran together, not knowing how many of them would be discovered and killed. All eighty-six days they ran while it rained five days without wind. Finally they came up near a Cherokee camp. Hi Man spoke for a moment to two Cherokee men who approached him. They went away and returned with a handful of axes to break away their chains. They called themselves Buffalo men. Weeks later, Paul D was the last man with the Buffalo hair among the ailing Cherokees—the rest of them had fled. Paul D inquired from one of the Cherokees about the way north. He asked him to follow the trees and flowers which finally brought him to Delaware. Here he lived with a woman for eighteen months. She was kind enough to offer him food and a place to live. It took him some time to forget his past, to keep it locked in "the tobacco tin" lodged in his chest. (113)

Chapter 11

Beloved moved Paul D and he didn't know how to contain himself. Beloved was compelling him to distance himself from Sethe, with whom he slept each day. He first moves away from Sethe's room and sleeps in the rocking chair. Sethe does not object to his sleeping separately, with two young girls in the house and Paul D not being her true-to-life husband. Paul D then moves to Baby Suggs' room. But he still feels that he is having house fits, so he goes to the storeroom. From the storeroom, he shifts to the coldhouse outside. Finally he realizes that this moving was involuntary and he was almost being prevented from his relationship with Sethe. He now visited Sethe in the morning, slept in the cold room at night and waited. After being forced out of 124 into a shed behind the house one chilly night, he hears the door open. Even before he turns to look he knows it was Beloved. Paul D asks the reason of her coming and she replies: "I want you to touch me on the inside part and call me my name." (116) When she hoists her skirt and turns her head over her shoulder, he chastises her saying "When good people take you in and treat you good, you ought to try to be good back. . . . Sethe loves you. Much as her own daughter you know that." Beloved's reply is: "She don't love me like I love her." She seduces Paul D, who reaches out to her calling "Red Heart, Red Heart, Red Heart." (117)

Valerie Smith writes that one might read Beloved's sexual relations with Paul D as a bodily cure: "His refusal reflects his sense that his secrets are located in what might remain of his heart, in that tobacco tin buried in his chest where a red heart used to be. Its lid rusted shut. The description of this scene suggests that the act of intercourse with Beloved restores Paul D to himself, restores his heart to him! In a variety of ways, then Morrison calls attention to the suffering that bodies endured under slavery. The project of the novel, much like Baby Suggs' project, seemed to be to reclaim those bodies to find a way to tell the story of the slave body in pain."[5]

Chapter 12

Sethe occasionally questions Beloved about her past. She says: "You disremember everything? I never knew my mother neither, but I saw her a couple of times." She asks if Beloved can recall anything about her own past. Beloved, scratching the back of hand replies that she could remember a woman who was her mother, and recalls being snatched away from her. Her clearest memory is one of standing on the bridge where she saw one white man. When asked how she had obtained new dress and shoes, her answer is, she does not remember. Sethe believed and told Denver that Beloved had probably been locked by some white man for his own purposes, and never let out of the door. She had probably escaped to a bridge and she cannot recall the rest of it. Something similar had happened to Ella, except that it was two men—a father and a son who had locked Ella in a room for themselves but Ella remembered every bit of it. Sethe thought this explained her behaviour about Paul D whom she hated.

Denver's devotion to Beloved was complete. She neither believed nor commented on Sethe's speculations; she lowered her eyes and never said a word about the cold house. She was certain that Beloved was the white dress that had knelt with her mother in the keeping room, she was the true-to-life presence of the baby that had kept her company most of her life. Beloved shared with Denver the stories about her past, about her grandfather, her brothers, her teacher Lady Jones.

On one occasion, dancing around the room with Denver, Beloved is thirsty, and asks for water. Denver suggests warming up some cider. It was noon, but there was little light outside, and it was dark inside. The door bangs shut, but Denver cannot make out where Beloved is standing. The ghost child performs an act of "magical disappearance." Beloved's disappearance pains Denver and she is hit by a sense of loneliness and she cries into the stove. At this moment Beloved appears again, standing in front of Denver and smiling. Beloved explains to Denver her essence by pointing to a sunlit crack, in the ceiling.

Chapter 13

Paul D grew up thinking that only Mr. Garner spared his slaves their manhood. He did what other whites had prohibited to slaves, i.e., he gave them the privilege of decision making while buying a house, a wife or a mother and permitted them to read and write. The slaves "were believed, trusted and listened to by Garner." (125) But they had the status of human beings only inside Sweet Home, outside Sweet Home they were trespassers on human race.

Paul D was not a weak man—he had lived through most difficult times, watched the men he loved die before his eyes. But he felt helpless over the power Beloved exercised on him. He felt like a ragdoll—picked up and put down anywhere, anytime by a girl young enough to be his daughter. Although he did not have a command over his feet, he felt he could talk and explain to Sethe how Beloved was moving him. He goes and stands outside the restaurant where Sethe cooks, so that they could walk back home. He stands there rehearsing what he would say to Sethe.

He begins by telling Sethe: "Sethe, you won't like what I'm 'bout to say." (128) Somehow he could not muster up courage to tell Sethe what he had come to explain. So he ends up saying something which he didn't know was on his mind, that is, "I want you pregnant, Sethe, would you do that for me?" (128) It now occurs to him that it was really one of the ways to hold on to Sethe. They walk back home weak and breathless from laughter at what Paul D said. Beloved is waiting outside the house carrying a shawl for Sethe since it was snowing. Paul D fought anger on seeing Beloved.

He feels grateful to Sethe when she invites him to stay in her room. Sethe, recalling Paul D's face in the street, wonders: "what he wanted her pregnant for? To hold on to her? have a sign that he passed this way?" (132) But she was in love with Paul D and had longed for his company for years, and wished him to stay.

Chapter 14

Beloved is jealous of the union of Paul D and Sethe. She asks Denver to drive him out. What she did next was to insert a thumb and forefinger in her mouth, and she pulled out a black tooth; but there was no blood. The author demonstrates Beloved's fear of death through her stream-of-consciousness.

> Beloved looked at the tooth and thought, this is it. Next would be her arm, her hand, a toe. Pieces of her would drop maybe one at a time, maybe all at once. . . . She had two dreams: exploding and being swallowed. When her tooth came out . . . she thought it was starting. (134)

She then cries out of the fear of losing Sethe.

Beloved's fear of being swallowed or exploding to pieces demonstrates her fear of violence. She was simply two when her mother had cut her throat. Her crouching position, which she demonstrates twice to Denver, also suggests "middle passage."

Chapter 15

Baby Suggs is grateful that her grandchildren have made it safely to Bluestone. There were two boys and a little girl. She was now waiting for the arrival of Sethe and Halle. Sethe arrives badly battered, with another new born. There is no sign of Halle but they are hopeful, he would make it too.

Baby Suggs feels obliged to throw a party when Stamp Paid brings two bucketful of blackberries to celebrate Baby's reunion with her daughter-in-law and grandchildren. More than ninety people are invited and there is an overabundance of food, cakes and punch. This overabundance makes the town furious. They are outraged at the poverty of their own lives and Baby's excesses. The scent of disapproval was high in the air. Baby could sense that something was wrong. She is fearful of Halle's well-being.

Baby Suggs' stream-of-consciousness reveals the agony of a slave mother. Halle's love for his mother is remarkable in the institution of slavery which impaired any such bonding. She recalls that on Halle's birth, she had barely glanced at him, thinking "it wasn't worth the trouble to try and learn features she would never see change into adulthood." (139) Seven of her children had been forcibly sold away from her.

When she hurt her hip, she was a cheap bargain for Mr. Garner because of her ungainly walk. He brought her to work in his farm in Kentucky, called Sweet Home. Her master Mr. Garner and his wife were nice to her and never knocked her down.

Her hip hurt but she never complained. Only Halle, who had watched her movements closely for several years, knew that she was in acute distress. So he speaks to Mr. Garner about buying his mother out for extra labour. When Halle paid Mr. Garner for his mother's freedom, she had wondered: "What does a sixty-year old slave woman who walks like a three-legged dog need freedom for?" (141) But on setting her foot on a free ground, she wondered how Halle who had never drawn a free breath knew how valuable it was. There was nothing like it in the world.

Baby Suggs experiences the wonder of possessing her own body, of recognizing the pounding of "her own heart." She renames herself Suggs (her husband's name), rejecting Garner's defence of the legal name on her bill of sale, Jenny Whitlow.

This division followed by the next division in the novel is in the form of a flashback. We are given an insight into Baby's life and Beloved's murder. A tragedy barely hinted at until the book is half over, it sheds a new light on things. It explains why Baby Suggs had stopped preaching, and her tough spirit slowly failed. It explains why Sethe's boys always slept holding hands until they were old enough to flee, and why Denver is afraid of going out of the house.

Chapter 16

Sethe, with her four children, was a piece of property too precious for the schoolteacher to let go easily. He traces them to Ohio and comes with the nephew and the sheriff, to capture them. Seeing her hopes of freedom dashed, Sethe picks up a knife and cuts the throat of her daughter whom she loves the best. The schoolteacher retreats, thinking that she had gone wild due to mishandling of a nephew who'd overbeat her and made her 'cut and run.' They are frightened with the sight of a slave woman, holding a baby she had just slaughtered.

Sethe is so shocked by her own action that she does not allow anyone to take away the dead child. In order to distract her, Baby holds a wailing Denver in front of her. Blood-soaked Sethe takes and feeds her, without cleaning herself up. So, Denver took her mother's milk along with the blood of her sister. Sethe prefers death for both herself and her most beloved, rather than a return to slavery, and have her children suffer institutionalized dehumanization.

Chapter 17

Stamp Paid informs Paul D of the heinous crime Sethe had committed by unfolding the newspaper clipping with Sethe's picture to him. Nothing could convince him that it is Sethe's face. A whip of fear broke through him, the appearance of the face meant that the face was there not because the person had a healthy baby or outran a street mob. A black never made news even if the person was killed or maimed, caught or burned, jailed, wiped, evicted, stomped or raped. This could hardly qualify as news in a newspaper. If the face was there, it was because of something extraordinary—something white people would find interesting.

Stamp Paid dashes Sethe's hopes of happiness with Paul D. Morrison is critical of the community's failure to love and forgive. She portrays the community's failure to grasp the broader context of Sethe's act or to empathize with her.

Chapter 18

Paul D questions Sethe after showing her the newspaper clipping. Sethe does not give a straight answer. She beats about the bush, telling him about the sacrifice motherhood demanded from her. She explains to him that she loved her children more when she arrived at Bluestone because in Kentucky they didn't belong to her. Paul D understood what she meant "to get to a place where you could love anything you chose—not to need permission for desire—well now, that was freedom." (162) Her only explanation is "I took and put my babies where they'd be safe." She defends herself: "I couldn't let all that go back to where it was, and I couldn't let her nor any of them live under schoolteacher." (169)

Paul D had earlier thought that Sethe lived in helpless and apologetic resignation because she had no choice, that in the absence of husbands, sons and mother-in-law, she was compelled to stay in this manner. But he was wrong—this was a new Sethe. She talked about safety with a handsaw. All Paul D could muster in response is "your love was too thick." When he asks her what she had gained by her act, she answers "they ain't at Sweet Home. Schoolteacher ain't got them. . . . It's my job to know what is and keep them away from what I know is terrible. I did that." (165) Paul D deserts her saying "you got two feet Sethe not four," and right then a forest sprang up between them "trackless and quiet."

Section Two

Chapter 19

Stamp Paid was feeling uneasy after showing the newspaper clipping to Paul D. He feels responsible for having stopped the one shot of happiness that a good man like Paul D could bring in her life. Denver too needed somebody normal in her life. So with a guilty feeling he approached 124 to talk to Sethe. The last time he had set his foot in the house was when Baby Suggs died.

Since people had refused to enter 124, the funeral service was held in the Yard. Sethe returned their contempt by not attending the service Revered Pike presided over. With a heavy heart, he approaches the yard of 124, but he does not have the courage to knock.

Sethe is lonely after few months of sun splashed life. Her twenty-eight days in freedom were followed by eighteen years of disapproval and solitary life. Paul D's company had changed everything but now he has left her. Sethe decided to take Baby Suggs' advice to 'lay it all down.' She searched for her ice-skates. Anyone who peeped in to see how she was getting along would discover that the woman junk-heaped for the third time for the love of her children was sailing happily over ice. All three holding hands swirled over the ice. Sethe laughed and laughed, making her eyes wet, but when laughter died tears did not. The following day, Sethe is late for work for the first time.

Stamp Paid, fingering a ribbon and smelling the skin, approached 124 again. He was thinking of Baby Suggs again. The black community, to which Baby preached her gospel of love, had failed to protect her and her grandchildren. He feels he had no right to act as "a high minded soldier of Christ" (170) and ruin Sethe's happiness.

He thinks of the atrocities against Blacks: eighty-seven lynchings in Kentucky, four coloured schools burned to the ground, black women raped by crew. But news of all these incidents had not moved him as much as the red ribbon floating on water. The red ribbon knotted around a curl with wet and woolly hair "clinging to a bit of scalp," the smell of skin nearly broke him down. It must have come from the head of a lynched (possibly raped) young black girl. It reminds him probably of his gift of his wife to his master. His wife Vashti had worn a black ribbon to all meetings with her seducer owner. He is wrapped up with the feeling of victimization of his wife and the young girl and the knowledge that their debtors did not pay. And also the debt he owes Sethe for having threatened her future. When he peeps into Sethe's house, he sees two girls asleep with their backs turned away from the window.

This is followed by Sethe's reverie. She remembers the days she had spent in jail. Baby had come to meet her in the jail and told her how coloured ladies of Delaware, Ohio, had drawn up a petition to keep her from being hanged. She recalls how after coming out of prison she had gone directly to Beloved's grave. Now her daughter has come back to her and all she wanted to know was "How bad is the scar."

Chapter 20

This chapter comprises Sethe's rememory. Sethe has now recognized her daughter Beloved who, she feels, has come back to her of her own free will, because her love was tough. She feels that she can persuade her daughter to understand what had compelled her to kill her. Her stolen milk had hurt her more than all the atrocities she has suffered in slavery. Sethe's own mother couldn't nurse her because she worked in the field. Instead, a woman called Nan nursed her. So she knows what it means to go without milk, "to fight and holler for it."

Sethe felt that she would have recognized Beloved immediately if Paul D had not distracted her. Sethe's fingernail prints when she held her head in the shed were still on her forehead. She didn't recognize her in spite of her mention of earrings, which she dangled for Beloved to play with. She recalls Paul D's departing words that "her love was too thick," and wonders "who in the world is he willing to die for? Would he give his privates to a stranger in return for a carving?" (203) If it had not been for Buglar, Howard and Denver, she would have ended her life. Her thoughts turn to her mother who was caught escaping. She wonders what compelled her to do so because nobody's ma'am would leave her daughter. She recalls the women she had seen in the jail. Some of them drank liquor to get over their depression, some gave that liquor to Phelps to pay for their children's requirements. After she came out of the jail and traded for Beloved's name, she realized what sacrifice these women were making.

Chapter 21

This chapter consists of Denver's rememory. Denver feels grateful for Beloved's company and is protective towards her. She says that she had recognized her sister the moment she had spelt her name. Denver's subconscious mind reveals her fear of her mother because Sethe is a killer. Her brothers have fled for the same reason. Denver is fearful that something terrible might happen to make her repeat her act. As a child she had attended Lady Jones's school until Nelson Lord's question (if her mother was in jail) put an end to it. She has not left 124 since then except twice: once when Baby Suggs was laid to rest, and the second time when Paul D took them to the carnival.

Denver's rememory shows her longing for her grandmother and her father. Grandma Baby taught her to listen to her body and love it. She talked affectionately about her father, who was an unusual person. He was the only slave on Garner's plantation who learnt to read and write. He could count on paper, and this helped him to buy his mother out. Denver dislikes Paul D, who has taken away his mother's company from her. She longs for her father who, she still believes, would make it to 124 if Paul D could.

Chapter 22

Through a series of interior monologues, Morrison reveals the internal conflict of the three central female characters. The first was Sethe's rememory, the second was Denver's and the third one is Beloved's, and the last one is a merging of all three. Beloved's interior monologue is the most intriguing of all three. There are no punctuation marks in her monologue, the group of words here are separated by literal spaces.

Beloved's disjoint thoughts in this chapter tell the story of her capture by white slave traders. She describes how white slave traders, 'men without skin,' captured the girl and her mother as the older women picked flowers. The place where green grass grows here refers to Africa.

The first scene talks about the girl watching her mother as she takes "flowers away from leaves give some space she puts them in a round basket . . . she opens the grass." This opening of the grass is probably caused by the mother falling down.

The following paragraph recounts the horrors faced by Africans during the "Middle Passage." She refers to people crouching, and dying of suffocation. Daylight here comes only through the cracks and they are bitten by rats. The men without skin bring water for them. There are images of people trembling, dying and vomiting.

In the next passage, she says that they were no longer crouching but standing with the men without skin, making loud noises. The pile of dead men is being pushed into the sea. Once captured, Beloved notices the change in her mother. She remembers seeing the diamond earrings 'shining in her ear,' as they were picking flowers. Now, on the ship, her mother 'has nothing in her ears,' but she has an iron collar around her neck, and she says: "she would bite the circle around her neck."

Beloved could have helped her but "clouds were in the way." Clouds here refer to gun-smoke. She refers to a man whom she liked because of his song but he died soon after. They were no longer crouching but floating on water. She recalls herself waiting on the bridge because her mother is under it. The men without skin are no longer following her. She repeatedly refers to her mother "chewing and swallowing." These words bring to our mind the African women who did not survive the Middle Passage—those who were chewed up, spit out and swallowed by the sea—ones whose bodies and stories were never recovered.

Chapter 23

This chapter begins with Beloved's interior monologue, but in the later half of the chapter, Beloved's, Sethe's and Denver's voices merge in an unusual form of poetry. Beloved's interior monologue begins like the previous chapter with the words, "I AM BELOVED and she is mine." Her disjoint thoughts here are conveyed by spaces between words with no punctuation marks. A story can be pieced together that describes how white slave traders, "men without skin," captured the girl and her mother as the older women picked flowers in Africa. Beloved remembers how she and her mother along with many other Africans were put aboard an abysmally crowded slave ship. Here they were given little food and water. Many blacks lost their lives in these inhuman conditions. To escape this living hell, Beloved's mother leaped into the ocean and, thus, in the eyes of the girl her mother willingly deserted her.

Beloved's, Sethe's and Denver's stream-of-consciousness merges here in the form of poetry. The use of poetry as narrative technique simulates the unnatural state of affairs that exist at 124. Sethe is happy that her daughter has come back to her, because her love was tough. Here she can protect her daughter; men without skin can no longer get her. Beloved notices that her mother's earrings are gone, but she no longer has an iron circle around her neck.

Denver's rememory merges with that of Beloved. She is happy that Beloved has come back to her. Denver warns her against Sethe who "chews and swallows" and asks her not to fall asleep when she braids her hair. Beloved, on the other hand, says that she loves her mother too much," she is her "hot thing." The three voices merge into poetry saying:

> Beloved
> You are my sister
> You are my daughter
> You are my face; you are me
> I have found you again; you have come back to me.
> You are my Beloved
> You are mine
> You are mine
> You are mine (216)

Chapter 24

This chapter describes a small church for the blacks where Paul D had taken refuge. Paul D sat on the porch steps rememorying his past. He was the youngest of three half-brothers (same mother—different fathers) sold to Garner, where he lived for twenty years. Once in Maryland, he met four families of slaves who had been together for a hundred years: great-grands, grands, mothers, fathers, aunts, uncles, cousins and children, and he watched them in awe. It was unusual for a slave to have static family ties since members of a family were usually sold to people staying away from each other.

Staying in Sweet Home, he was happy because he had everything a slave could ask for. He lived like a family, with his two brothers, two friends, Baby Suggs and a boss who was kind to them. After Mr. Garner's death, the schoolteacher came and broke this cradle. He constantly complained that the slaves "ate too much, rested too much and talked too much." (220) Paul D believes that schoolteacher broke into children what Garner had raised into men.

He recalls their elaborate plans of escape. They were only waiting for the spring when the corn was ripe and high, and would make their escape easier. At the last moment their plans had failed: only Paul D and the thirty-mile woman make it to the creek. There is no sign of Halle, Sethe or Paul A. Sixo joins them but he is purused by the schoolteacher, his pupils and four other white horsemen, carrying guns. He recalls how Sixo sung when five rifles were trained on him. Sixo was happy because his thirty-mile woman had escaped with his "blossoming seed."

He remembers his last meeting with Sethe at "Sweet Home." She had come to tell him that she was escaping without Halle since he could not be found. He felt sure that Sethe would not be able to make it; her pregnancy would foil her plans of escape. He was sure that this was his last meeting with Sethe, and "right then and there his heart stopped." (228)

Chapter 25

Stamp Paid apologises to Paul D for his retreat into isolation in the old church cellar after leaving 124. He invites him to stay at his house or any other house of the coloured ones in Cincinnati.

He narrates the story of his life to Paul D. Called by the slave name Joshua earlier, Stamp Paid is a man who has earned his freedom by acquiescing in the repeated rape of his young wife Vashti by the young heir to the plantation where he grew up. He has without violence or verbal objection handed over his wife to his master's son.

Joshua had remained quiet, at his wife's insistence, during the period of her degradation. Vashti felt that he should not risk his life defending her, so that she can have someone to turn to when the white man tires of her. His silence was an additional burden on his soul. The master's son uses Vashti to assert his manhood. That act signals to Joshua that he can never be a man. Joshua can neither claim nor protect his wife, for the ownership of the wife's most private parts are the privilege of the slave owner.

Joshua goes begging to the white woman to persuade her husband to return his wife back to him. He had at this point tried unsuccessfully to turn his anger at Vashti and kill her for a set of circumstances over which she had no control. But his fleeting desire to kill her is really his longing for suicide, a desire to destroy himself when he sees the same powerlessness in himself. At the end of the year, the master's son dismissed Vashti from his bed. Joshua too leaves her. Instead of snapping her neck, he changed his name, thereby sparing her life as well as his own.

Stamp Paid now attempts to humanize Sethe's act of killing her daughter to Paul D. He feels that Sethe killed the baby only for protecting her children from slavery. She, according to Stamp Paid, was trying to "outhurt the hurter." Their talk then turns to Beloved, the new girl in the house. Since Stamp Paid has never laid eyes on the girl before, he suspects that the girl was probably the one locked up in the house by a whiteman for his own purpose. "Folks say he had her in there since she was a pup." (235) This Whiteman was found dead last summer and the girl gone. He suspects that Beloved is the same girl.

Section Three

Chapter 26

The day Sethe noticed the scar under Beloved's chin, she had fingered it and closed her eyes for a long time. Sethe had come to realize that her daughter has come back to her. She now became totally oblivious to Denver's presence and devoted her entire attention to Beloved. Sethe loses her job at Sawyer, but instead of looking for another job she spent her entire time trying to make Beloved happy. All the thirty-eight dollars of Sethe's life saving went in indulging Beloved with best of food and clothes. She always had the best of everything first, the best chair, the biggest piece, the prettiest plate, the brightest ribbon: "Anything she wanted she got, and when Sethe ran out of things to give her, Beloved invented desire." (240)

Initially Denver had set out defending Beloved, to see if any harm can come to her from Sethe, but she ends up defending her mother from Beloved. She watches Sethe's health deteriorate, overwhelmed by her guilt and her all-consuming love for Beloved. Beloved accuses her of leaving her behind, alone with the dead, of not smiling at her. Sethe bends down asking for forgiveness. She says she would give her life to take back just one of Beloved's tears. She tells her that when she was a baby she slept each day on her chest. Once or twice when Sethe tries to assert herself, Beloved slammed things, wiped the table clean of plates, threw salt on the floor and broke a windowpane. Denver thought she understood the connection between her mother and Beloved: "Sethe was trying to make up for the handsaw; Beloved was making her pay for it." (251)

Beloved becomes mean-spirited and exploits her mother's pain. Sethe gives her a number of explanations to show that her children are her "best thing." She tells her, how nothing was more important than getting her milk to her children, how it pained to see her baby bitten by a mosquito. She tries to explain to Beloved how slavery made it impossible for her to be the mother she wanted to be.

Starvation forces Denver out of her mother's porch. The first person she turns for help is Lady Jones. She requests her to help her in seeking a job. Lady Jones gives her some food, and recommends her to church committee, formed to prevent people from starving. Every now and then women dropped gifts of food at her doorstep. Denver in turn goes to thank them for their generosity. All of them knew her grandmother and some had even danced with her in the clearing. Denver turns to the Bodwins for finding work. She tells their housekeeper Janey how Beloved's presence plagued her mother.

The news soon spreads among the coloured community that Sethe's daughter, whose throat she had cut, had come back to revenge her and in fact threatened her life. A group of thirty black women come to her rescue. "For Sethe it was as though the clearing had come to her with all its heat and simmering leaves." (261) The singing women saw the devil-child standing in the shape of a pregnant woman, naked and smiling. At this moment, Bodwin, a white, comes to pick up Denver. Sethe and Denver run towards the singing women, leaving the ghost-child alone. The ghost-child, left alone, watches Sethe run "away from her to the pile of people out there. They make a hill." She is terrified at the sight of Bodwin, a "man without skin." (261)

Chapter 27

Beloved has disappeared from 124—she exploded right in front of the eyes of black women, the coloured women, who had come to the spiritual assistance of Sethe and to rescue Sethe from the ghost-child. At this moment, Bodwin, now Denver's employee, comes to pick her up. Sethe is terrified on seeing Bodwin's hat because she associates Bodwin with the schoolteacher. She forgets where she is and who he is, and tries to kill him. But Denver and a group of black women overpower her. Beloved too looks at Bodwin and sees him as a slave driver. Terrified, she disappears, "cutting through the woods, a naked woman with fish for hair." (267)

Paul D meets Denver, who has matured into a fine young woman, fending for herself and her mother. He learns of Sethe's illness and goes to meet her. Entering the house, he recalls his encounter with Beloved. "Coupling with her wasn't even fun. It was more like a brainless urge to stay alive. Each time she came and pulled up her skirts, a life hunger overwhelmed him and he had no more control over it than over his lungs." (624) He finds Sethe in Baby Sugg's bed. He is angry to see her dying, and shouts at her "Don't you die on me! . . . Is that what you are planning?" (271-72)

Sitting down near her in the rocking chair, Paul D recalls what Sixo had said of his thirty-mile woman: "she is a friend of my mind. She gather me, man. The pieces I am, she gather them and give them back to me in all the right order." (272-73) Paul D feels the same for Sethe—she is the only one who spared him his manhood. Close to her, he never felt the shame of being collared like a beast. He wanted to put his story next to hers. He bends down, takes her hand and tells her: "me and you, we got more yesterday than anybody. We need some kind of tomorrow." (273)

Chapter 28

Reclaiming the history of slavery and reconstruction through the story of Beloved, Morrison re-emphasizes the importance of Beloved, and thousands of such slaves whose story has gone unaccounted for. In the last chapter, she writes: "Everybody knew what she was called, but nobody anywhere knew her name. Disremembered and unaccounted for, she cannot be lost because no one is looking for her." (274)

Morrison repeats the line "It was not a story to pass on" thrice in the last chapter. This line contradicts what Morrison is saying in the first part of the chapter. Through this contradiction, Morrison wants to re-emphasize the pain involved in the process of rememory or rediscovery for the blacks whose history is a painful one. She calls Beloved's story "an unpleasant dream during a troubling sleep." (275)

After narrating the story in the 275 pages of the novel, Morrison repeatedly warns: "it is not a story to pass on." The repeated warning implies that the story cannot be rejected (forgotten or ignored) or passed over (overlooked). "Pass on" here signifies both rejection and acceptance.

Black Feminist Criticism and *Beloved*

Black women were brought to America to breed slaves, and to attend to the personal needs of slave holders, to care for their families and to work in the fields. Women of African descent have struggled with the reality of gender, racial and economic oppression. The autobiographies of black women are rich sources of their poignant, sensitive definitions of self and compelling expression of needs and ideals of black people. Black women's autobiographies and political writings have created an extraordinary body of literature. During the antebellum years, there were prominent abolitionists like Sojourner Truth and Harriet Tubman, who led a number of slaves to freedom. Their autobiographies throw light on black women's struggle for power and equality in America.

In the antebellum years, self-named and self-emancipated former slave Sojourner Truth is best recognized. Truth had a profound impact on the expanding notions of womanhood and delivered two significant speeches: in 1851 on "Women's Rights" and in 1867 "When Woman gets her Right, Man will be Right."[6] Another escaped slave, Harriet Tubman, a contemporary of Sojourner Truth, led thousands of slaves to freedom, through the underground railroad, before the war. She became the first American woman to lead black and white troops in battle when she headed the intelligence service department. She was often called "Black Moses," for leading black slaves from bondage to freedom.

The period of civil war, followed by military emancipation and campaigns of the nineteenth century in which black slave women played an important role, feminist literature was born. The slave narratives are rich and valid sources for study and critical enquiry into lives of black women. Harriet Jacob's novel *Incidents in the Life of a Slave Girl* and Francis E.W. Harper's *Iola Leroy* challenged Victorian notions of true womanhood and rigid social categories.

During the decades following Reconstruction, a new generation of African-American women was born. African-American women became chroniclers of society, politics and equality. In 1892, educator Anna Cooper published *A Voice from the South: By a Black Woman from the South.* She became one of the two black women delegates from the U.S to attend the first Pan-

African Congress held in 1900 in London. She later became principal of celebrated M. Street High School in Washington, D.C. Her contemporaries Ida B. Wells and Mary Church Ferell were important anti-lynching and anti-racist crusaders, who achieved international prominence. Their political speeches on the Negro question branded them as critical intellectuals and activists of their era.

The "Harlem Renaissance"[7] (1919-40) marked another milestone in black women's literary production. The works of Jessie Redmon Fauset, Nella Larsen and Zora Neale Hurston threw light on the issues of race, class, sex and colour. The era following the Second World War witnessed another boom in literary writings by black women. Experiments in literary tradition such as realism and modernism revealed to them another dimension of feminist interpretation. Important black women writers who experimented with this technique are short-story writer, novelist and editor Dorothy West, poet Gwendolyn Brooks whose *Annie Allen* won the Pulitzer in 1950. Playwright Lorraine Hansberry's play *A Raisin in the Sun* (1959) became the first play written by an African-American woman to debut on Broadway. Such creative endeavours helped to highlight the struggles of Black people and Black women, to the Americans and people outside America. The literary inventions and interventions of the 1920s through the 1950s co-existed with civil rights activism fostered by organisations like "National Association for the Advancement of Colored People" (NAACP) and "Southern Christian Leadership Council" (SCLC) headed by Dr. Martin Luther King, Jr.

The writings of Black women during the 1960s and 1970s highlight their socio-economic and political concerns. Although the words "black feminism" were rarely used, their writings raised questions and debates about black women's sexuality. Important writers of this period are Sonia Sanchez, June Jordan and Audre Lorde. Toni Cade edited *The Black Women: An Anthology* and Angela Davis wrote *Women, Race and Class.*

The political activities of black leaders and Civil Rights movement gave further boost to the black Arts Movement. This is evident in the wealth of African-American literary achievements, black studies and women studies programs which became an important part of university education by late 1970s and early 1980s. A flurry of writings by black women sought to correct the racial bias of black studies within and outside the academy. Important writers of this period are Toni Morrison, who published her first novel *The Bluest Eye*, Alice Walker wrote *In Search of Our Mother's Gardens: Womanist Prose* and *The Color Purple.* Bell Hooks wrote *Ain't I a Woman.* Gloria T. Hull, Patricia Bell Scott and Barbara Smith together edited an anthology *All the Women are White, All the Blacks are Men, But Some of Us are Brave: Black Women's Studies.* Barbara Smith edited another collection of Black women's writings: *Home Girls: A Black Feminist Anthology.*

In the 1980s, male academics promoted works by black women writers and Feminists. Important among them is Henry Louis Gates, Jr., who edited an anthology *Reading Black, Reading Feminist.* He introduced readers to relatively obscure women writers from nineteenth to mid-twentieth century who embodied black feminist sensibilities and politics.

The writings of black women generated a body of black feminist criticism. The theories of reading and notions of tradition were created by significant black feminist works like Barbara Christian's *Black Women Novelists: The Development of Tradition* (1892-1976), Mac Gwendolyn Henderson's "Speaking in Tongues," Barbara Smith's "Towards a Black Feminist Criticism" and Shirley Anne William's "Some Implications of Womanist Theory."

The noted author Alice Walker in the 1980s contrasted black feminism with white or Euro-Centric feminism, using the term "womanist" to render superfluous the adjective "black" for gender progressive "woman of color." She posited a culturally specific womanism that extends beyond women of African descent, but is different from dominant feminism of white (bourgeois) women.

In the mid to late 1990s, it became evident that varied ideological, cultural and literary contributions by black women belie any attempt to formulate a monolithic or homogenous black feminism. A diversity in outlook and writing, and lack of ideological uniformity despite shared concerns for racial and gender equality, gives this school of thought its complexity. Nevertheless, the influence of historical women on black feminism has proved enduring. As the "Combahee River Collective," a militant black feminist group, maintain in their 1977 Black feminist statement:

> There have always been Black woman activists—some known like Sojourner Truth, Harriet Tubman, Francis E.W Harper, Ida B. Wells Barnett and Mary Church Ferell, and thousands upon thousands unknown—who have shared awareness of how their sexual identity combined with their racial identity to make their whole life situation and the focus of their political struggle unique. Contemporary Black feminism is the outgrowth of countless generations of personal sacrifice, militancy and work by our mothers and sisters.[8]

Increasingly, new literature and activism explore black feminist contributions, creativity and ideological debates. Growing amid diverse tendencies and tensions, which fuel its insights, one cannot deny the significance of Black feminism as a tool for critical inquiry within American and global culture.

Beloved: A Feminist Perspective

Morrison, dedicating her novel *Beloved* "to sixty million or more," who failed to survive the "Middle Passage," sets out to give voice to "disremembered and unaccounted for"—the women and children who left no written records. The epigraph from Romans 9:25 prefigures the writer's purpose to reclaim the "lost tribe."

> I will call them my people,
> Which were not my people,
> And her beloved,
> Which was not beloved.

Mae G. Henderson points out: "In her citation of a 'New Testament' passage that repeats with little difference a passage from 'Old Testament,' the author not only problematizes the relationship between the past and present but also thematizes the importance of historical Reclamation and Repossession. As Jehovah reclaims the Israelites after their apostasy, so Morrison seeks to repossess the African and slave ancestors after their historic inflation (figured in *Beloved* as physical rape)."[9]

Morrison further elaborates this point in a conversation with Gloria Naylor. Morrison identifies the project which has dominated her own imaginative world as bringing to life of the "dead girl." This ongoing literary construction of black female identity has been part excavation, part recreation: "rescuing her from the grave of time and inattention . . .bringing her back to living life."[10] Clearly, Morrison is using her creative writing to bring the attention of people to issues of mothering and tensions between community and individuation.

Beloved is a novel that speaks multiply. It reflects the harsh reality of being a black mother and voices the positions of daughters, grandmothers, fathers, male friends, neighbours, community and the mother herself. Sethe's actions are measured and weighed against numerous atrocities and destructions and possible responses to them. The text therefore deliberately centres on the historical fact that there were black women during slavery who suffocated their babies rather than allow them to be offered up to destruction by slavery. In other words, the spectre of Beloved, the living embodiment of Sethe's mother love and painful past of enslavement which she represents is never really destroyed. That past is allowed to dissolve into mythology and history of the community. Read as Morrison's bringing to life of "the dead girl," then she will manifest herself elsewhere.

Morrison draws the attention of people to the crucial position of black women in the U.S. In an interview with Nellie Y. Mckay, she says:

> I think black women are in a very special position regarding black feminism as advantageous one, white women generally define black women's role as the most repressed because they are both black and female, and these two categories invite a kind of repression that is pernicious. But in an interesting way, black women are much more suited to aggressiveness in the mode that feminists are recommending, because they have always been both mothers and

> laborers, mother and worker and the history of black women in the states is an extremely painful and unattractive one but there are parts of that history that were conducive to doing more rather than less, in the days of slavery. We think of slave women as women in the house, but they were not, most of them worked in the fields along with the men. They were required to do physical labor in competition with them, so that their relations with each other turned out to be more comradeship than male dominance/female subordination. When they were in the field plowing or collecting cotton or doing whatever the owner or slaves didn't care. Whether they were women or men—the punishment they have varied: they could beat both, rape one, so that women could receive punishment but the requirements were the same, the physical work requirements.[11]

What Morrison does in *Beloved* is that she unearths at the excavation site "the silenced voice" of the black slave woman, whose story more often has been told by the black male narrator whose focus was primarily upon his journey to wholeness. The women who appear are not mere fixtures; through them the horrors of slavery are unravelled. The structure of the novel foregrounds the ambivalences of slave women about motherhood which violates their personal integrity and that of their family. Foregrounding the theme of motherhood, Morrison divides the text into twenty-eight unnumbered, mini-sections, the usual number of days in a woman's monthly menstrual cycle.

Beloved develops the idea that maternal bonds can harm a woman's sense of self. The book both thematizes and problematizes the conflict between history, culture and maternal instincts. Morrison said in a national broadcast after receiving the Pulitzer Prize: "motherhood is not history. It is a timeless, a historical force with all the glories and limitations that pure nature imposes, even when colored, camouflaged by its many cultural versions."[12]

With *Beloved*, Morrison probes deeper into the psychological effects of missing mother-infant bond and unearths the psychological damage of slavery to the mother-child relationship. Hortense Spillers in an essay appropriately titled "Mama's Baby, Papa's Maybe! An American Grammar Book" quotes Meillassoux who contends that "femininity loses its sacredness in slavery." Spillers points out that for African-Americans

1. motherhood as female blood site is outraged, is denied at the very same time that it becomes the founding term of human and social enactment
2. a dual fatherhood is set in motion, comprised of the African father's banished name and body and the captor father's mocking presence. In this play of paradox, only the female stands in the flesh, both mother and mother dispossessed. This problematizing of gender places her, in my view, out of the traditional symbolics of female gender, and it is our task to make a place for this different social subject.[13]

Beloved provides an insight into the structure and working of the plantocracy that denied a woman her basic human and political rights. In committing her brutal act, Sethe believed she was sparing the child from the "unspeakable" fate to which most female slaves were heiress. The slave women were not recognized as mothers having bonds with their children but considered only "breeders" and workers. Their slave owners had no scruples about selling children away from their mothers. The infant children could be sold away from them like calves and cows.

Beloved is characterized by mothers losing their children: Sethe's mother-in-law barely glanced at last of her eight children, "because it wasn't worth the trouble." (139) Baby Suggs asks Sethe to be thankful to have all her children with her, and also of the fact that all her children had been fathered by the same man. "Be thankful why don't you? I had eight. Everyone of them gone away from me." (5) Sethe's own mother was hanged when Sethe was a small child, and she had not been allowed to nurse Sethe. Even eighteen years after her escape, Paul D recognized that Sethe's mother love is risky. "For a used to be slave woman to love anything was dangerous especially if it was her children she had settled on to love." (45)

In the community of former slaves, there is Ella who spent her puberty locked in a house and shared by a father and son whom she called "the lowest yet." (256) Ella had been "beaten every way but down . . . she had delivered, but would not nurse, a hairy white thing fathered by the lowest yet." Ella's rejection of enforced motherhood is echoed in Sethe's faint memory of her own mother's life, a woman she hardly knew, the only sign of recognition she could recall being the brand in her flesh. The woman's story stretches back to the horrors she experienced during the "Middle Passage." She and the woman Nan bore children to the crew on the ship and to other white men but "threw them all away," (62) keeping only Sethe, the child she conceived with the black man she loved.

So Ella and Sethe's mother did exercise choice of some sort, one that provokes in Sethe a wave of anger and shame she cannot comprehend. Thus Sethe's definition of motherhood is a defiant answer to slavery's brutal destruction of maternal connections. It was to avoid a future in slavery for her children that led Sethe to plan escape and to get her milk to her baby, she sent ahead with the other children—that made her attempt it alone. She experiences having her milk stolen from her by the nephews of her slave master as the ultimate brutality, even worse than the savage beating she received just before escaping.

When Beloved comes back to pass judgement on Sethe, and Sethe realizes that Beloved is the ghost of her third child, she wants desperately to make her understand that she tried to kill her babies so that they would be protected from captivity forever. Sethe assumes that Beloved will forgive her but the latter does not do so. Beloved becomes mean-spirited and exploits her mother's pain. Sethe gives Beloved story after story of her love and devotion to her. She tells her how nothing was more important than getting her milk to her, how she waved flies away from her in the grape arbour, how it pained her to see her baby bitten by a mosquito, and how she would trade her own life for Beloved's. Sethe tries to impress upon her how slavery made it impossible for her to be the mother she wanted to be.

Morrison interweaves racial and sexual consciousness in *Beloved.* The structure and style of the text foregrounds the ambivalence of slave women about motherhood that violates their personal integrity and that of their family. It shows their desire to be complete individuals. To conclude, one can say that Beloved is a ghost story that frames embedded narratives of the impact of slavery, racism and sexism on the capacity for love, faith and community of black families, especially the black women, during slavery and Reconstruction period.

Self-Discovery and the Role of History and Community

Black theorists like Henry Louis Gates have discussed the theoretical basis of black literature. His work has placed in new light a tired issue: what distinguishes black literary production in America from other literary works? He positions the question saying: "Can it be a legitimate exercise to translate theories drawn from a literary tradition that has often been perpetuated by white males who represent blacks in their fiction as barely human, if they deem it necessary to figure blacks at all? Aren't we justified in being suspicious of a discourse in which blacks are signs of absence?"[14] The question from this view becomes not how African-American literary production distinguishes itself from other forms, but rather how given socio-historical conditions which are compelling it towards silence, the literature manages to speak at all. Gates in *Figures in Black* and *Signifying Monkey* looks at ways in which linguistic structures at once mask and reveal the social and political structures from which they arise and which they create.

The problem for black writers, as Gates points out, is to use a language in which blackness signifies absence, and then to write about their own 'blackness' as a source of identity. Gates has finally come to argue that black writers have had to digest both western and non-western forms of literary production. Out of this process they forge a literary discourse that transforms notions of blackness. Rafael Perez Torres points out:

> The blackness of a black literary text, historically read to signify a lack in western discourse, becomes in Morrison's hands an important thread tying together something, all too disparate reclaims of politics and aesthetics. The 'not' signified by blackness becomes for Morrison a means by which to weave her tale. A process of interpretation and reinterpretation in *Beloved* serves to form an 'is' out of 'nots'; helps to unite the tangled threads by which Morrison

> knits together her novel. *Beloved* challenges us to rethink the relationship between post-modern and marginal to bind together the seemingly separate cultural realms. The novel forces us to retrace the distinct threads of historically marginal that colour the weave of post-modern culture.[15]

Morrison is both participant and theorist of black aesthetic of remembering, and her works have laid down the mandates for establishing a form of literary theory that will truly accommodate African-American literature. A theory based on an inherited 'culture,' and inherited 'history' and one can understand the relationship between any artistic work and the cultural and historical world that it inhabits.

Morrison had assumed that *Beloved* would be the least read of her novels because it deals with slavery, an institution that is willingly placed under erasure by what she calls a "national amnesia." Morrison says: "I thought this had got to be the least read of all the books I'd written because it is about something that characters don't want to remember, I don't want to remember, black people don't want to remember, white people don't want to remember. But *Beloved* is not about slavery as an institution, it is about those anonymous people called slaves."[16]

Morison's sense of ambivalence of wishing to forget and remember at the same time is enacted in her attitude to the story and its characters. Speaking about the writing of *Beloved*, she declares her wish to invoke all those people who are "unburied" or at least unceremoniously buried. However this burial-purpose, it would appear, is to bring them back into 'living life.' This tension between needing to bury the past as well as needing to revive it, between a necessary remembering and an equally necessary forgetting exists in both the author and her narrative.

Despite the dangers of remembering the past, African-American artists have insistently based a large part of their aesthetic ideal on precisely that activity. As Morrison puts it, "if we don't keep in touch with the ancestor—we are, in fact lost." Keeping in touch with the ancestor, she adds, "is the work of a reconstructive memory. Memory (the deliberate act of remembering) is the form of willed creation. It is not an effort to find out the way it really was—the point is to dwell on the way it appeared and why it appeared in that particular way. Eventually, her work, she states, must bear witness and identify that which is useful form, that past and that which ought to be discarded."[17]

The story of *Beloved*, according to Morrison, was inspired by "two or three fragments of stories" that she had "heard from different places." The first was the story of Margaret Garner, a slave, who in January 1856 escaped from her owner Archibald K. Gaines of Kentucky, crossed the Ohio river, and attempted to find refuge in Cincinnati. She was pursued by Gaines and a posse of officers. They surrounded the house where she, her husband Robert, and their four children lived. At this moment, Margaret Garner seized a butcher's knife that lay on the table, and with one stroke cut the throat of her little daughter, whom she probably loved the best. Margaret Garner chose death for both herself and her most beloved rather than accepting a return to slavery, and have her children suffer institutionalized dehumanization. The story of Margaret Garner was eventually to become the historical analogue of the plot of *Beloved.*

What Morrison does is to pick this historical personage—a faintly famous African-American victim of racist ideology and construct her as a hopeful presence in a contemporary setting. Morrison makes us rethink American history from the point of view of slaves. She makes articulate a victim of patriarchal order in order to criticize that order. Yet she portrays an unrelenting hopefulness in that critique. And she does not reduce her narrative to anything resembling what Henry Louis Gates, Jr. has called a "master plot of victim and victimiser."[18] She, like Alex Haley, returns to history not to find claims for separation or reason for despair, but to find something subjective and complexly and compellingly human. What Morrison does according to Ashraf. A. Rushdy is: "Construct(ing) and reconstruct(ing) repertoires of usage out of the most painful human/historical experience. In articulating a reconstructive—critical and hopeful—feminist voice within the field of revisionist historiography and contemporary fiction—what Morrison does is create daughters signifyin(g) history."[19]

In *Beloved,* Morrison goes further in giving the dead voice in remembering the forgotten. *Beloved* symbolizes the resurrection of dead spirit. Beloved in the novel is the ghost of Margaret Garner's unnamed child. Morrison says: "So I just imagined the life of a dead girl, which was the girl that Margaret Garner killed, the baby girl that she killed—And I called her Beloved so that I can filter all those confrontations and questions that she has in that situation."[20] Beloved is more than just a character in the novel, she is the embodiment of the past that must be remembered in order to be forgotten. She symbolizes what must be reincarnated in order to be buried properly. Morrison says: "Everybody knew what she was called, but nobody anywhere knew her name. Disremembered and unaccounted for, she cannot be lost because no one is looking for her."[21]

Beloved contributes to black American history which is being recovered and written. The debate currently ranges between those who argue that slavery led to the 'infantilisation' of adult Africans but the most significant relationship in any slave life was that between the slave and master, and those who argue that slaves formed viable internal communities, family structures, and protective personae that allow them to live rich, coherent lives within their own system of values. One premise underlying this debate is the question whether slaves were acquiescent or resistant to the institution, whether they confirmed to the 'Sambo' or 'Mammy' stereotypes or whether they were in perpetual opposition to them. It is within this revisionary fray that *Beloved* may profitably be examined. The novel both remembers the victimization of ex-slaves and asserts the healing wholeness in their communal lives.

This novel uses the conception of history derived from call and the response patterns and the communal nature of art, that is an important part of Black American tradition. In contrast to master versions of history, which erroneously present themselves as independent of the makers, and so any particular perspective, the history created in *Beloved* both emphasizes the importance of perspective and requires the articulation of multiple perspective. As Maggie Sale points out: "Because it is performative in nature and community based, this kind of hi(story) depends upon the repeated interaction of one and many, recognition, authority and responsibility. For this hi(story) not only requires but relish audience participation, the contributions of many tellers (writers) and listeners (readers)."[22]

These principles from African-American oral traditions have a powerful effect when used to evoke the sense of an enslaved past. *Beloved*'s black characters are by and large "illiterate." The Sweet Home men are not interested in learning how to read because "nothing important to them could be put down on paper." Others can write only their names, Sethe can recognize seventy-five written words, only Stamp Paid, Lady Jones and eventually Denver can actually read. The picture of Sethe accompanying the newspaper article detailing her crime is emblematic of how the majority of African-Americans in the nineteenth century were objects of writing, rather than its producers and consumers. *Beloved* cannot be said to recreate the 'actual' oral traditions of the enslaved African-Americans. But Morrison uses these principles in her representations of an enslaved and formerly enslaved past. These principles are, in some form, descendants of African and enslaved cultures. Morrison, while using these forms, is creating a text, and a sense of the past that are, in her words, "irrevocably indisputably black."[23]

A number of elements from these oral traditions influence the narrative strategies and thematics of *Beloved*, and significant among them are the ways in which call and response patterns are "translated into print." According to Maggie Sale, "call and response patterns are both structure and the theme of Sethe and Beloved's relationship. Sethe's guilt, which she acknowledges, only to her murdered child, keeps that alive and eventually calls her back into the physical world. Beloved calls Sethe to account once Sethe realizes who she is, and Sethe responds endlessly but uselessly, since the healing response is not reciprocal."[24]

When Sethe and Beloved become locked in a narrowing spiral, that threatens to destroy the mother even as it feeds the child, Denver leaves her self-imposed exile, calling the women of the community, who respond with food and later with spiritual assistance. When considered on a larger frame, "call and response patterns are related to audience (reader) participation in that the text suggests or calls implicitly asking for a response. One example is how stories are left unfinished or unclarified. We never learn exactly what happened to Halle, either before Sethe was attacked or afterwards, or what happened to Howard and Buglar—or even finally to Beloved."[25]

But in the cases such as Sethe's sons, one feels there is no participation on the part of the reader because the boys leave the narrative ambiguously and speculation is not called for. But Morrison's representations of Beloved invite readers to respond, to think over her appearance, her disappearance and her symbolic being which gives meaning to this text. Morrison's representations of Sethe and her act of infanticide challenge the reader to examine their own responses to this event and circumstances surrounding it. "Beloved presents and clarifies social problems without resolving them, and so raises, or calls out, issues to be discussed or to be responded to by readers or the community. This call for communal response is part of the contemporary healing process that this text is involved in."[26]

For those who were specifically oppressed by the nineteenth century ideology of white supremacy, traditional and "mainstream representations of slavery have continued the legacy oppression by distorting and ignoring their experiences. *Beloved* grows out of and joins with a contemporary movement begun by scholars such as John Blassingame and Herbert Gutman to shift the terms of representations of slavery by re-envisioning this vexed past from the perspective of the enslaved.

Beloved should also be seen as entering into contemporary dialogue, this complex call and response—all of which respond not only to the negative stereotyping of African-American in the traditional histories of slavery, but also to the lack of attention paid specifically to the importance of gender and the experience of the enslaved women in the first wave of revisionist histories. Like other revisionist projects of the past two decades, *Beloved* shifts the terms of representation by moving those marginalized by traditional "mainstream' histories to the centre, and forcing those traditionally at the centre to the margins.

Narrative Technique in *Beloved*

Morrison in her writings privileges all the important aesthetic traditions of African-American writings which she details in the following passage:

> If my work is faithfully to reflect the aesthetic tradition of Afro-American culture, it must make conscious use of the characteristics of its art forms and translate them into print: antiphony the group nature of art, its functionality, its improvisational nature, its relationship to audience performance.[27]

Maggie Sale points out that "the characteristics listed here are aspects of African-American oral traditions and are interrelated rather than discrete. Antiphony or call and response, function improvisation and audience performance can all be thought of as part of group or communal nature of art."[28] Morrison's theory of art is interactive or process oriented. "Call and response" patterns that thrive on audience performance ensure that the art will be meaningful and functional to the community. For Maggie Sale, "*Beloved* is an oral text shaped by the principles outlined above, with a special emphasis on improvisation and call and response patterns. Such a reading goes beyond the vexed question of authorial intent—i.e., reading *Beloved* the way that Morrison says that we should—by showing the importance of incorporating the above stated principles of African-American oral traditions into ways of thinking about history and systems of critical inquiry. *Beloved* not only presents 'new' perspectives but foregrounds the power and problematic of perspective itself. This text suggests a complex method of reading and interpreting . . . refusing the problematic notion that all positions are equally valid."[29]

Call and response patterns, developed in spirituals and play and work songs of the slaves are related to the group or communal nature of art. These characteristics suggest that importance lies not only in what is said, but also in how it is said. The assumption is that a story will be repeated and will change with every telling. And so the significance of a particular story resides not so much in its similarity to the original, as to its individual nuances and its ability to involve others. Improvisation shows how well he or she recreates the story to fit individual and group needs. Such a theory of art demands and values change over continuity, within a given, agreed upon structure.

Beloved is unique as far as the linguistic expression is concerned. As pointed out earlier, it has made use of both oral and written discourses. The narrative voice shifts from third person narration to omniscient narration to interior monologue. There is a constant repetition of words, phrases and passages. The metaphors of personal and communal wholeness in the text heighten the psychological realism of its womanist themes of black kinship, motherhood, sisterhood and love. Besides, the structural analogue to a woman's natural reproductive cycle (there are twenty-eight chapters in the book equal to the days in a menstrual cycle), the text frequently highlights metaphors and metonyms for agony and ecstasy, despair and hope of loving, birthing, nurturing, bonding (heart, breasts, milk, butter, water and trees).

The structure of *Beloved* is designed by Morrison in a way that it matches form with substance. On one hand, the novel's inscription "Sixty million and more," gives us a framework for analyzing the text: sixty million or more stands for the Africans who perished during the middle passage and whose names and identities remain unknown. The number sixty million refers to a theft of sizable portion. The writer wants us to see African people as a collective. We are introduced to unmarked chapters throughout a Morrison novel. The absence of passages, dates and numbers reflects a negation of time in regard to African people.

Another skilful structural device that Morrison uses to reflect the unchanging status of African people is the repetition of key words, phrases or sentences. Sometimes whole chapters take up where the preceding ones left off. On page 209, the chapter ends with the lines: "she is mine, Beloved, she's mine." The next chapter which begins on page 210 uses a similar sentence construction and utilizes three of the same words: "I AM BELOVED and she is mine."

Within chapters, Morrison uses repetition to achieve structural coherence as well as to reflect, thematically, the African's unchanging reality. Also, from the traditional African perspective, time is cyclic, not linear as in Western culture. The past, present and future merge into one continuum, allowing African people to move forward and backward in time as they please and allowing their 'dead' ancestors to remain among them as guiding forces. Baby Suggs in this novel is remembered through the consciousness of Sethe, Denver, Paul D and Stamp Paid as a preacher who taught the gospel of love. The women of her community too recognize her role as a preacher and their saviour who taught them to love their bodies.

Just as thematically the character of Beloved represents isolation, chaos and disunity, so structurally the sections in the novel that describe her thoughts are symbolic of isolation, chaos and disunity. Her words are out of order or important words are omitted altogether (tell me your earrings) and her names for things are incorrect (your woman, she never fix up your hair). Words are not capitalized, and whole passages are left unpunctuated. Furthermore, when Beloved becomes the dominant force at 124, Bluestone, communication takes on the unnatural form of disintegrated thoughts. The use of disconnected statements, simulates the unnatural state of affairs that exist at 124.

> In the beginning I would see her   I could not help her because the clouds were in the way   in the beginning I could see her   the shining in her ears   she does not like the circle around her neck   I know this   I look hard at her so she will know clouds are in the way. (211)

Gates in *Black Literature and Literary Theory* points out that the signifyin(g) of black narratives—the linguistic playing, punning, coding, decoding and recoding found in African-American texts—emerges from the pressing necessity for political, social and economic survival: "Black people have always been masters of the figurative: saying one thing to mean something quite other, has been basic to black survival in oppressive western cultures. Misreading signs could be and indeed often was fatal. 'Reading' in this sense, was not play, it was an essential aspect of the 'literacy' training of a child. This sort of metaphorical literacy, the learning to decipher codes, is just about the blackest aspect of black tradition."[30]

For example, the reader is told several times that Beloved's story "is not a story to pass on." The repeated warning implies that the story cannot be rejected (forgotten or ignored) or "passed on." "Pass on" signifies both rejection and acceptance.

Beloved reflects Morrison's skill in bringing to life the facts about slavery. It shows Morrison's adeptness at correcting myths about slavery, the foremost of which is that slave life for some was good. Slavery was slavery, on Sweet Home, as well as any other plantation. Baby Suggs testifies to this truism when Mr. Garner takes her to the European abolitionists, the Bodwins, after she is bought out of slavery by her son Halle. Mr. Garner's attempts to distinguish himself from the collective of slaveholders is regarded as hypocritical distinction:

> "Tell em, Jenny. You live any better on any place before mine?"
>
> "No, sir," she said. "No place."
>
> "How long was you at Sweet Home?"
>
> "Ten years, I believe."
>
> "Ever go hungry?"
>
> "No, sir."
>
> "Cold?"
>
> "No Sir."
>
> "Anybody lay a hand on you?"
>
> "No, Sir."
>
> "Did I let Halle buy you or not?"
>
> "Yes, sir, you did," she said thinking. "But you got my boy and I'm all broke down. You be renting him out to pay for me way after I'm gone to Glory." (146)

Not only were conditions in slavery quantitatively indistinguishable, no matter whether you had a "good" master or a "bad" master, but also, in or out of slavery. Baby Suggs, a free slave, feels that life for her has been a continuous cycle of oppression: "Her past has been like her present—intolerable." For a 'free African-American living in a slave society,' life is not qualitatively different either.

Morrison shows how lack of communication is the cause of major disasters in any community. The African community does not warn Baby Suggs and Sethe of slave trapper's approach. ("Not Ella, not John, not anybody ran down to Bluestone Road, to say some new white folks with the look rode in"). Sethe does not tell Denver the reason for her murder of Beloved. ("All the time, I'm afraid, the thing that happened that made it right for my mother to kill my sister could happen again" [205]), and neither does Sethe ask the community for help once she is released from the jail. (She returned their disapproval with the potent pride of the mistreated." [96])

On the other hand, communication, the sharing of ideas through the word, creates unity in the novel. Songs, gestures and signs of slaves, the word from Hi Man as well as Baby Suggs speaking of the word. Dorothea Drummond Mbalia comments: "It is as if Morrison is advising African people to speak the word of their common history, their common plight, their common struggle, their common destiny. And she matches her theory with practice because it is through her 'Word' that Africans become a more conscious people."[31]

Describing the nineteenth century slave narratives, Morrison has said: "no slave society in the history of the world wrote more or thought more fully about its own enslavement."[32] At the same time, Morrison commenting upon *Beloved* reveals a repression in the minds of characters, a desire to put a veil on their intolerable lives. Morrison's task in this novel is to move that veil aside in order to penetrate the memories within. These memories—personal and collective—constitute the background of her work. She makes the readers and the characters realize the importance of their unwritten interior life.

Like Morrison, the principal characters in *Beloved* are in struggle with a past that is part of white/male historical discourse. Sethe's task in the novel is to transform the rememories of her past into a historical discourse. Lacking a discourse of her own, Sethe's task is to transform the residual images (re-memories) of her past into a historical discourse, by narrating these stories. These images, however, remain for a time disembodied—without form, sequence or meaning. We see that the challenge of the slave as victim of enforced illiteracy is similar to that of the highly literate contemporary historian or novelist—and that is to discover a way of organizing memory, of contriving a narrative configuration in the absence of written records. If it is true, as Henry Louis Gates, Jr. argues, that our sense of the self, as we have defined it in the West since the Enlightenment, "turns in part upon written records," if "our idea of the self . . . is . . . inextricably interwoven with our idea . . . of (writing)," then what are the consequences of an absence of written records. Quite simply and perhaps startlingly, as a slave "one's sense of one's existence . . . dependent upon memory." It was memory, above all else," according to Gates, "that gave shape to being itself."[33] Like Morrison, Sethe must learn to represent the unspeakable and unspoken memories in language.

Morrison uses the trope of memory to revise the genre of the slave narratives and thereby makes the slave experience it inscribes more accessible to the contemporary readers. In other words, she uses memory as the metaphor or sign of the psychological realities of slave life, and to explore and represent dimensions of slave life that the classic slave narratives have omitted. By doing so, she seeks to make slavery accessible to readers for whom slavery is not a memory, but a remote historical fact to be ignored, repressed or forgotten.

Through the trope of memory, Morrison moves into the psychic consequences of slavery for women who, by their very existence, were both the means and the source of production. In the words of the text, the slave woman was "property that reproduced itself without cost." The text of *Beloved* moves through a series of narrative starts and stops that are complicated by Sethe's desire to forget or "disremember" the past. Thus, at the same time that the reader seeks to know "the how and why" of Sethe's infanticide, Sethe seeks to withhold that information not only from every-one else, but even from herself. Thus, the early sections of the novel reveal the complex ways in which memories of the past disrupt Sethe's concerted attempt to forget.

Throughout the novel, there are similar passages that signal the narrative tension between remembering and forgetting. At various points in the text, a single phrase, a look or the most trivial incident rivets Sethe's attention to the very details of the past she is ready to confront. In the words of the text, "she worked hard to remember as close to nothing was safe." At another place, the text refers to Sethe's "serious work of beating back the past." (173) Moreover, a mindless task such as folding clothes takes on grave significance, as the following passage suggests: "she had to do something with her hands because she was remembering something she had forgotten she knew, something privately shameful that had seeped into a slit in her mind." (61)

The meaning of Morrison's complex use of trope of memory becomes clearer in what many readers regard as the most poetic passage in the text. These passages appear in the section two of the novel where we have a series of interior monologues that become a dialogue among the three central female characters: the first is Sethe's, the second is Denver's, the third is Beloved's and the last one is a merging of all three.

> Beloved
> You are my sister
> You are my daughter
> You are my face; You are mine
> I have found you again, you have come to back to me
> You are my Beloved.
> You are mine. (216)

One can conclude that Morrison has managed to write a "Black book" which uses the African-American traditions. *Beloved* is unique in bringing to life the significance of oral literature she privileges a group nature of art, her use of "call and response" pattern calls for an "effective and participatory" relationship on the part of audience. An extremely painful and unattractive history of black women in America is passed on to the readers in an interesting fashion. Importance of Black literature lies in creating an acute sense of consciousness among Black people against social injustice. Thus it raises a demand for the recognition and redress of their genuine grievances.

NOTES

1. Toni Morrison, *Beloved* (U.K.: Vintage, 1967), p. 61.
2. Marc C. Conner, *The Aesthetics of Toni Morrison* (U.S.A.: University Press of Mississippi, 2000), p. 43.
3. Marsha Darling, "In the Realm of Responsibility: A Conversation with Toni Morrison," *Women's Review of Books* (U.S.A., 1998), p. 6.
4. Maggie Sale, "Call and Response as Critical Method: African-American Oral Traditions and *Beloved*," *African-American Review*, vol. 26, no. 1, 1992.
5. Valerie Smith, *Toni Morrison: Critical Perspectives: Past and Present*, ed. Gates and Appiah (New York: Amistad Press, 1993), p. 348.
6. Sojurner Truth's speeches are reprinted in Beverly Guy Sheftall, ed., *Words of Fire: An Anthology of African-American Feminist Thought* (New York: The New Press, 1995), pp. 36-38.
7. In 1926, a renaissance in the arts created by a group of writers calling themselves "New Negroes and Centered in and about Harlem," was at its zenith. Wealthy white patrons and mainstream New York publishers were sponsoring young black writers as never before. Civil rights and political leaders had come to believe that it would be through arts that full social, political and eventually economic liberation for black elite would come.
8. Combahee-River Collective, "Black Feminist Statements," in Gloria T. Hull, Patricia Bell Scott, and Barbara Smith, ed., *All the Women are White, All the Blacks are men, But Some of Us are Brave: Black Women Studies* (Westbury, New York: Feminist Press, 1982), p. 273.
9. Mae G. Henderson, "Toni Morrison's *Beloved*: Re-Membering the Body as Historical Text," *Comparative American Identities: Race, Sex and Nationality in the Modern Text*, ed. Hortense Spillers, (New York: Routledge, 1991).

10. Daily Brenda and Maureen T. Reddy, *Narrating Mothers: Theorizing Maternal Subjectivities* (Knoxville: University of Tennessee Press, 1991), p. 45.
11. Toni Morrison in an interview with Rosemarie K. Lester in Nellie Y. Mckay, *Critical Essays on Toni Morrison* (U.S.A.: Library of Congress Cataloging, 1988), pp. 48-49.
12. Stephanie A. Demetra quotes Morrison in "Maternal Bonds as Devourers of Women's Individuation in Toni Morrison's *Beloved*," *African-American Review*, vol. 26, No. 1, 1992.
13. Hortense J. Spillers, "Mama's Baby, Papa's Maybe," Joy-James and T. Denean Sharpley-Whitling, *The Black Feminist Reader* (U.S.A.: Blackwell, 2000), p. 76.
14. Henry Louis Gates, Jr., *Figures in Black: Words, Signs and the 'Racial' Self* (New York: Oxford University Press, 1987).
15. Linden Peach, qtd. Rafael P. Torrez, "Knitting and Knotting Narrative Threads: *Beloved* as Postmodern Novel," *New Casebooks: Toni Morrison* (London: Macmillan, 1998).
16. Bonnie Angleo in an interview with Morrison, "The Pain of Being Black: An Interview," *Times*, 22 May, pp. 48-50.
17. *Ibid.*
18. Henry Louis Gates, Jr., "Introduction," *Reading Black, Reading Feminist: A Critical Anthology* (New York, 1990), p. 16.
19. Linden Peach, qtd. Ashraf A Rushdy, "Daughters Signifying History," *New Casebooks: Toni Morrison.*
20. Mervyn Rothstein, "Toni Morrison in her New Novel Defends Women," *New York Times*, August 26, 1987, p. 17.
21. *Ibid.*
22. Maggie Sale, qtd.
23. Toni Morrison, qtd., "Rootedness: The Ancestor as Foundation," *Black Woman Writers*, ed. Mari Evans (Garden City: Anchor, 1984), p. 339.
24. Maggie Sale, qtd.
25. *Ibid.*
26. *Ibid.*
27. Robert B. Stepto, "'Intimate Things in Place': A Conversation with Toni Morrison," *Massachusetts Review*, vol. 8 (1977), pp. 473-89.
28. Maggie Sale, p. 41.
29. *Ibid.*
30. Henry Louis Gates, Jr., ed., *Black Literature and Literary Theory* (New York: Methuen, 1984).

31. Dorothea Drummond Mbalia, *Toni Morrison: Developing Class Consciousness* (U.S.A.: Associated University Press, 1991), p. 102.
32. Toni Morrison, "Site of Memory," *Inventing the Truth: The Art and Craft of Memoir*, ed. William Zinsser (Boston: Houghton-Mifflin, 1987), pp. 109-10.
33. Henry Louis Gates, Jr., "Fredrick Douglass and the Languages of Self," *The Yale Review*, vol. 70, No. 4 (July 1981).

Emergence of African American Literature and Toni Morrison

K. SUMANA

The comprehensive article by K. Sumana is divided into seven parts. The first part talks about how the hegemony of masculine perspective is challenged by Black women's literature. The second part traces the development of the tradition of black novelists like Francis Harper, Jessie Fauset, Nella Larsen and Ann Petry who present a tradition of heroines who want to pass for white. There is a considerable shift in black women's writing with Zora Neale Hurston, Gwendolyn Brooks, Paule Marshall and Alice Walker who dwell on a black woman's struggle with white values. The third part talks of the struggle of black women against triple oppression of racism, sexism and classism, upon which the societal definition of black women is based. The fourth part outlines the themes and concerns of all major black women novelists and their works. The fifth part talks of Morrison's family background, her development as a writer and her indebtedness to various African and African American writers who shaped her thought. The sixth part gives a brief account of the novels and critical essays written by Morrison. The last part focuses on how Morrison's writings combine her political commitment with aesthetic responsibility. She uses all the characteristics of black art, black music and black village and community life.

Editor

The Act of writing requires a constant plunging back into the shadow of the past where time hovers ghostlike.

Ralph Ellison, *Shadow and Act*

To read is to find meaning and to find meaning is to name them; but these named meanings are swept away toward further names; names invoke each other. . I name, I unname, I rename.

Ronald Barthes, *s/z*

In his now famous essay, "Blueprint for Negro Literature," Richard Wright asserts that a Marxist black male-oriented aesthetic and politic against racism and capitalism should be the all consuming perspective of the Negro writer.[1] Accordingly, the central character in all his novels and stories is a young black male, ensnared in the nightmare of a white racist, capitalistic world. Furthermore, the masculine perspective itself, concerning the manhood of the black race, has always occupied centre stage in the drama of African-American literature. The African-American male writers have been machoistic in their treatment of black women as fully debased creatures, evil castrates and immoral beings. They also portrayed black women as sex objects or merely an extension of the male ego with no autonomous individual self. In other words, black male writers have been no different from their white counterparts in their treatment of black women.

It is this hegemony of the masculine perspective, along with its male-centered aesthetic, that is now being challenged in and through the writings of Black American women. Black women in America being at once black, female and poor, have been victimized by the mountains of racism, sexism, and capitalism, not only from the white world but also from the men of the black world. Black women are bearers of what Barbara Smith calls "geometric oppression."[2] They are, therefore, bearers of a triple consciousness—race, gender and class.

Small wonder, therefore, if a black feminist perspective pervades contemporary African-American literature. Happily, the perspective governs the aesthetic and the aesthetic informs the landscape and the vision. The status of the black women writers is no longer relegated below the status of the males. Instead of being secondary to the literary dominance of black males, the literature of black women is expansive and, what is more, liberating. Unlike in the past when women were supposed to be seen but not heard, the women of today are recognized writers in all fields and genres. Most importantly, black women are dealing with the political machinations of the racial and sexual beliefs, feelings and actions that black men writers have maintained towards black females, in the street, in the family, and in the bedroom. Their perspective, which is consistent with the aesthetic, is faithful to the actual experiences of black women in America. As a result, we have in their works a woman-to-woman approach rather than a woman-to-man approach. It is, in brief, a black feminist aesthetic in which the form, language, syntax, sequence and metaphoric rendering of experience are markedly different and expansive in comparison to the male-authored literature. This can be meaningfully witnessed in the works of Toni Morrison, the richly deserving recipient of the Nobel Prize for literature for 1993.

Toni Morrison is, perhaps, the most formally sophisticated novelist in the history of African-American literature, whose work has been described as "amazingly high." She astutely describes aspects of the blacks' lives and especially of blacks as the people they are. There are many writers who are willing to describe the ugliness of the world as ugly, but the uniqueness of Toni Morrison lies in revealing the beauty and the hope beneath the surface of black America. Combining the aims of the Black Freedom Movement and Women's Liberation, she seeks to produce literature which is irrevocably and indisputably black. But the artistic excellence of Morrison's fiction lies in achieving a balance between writing a truly black literature and writing what is truly universal literature. Although firmly grounded in the cultural heritage and social concerns of black Americans, her work transcends narrowly prescribed conceptions of ethnic literature, exhibiting universal mythic patterns and overtones. To put it in Faulkner's phrase, her novels "grieve on universal bones."

The signal accomplishment of Toni Morrison as a writer is that she has managed uncannily to invert her own mode of literary representation. Her themes are often those expected of naturalist fiction—the burdens of history, the determining social effects of race, gender or class—but they are also the great themes of lyrical modernism—love, death, betrayal, and burden of individual responsibility for her or his own fate. Like Golding's, her novels have a fabulist quality as she has been directly influenced by Afro-American folktales. Like George Eliot she has a rare gift for characterization. She can compel her readers to learn about themselves by experiencing through her characters, states of mind which they would ordinarily disavow. Morrison's extraordinary distinction as a novelist also lies in restoring the language the black people speak to its original power.

As a result of her literary and artistic abilities and competence, Toni Morrison stands in the vanguard of contemporary writers of fiction, transcending both her racial identity and gender. Her acclaim is international as her novels are translated into many languages. Scholars the world over critique and assess her works, seeking to unravel the complexity that Morrison prides herself upon. An astute scholar as well as a uniquely creative writer, Morrison has won the deepest respect and admiration of both her fellow writers and populace at large. In addition to the feature coverage she has received from the popular media, from major national magazines and journals, she has been the recipient of several honorary degrees, literary awards and domestic recognitions. The numerous awards she has received, culminating in the Nobel Prize awarded to her in 1993 for her distinctive writing, bear testimony to her genius as a writer. With her powerful narratives set against a historical as well as mythical backdrop, Morrison has captivated the hearts of the common reader as well as scholars of literature. She enjoys today the unique distinction of being both a popular writer and an outstanding literary figure.

II

But in order to really understand the remarkable achievement of Toni Morrison as a novelist, one must go back and appreciate the black women's literary tradition to which she belongs and the conflict of images with which her foremothers have had to contend. For, what African-American women have expressed as part of the self is greatly affected by various other complex issues. As Barbara Christian rightly observes, "To be able to use the range of one's own voice, to attempt to express the totality of self, is a recurring struggle in the tradition of those writers from the nineteenth century to the present."[3]

Black women literary tradition can be traced back to Phillis Weatley in the eighteenth century down to the boom period—the Seventies and the Eighties with its remarkable talented writers like Paule Marshall, Alice Walker and Gloria Naylor, encompassing the pioneering work of Zora Neale Hurston in the Forties. Barbara Christian calls it the "Development of a Tradition" meaning that it has been a continuously evolving process, if one can trace the development of the black women's self from its infantile stage of invisibility to its present stage of self-definition and self-assertion. A survey of black women writers' tradition reveals that women writers could discover the positive-self in women and give a true picture of womanhood in all its density and complexity.

Women writers took it up as their bounden duty to discover black women's self entrapped in the white society. The urge to discover one's self and its relation to the world have become the important thrusts of these novelists. About this Alexis De Veau says: "I see a greater commitment among black women writers to understand self multiplied in terms of the community, that community multiplied in terms of the world."[4]

Barbara Christian explains how difficult it has been for them to achieve such "an overtly self-centered point of view," because of the way in which they have been conceptualized by black as well as white society. She says: "The extent to which Afro-American woman writers like Alice Walker, Paule Marshall, Gloria Naylor, Alexis De Veau, in the Seventies and Eighties have been able to make a commitment to an exploration of self, as central rather than marginal, is a tribute to the insights they have called in a century or so of literary activity.[5] Their predecessors were not permitted to contemplate and express their views on their self, because their self was not their own but something gravely affected by other complex issues. They had to struggle hard to evolve a self which was deeply afflicted by racism and sexism. They found it even harder to give self-expression to the unheard voice of their self.

Early African-American women novelists like Frances Harper, Jessie Fauset, Nella Larsen and Ann Petry indicate their stated intentions and their primary reasons for writing their works. Frances Harper in her preface to *Iola Leroy* makes her purpose clear when she writes that "her story's mission would not be in vain if it awakens in the hearts of our countrymen a strong sense of justice and a more Christian like humanity."[6] Harper, thus, pleads for the justice for African-Americans, who, in the 1890s, were being lynched, burned out, raped, and deprived of their rights as citizens in the wake of the failure of Reconstruction. However, her intention is to impress and to please the white readers by creating a lady-like version of the heroine, Iola Leroy, whom the Americans are expected to respect even though she is black. Jessie Fauset (1884-1961), a woman novelist of the Harlem Renaissance, also writes with a craving for white acceptance. She wants to correct the impression most white people have about black people. In her preface to *The Chinaberry Tree* (1931), she says that her novel is about "those breathing spells in-between spaces where coloured men and women work and live and go their ways in no thought of the problem."[7] Both Harper and Fauset were thus aware of the negative images of the black people that predominated in the minds of white Americans. Nella Larsen (1893-1963) too creates such heroines who wish to 'pass' for whites. They look like whites and act like whites. She felt that creation of assimilated women and a new bourgeois class in the black community would take the race closer to power and white acceptance. For example, her heroine, Helga Crane in *Quicksand* (1928), identifies herself with the white value structure so much so that she gets herself alienated from the common Negro mass socially and culturally. Ann Petry (1908) continues the tradition of the heroines who want to 'pass' for white. For example, Lutie Johnson in *The Street* (1946) is frustrated and alienated from self because she tries to live by the female version of the American Dream as pure, protected and well-provided for. However, Petry's contribution to the development of black women's literary tradition is that she presents women and mothers struggling against the social and economic hostilities stacked against them.

We have, however, one notable exception to this trend in early African-American women writers' works in Zora Neale Hurston's *Their Eyes Were Watching God* (1937). It appeared eight years after Nella Larsen's *Passing* and new winds began to blow across the black women s fictional landscape. Hurston was not only the group's best woman writer, but one of the first black women writers to attempt serious study of the black folklore and folk history. The major themes that emerge in the novels of Hurston are search for black woman's self-fulfillment through community, quest for the ideal relationship between man and woman, black sisterhood, and significance of fidelity in interpersonal relationships.

Hurston not only preserves black folk culture but even contributes to the definition of woman's selfhood. Like Jessie Fauset or Nella Larsen, Hurston does not employ the 'passing' theme or the white emulative motif, nor does she show crude bitterness toward the white society, nor any extrovert reaction to the external forces, but rather an "opposition to various forms of repression which are more generally human, and sometimes self-manufactured."[8] Unlike her predecessors' heroines, Hurston's women continually quest for personal freedom and self-love by placing themselves in relation to the community they live in. By presenting black women with all the ordinariness of their lives, their aspirations, their dreams, Hurston not only rescues them from the stereotypical upper middle-class bourgeois traps but comes close to probing the dimensions representing the general female condition as well. Thus, in its radical envisioning of the self as central, and "in its use of language as a means of exploring the self as female and black, *Their Eyes Were Watching God* is a forerunner of fiction of the Seventies and Eighties."[9] A 'transitional' writer, Hurston, shows considerable talent in revising the preceding models of black womanhood and leading the way a bit further up. Her writings signalled that the dawn was not far off and the 'new black woman' would soon knock at the doors of African-American literature.

But the attempt on the part of Hurston to present positive images of black woman did not result in any improvement in her image or in her condition. On the other hand, refutation of negative images created a series of contradictions between the image that black women could not attain and the reality of their existence. That kind of tension increased throughout the first half of the century till the 1940s when the destruction it created becomes apparent in the fiction written by black women. The heroines in the fiction of the Forties like Lutie Johnson in Ann Petry's *The Street* (1946) and Cleo Judson in Dorothy West's *The Living Is Easy* (1948) are defeated both by social reality and by their black self-knowledge.

However, there was a definite shift in the African-American women's writings towards the process of self-definition beginning with Gwendolyn Brooks' *Maud Martha* (1953). The protagonist of the novel, a very ordinary black woman, manages to transform her 'little life' into something significant in spite of the limitations set by her husband, her family, her race, her class and by society in general. She manages to be her own creator. Thus, while presenting a young black girl coming into womanhood, Brooks never employs the stereotypes used by her predecessors. For the first time in African-American literature, we come across a black female character who is neither a tragic victim consumed by the deterministic socio-economic conditions, nor a pariah obsessed by any cult. Barbara Christian critiques Brooks' protagonist: "She [Maud Martha] is no Iola Leroy. Nor is she, like Fauset's heroine, merely conventional. . . Nor is Maud Martha a beautiful Lutie Johnson, tragically destroyed by her environment. . . . It is just that she is not reduced to a stereotype either in the grand heroic style or the mean downtrodden mode."[10] Thus, signifying the end of an era of 'contradictory instincts' characterized by the malady of suspendedness and soul-stifling black bourgeoism, *Maud Martha* heralded the long-awaited moment in African-American literary history which was to establish the authenticity of black woman's true self by placing her life in the context of black culture and community.

The African-American women's literary tradition took a qualitative leap into the world of ontological transmutation of black women's existential conditions in America with Paule Marshall's first novel, *Brown Girl, Brownstones* (1981). The novel opened the creative floodgates and black women's words poured forth from the depths of their souls in an undiminished stream. The creative outpouring indicated the coming of age of black women's literary tradition. The novel clearly demonstrates black women's determination to revise history, to carve out a place for themselves and to announce to the whole world their existence as "a person and as a presence, as someone autonomous and as someone responsible to a community."[11] Unlike her predecessors, who spoke to others, Marshall's women speak to their own self and try to articulate that self with a great force.

Paule Marshall meaningfully engaged herself to the task of reconstructing black womanhood. She is the first black woman novelist who sculpts black female characters in relation to their culture and community. Barbara Christian writes: "She [Marshall] veers sharply away from much of the preceding literature, which emphasized advancement for black women in terms of white American values."[12] One of the reasons why she felt impelled to write *Brown Girl, Brownstones* was also to seek corrective measures against the prevalent derogatory image about black woman. In her interview with Sabine Brock, Paule Marshall states: "One of the reasons I wanted to write the story of a Selina Boyce was to give an answer to the prevailing image, to say that she was not a topsy, she was not any of the characters . . . or any of the stereotypes. . . . I wanted Selina to be a departure from all that."[13] Marshall charges that such a truthful reflection of black women's realities was not chronicled both in American and African-American literature.

Paule Marshall, thus, stands out as a pioneer of the black women's renaissance. Until her arrival on the literary scene, most writers approached the major themes like history, colonialism, slavery, racism from a male perspective. Marshall is the first black woman writer who treated these ideas from a black feminist point of view. Helene Christol writes that Marshall's

Brown Girl, Brownstones, became "the starting point for the contemporary black women writer's thrust forward to a courageous revision of American history, society and literature from a black feminist perspective."[14]

During the Sixties there was a perceptible change in the attitude of writers on account of the cultural renaissance. For a long time, many blacks deliberately attempted to forget their painful past or leave it to the deliberations of the white writers. But, after the cultural upheaval, African-American literary traditions took a new direction. Writers started making conscious attempts to go to the roots and re-link the present with the past. This radical change in the attitude of the writers in the late Sixties manifested especially in the works of Alice Walker.

Alice Walker prefers to call herself a 'womanist' because 'womanism,' in her opinion, expresses women's concerns better than 'feminism.' It appreciates "women's culture, women's emotional flexibility . . . and women's strength."[15] As a womanist she is certainly concerned with the liberation of all womankind from the psychology of oppression. But as an African-American woman writer, she is more "committed to exploring the oppressions, the insanities, the loyalties, and the triumphs of black women"[16] This is made clear when, in an interview with John O'Brien, she unequivocally expresses: "I am preoccupied with the spiritual survival, the survival of whole of my people. But beyond that, I am committed to exploring the oppressions, the insanities, the loyalties and the triumphs of black women."[17]

What Alice Walker professes in theory is practised in her novels. *The Third Life of Grange Copeland* (1970), for instance, demonstrates that the violence that the men and women and children of the Copeland family inflict on each other is the direct outcome of the internalization of racist hatred. The basic principle that Walker highlights is that the change in a person is linked with the change in the society. Walker gives expression to the tension that prevailed between the need for black man's self-love and his sense of shame. Her masterpiece, *Meridian* (1976), is about a woman protagonist who gradually awakens from her subordinate status as a black female, daughter, wife and mother to her own self and tries to become the maternal provider of the larger black community. She finally rejects the status of a biological mother, but tries to become the community's mother.

Thus, by the mid-Seventies, African-American women writers like Paule Marshall, Alice Walker, Toni Cade Bambara, Gayle Jones and Toni Morrison had not only defined their cultural context as a distinctly African-American one but also probed many facets of the interrelationship of racism, sexism and classism in their society. They not only demonstrated the fact that these three sources of oppression existed in black communities but also challenged the prevailing definition of woman in male-dominated American society, especially in relation to motherhood and sexuality. Furthermore, they insisted on the centrality of black women to African-American history as well as on their pivotal significance to the contemporary social and political developments in America. Their novels invariably look at ways in which the quality of black women's lives is affected by the interrelationship of racism, sexism and classism. Race, gender and class are not separate entities, at least in America, but closely linked with each other. As Barbara Christian observes, "like the images of a kaleidoscope, these elements are so organically connected that one must understand their interrelationship in spite of their ever-shifting appearance."[18]

III

Racism, sexism and classism signify the traumatic conditions under which African-Americans lived in white America. They are systems of societal and psychological restrictions that have critically affected the lives of blacks in general and African-American women in particular. Right from the days of slavery, the blacks, irrespective of sex, had realized the cruel reality of racism. Judged from the white man's standards of life and beauty, the black man's life became unbearable. Sexism more oppressive physically and mentally was cause of grievance to the black women who were sexually exploited by both the black and white men. Just as blacks as a group were relegated to an underclass by virtue of their race, so were women relegated to a separate caste by virtue of their sex. Confronted on all sides by racial and sexual discrimination, the black woman has no friends but only liabilities and responsibilities. Responsible for their own and their children's well-being and future, these women had to face daily the reality of their relationships with white men, with white women and, above all, with black men. But within the separate caste, a standard of woman was designed in terms of a class definition. The ideal southern lady image of eighteenth century America has been one of the dominant factors in America's conception of woman. She was expected to be beautiful in an ornamental way, chaste, pious, married and eventually, a mother. She was obviously a white, beautiful and rich woman who did not work. The ideal concept of woman in the society, then, is not only racist and sexist but also classist. And because black women were, by nature of their race, conceived of as lower class, they could hardly approximate the norm: "They had to work; most could not be ornamental or withdrawn from the world; and, according to the aesthetics of this country, they were not beautiful. But neither were the men. Any aggressiveness or intelligence on their part, qualities necessary for participation in the work world, were constructed as unwomanly and tasteless."[19] Thus, African women could not achieve the standard of womanhood on the one hand and on the other, they were biologically females, with all the societal restrictions associated with that state.

So, to be black and female is to suffer from the twin disadvantages of racial discrimination and pronounced gender bias. Possibly no other social group has been subjected to such an unedifying spectacle of human debasement and depravity. Being black, the African women suffered from racism; being females they were the victims of sexual atrocities at the hands of the white patriarchs as well as the blacks and being former slaves, the white establishment forced them to live on meagre resources and were compelled to remain poor. In short, the black women in America were made victims of triple jeopardy—racism, sexism, and classism.

As sources of oppression of blacks, racism and sexism are allied and have a parallel existence. They are mutually interdependent and hence they arise from the same set of circumstances. Gloria Wade-Gayles explains this interesting phenomenon through the imagery of circles:

> There are three major circles of reality in American society, which reflect degrees of power and powerlessness. There is a large circle in which white people, most of them men, experience influence and power. Far away from it there is a smaller circle, a narrow space, in which black people, regardless of sex, experience uncertainty, exploitation and powerlessness. Hidden in this second circle is a third, a small, dark enclosure in which black women experience pain, isolation, and vulnerability. These are the distinguishing marks of black womanhood in white America.[20]

What we see here is the omnipresent, all-embracing reality of racism as a common factor in the lives of all blacks, irrespective of sex. The black man faced with the hard fact and cruel reality of racism realised right from the days of slavery that his colour and physiognomy were terrible handicaps, and as such would mark him off as evil, despite all claims to the contrary. Judged by the white man's standards of life, behaviour and beauty, his life became unbearable. Universal codes of social and psychological praxis as laid down by the dominant white culture were forcibly thrust upon him.

Thus began the oppressive story of racism in America. It brought with it pain, sorrow, bloodshed, death and, above all, the negation of an entire race. The African-American race was ghettoized, persecuted and viciously outlawed from all avenues of decency, hope, progress and livelihood. Racism, as a life-threatening, non-nurturing force, exists even today, thus becoming the forum for all types of discussion.

Racism, as a man-made phenomenon, may be defined according to Hernton as "all of the learned behaviour and learned emotions on the part of a group of people towards another group whose physical characteristics are dissimilar to the former group; behaviour and emotions that compel one group to . . . treat the other on the basis of its physical characteristics alone, as if it did not belong to the human race."[21] The basic myth of racism, in other words, is that white skin brings with it cultural superiority—that the white are more intelligent and more virtuous than the black by the mere fact of being white. On the psychological level, whiteness is automatically equated with beauty and culture and blackness with ugliness and slavery.

Racism started in America when white masters of the land brought the first Africans in chains and used their labour to enrich their coffers. As a result, black people soon ceased to exist as human beings in the white world. In an illuminating study of the origin of racism in the United States, Joel Kovel says that the white master "first reduced the human self of his black slave to a body and then the body to a thing; he dehumanized his slave, made him quantifiable, and thereby absorbed him into a rising world market of productive exchange."[22]

All that was left to blacks was their African soul which was also taken away by imposing white values on them. With the breakdown of their native values, they lost their authentic self and almost invariably fostered feelings of inferiority. Whites created the institutions which blacks were finally ready to live by. This covert form of racism, Plakkoottam correctly maintains, "was doubly injurious to the black race in that not much notice was taken of its invisibly corrosive nature."[23] No wonder, it proved most devastating in its ultimate repercussions. Such was the first step toward the establishment of racism as an inseparable part of white American civilization.

Sexism, with its accompanying horrors, mutilated the backs and minds of slave women and defiled their sexual beings and scarred them psychologically for all time. Suffering at the hands of both black and white men, the African-American woman had to fight for survival both inside and outside her house. Thus, her story, even in modern America, is fraught with the perils of navigating between the Scylla of racism and the Charybdis of sexism. Impeded from attaining social, political and economic independence and prosperity, black women have had to fight hard for just the basics. With emancipation and induction at the lowest levels of the work force, these women have selected education as their one strong weapon for integration. Despite gradual progress, they are still far behind black men and white women. Racism and sexism should be blamed for this hapless situation.

Gloria Steiner, in her introduction to *Outrageous Acts and Everyday Rebellions*, states this equation very tersely thus: "Just as male was universal but female was limited, white was universal but black was limited."[24] A sense of inferiority and inadequacy was being cultivated by the white dominant group to deprive blacks of their genuine potential. Thus, race and gender, that is, 'black' and 'female' were juxtaposed against 'white' and 'male,' in the process creating a subjugated microcosm within a dominating microcosm. Just as racism deprived a group of people of their growth and happiness, so too sexism. Racism and sexism grew out of the same stultifying atmosphere of prejudice, discrimination and condescension. In the case of racism, discrimination was based on the differences of race and colour, in the case of sexism, on that of gender. But in spite of these differences, they create the same kind of negative currents which even today cause great harm. On the whole, it was the black woman who had the greater cause for grievance, being oppressed as both a black and a woman. It is her story which more vividly describes this horrendous tale and its accompanying woes. The entire Africa-America community was condemned to endless suffering, yet the black woman's condition was much worse than the black man's because "To be black and Female was to be in Double Jeopardy."[25]

There has ever been an unholy nexus between racism and sexism. They, in fact, originated from the same set of circumstances: "both are motivated by similar economic, social and psychological forces, it is only logical that those who sought to undermine Blacks were also most virulent anti-feminists. The means of oppression differed across race and sex lines, but the wellspring of that oppression was the same."[26] Because of her ability to do man's work and her extraordinary reproductive capacity, the black woman was treated by her white master as an indispensable commodity. Miscegenation played a vital role in their relationship during the days of slavery. White mercenary planters saw profit in it. The children born out of such a sordid union would be their sole property and, therefore, could be used to further their economic interest. The black woman was also seen as a wanton creature easily available for instant sexual gratification. Thus, she became the double victim of racist and sexist oppression including lynching and rape.

The other side of the coin tells of the disgrace the black woman suffered at the hands of her own man. Despite all sympathy for his abused wife, the black man gradually developed a kind of aversion to her. He also began to see her as a loose woman who preferred extramarital adventures to marital permanence. The stigma attached to the black woman by her white slaver ironically received the black man's sanction. He felt sexually neglected and took his woman to be his enemy. The white man's clever manipulation of the social situation thus escaped black man's attention. On the other hand, one discovers the latter's helplessness. Being a slave himself, he was absolutely powerless to question the scheme of things. Either way, "the black woman was deprived of a strong black man on whom . he could rely for protection."[27] So, her awful predicament continued.

But then, the alternate voices of the oppressed are not those of race and gender alone. Class exploitation is, perhaps, the greatest source of oppression of blacks in white America. After the Civil War, during which blacks were liberated, there was some improvement in the condition of their lives. But the First World War again hit them hard as it precipitated a global crisis. The Great Depression posed further threats to the African-American population. As a matter of fact, to millions of common people in America, irrespective of race, nothing seemed so urgent as survival in a world of unemployment and economic collapse. Yet, blacks were worst affected as racial discrimination reached its apex.

Even if it is true that the class struggle has not been a major theme in the history of the African-American freedom movement, we cannot possibly negate the class issue. Nor can we agree with critics like Wade-Gayles who see class "not as urgent as race and sex in black women's reality for class oppression cuts across racial and sexual lines and is, therefore, not unique to black women."[28] Even if we do not see ethnicity as a mask behind which people conceal their class position both from each other and from themselves, even if we realize the importance of racial and ethnic values, we cannot ignore the class issue—capitalism.

Capitalism is an economic system characterized by the concentration in a few hands of the ownership of the means of producing wealth and by unequal distribution of the products of human labour. Thus, it is a system which "divides society into classes [sections of people who get their living in the same way], one which carries out the actual process of production [slave, serf, wage-worker], while the other (slave-owner, lord, capitalist employer] enjoys a part of the product without having to work to produce it."[29] The class that owns and controls the means of production is called the ruling or capitalist class. To rule society simply means organizing it to serve the interests of only one class of people and imposing the will of this group on all other groups, whether they agree or not. Ultimately, the objective of the ruling class is to convince others that its rule is the most just. If the objective is accomplished, the ruling class secures its place in the society and thus continues its exploitation with few opposing disturbances. In any society in which the interests of only a small sector of the population are considered, gross injustices are present. Under capitalism, for example, there exists a permanent sector of unemployed people, and periodic economic crisis: "incredible poverty in the midst of wealth and wastage, deviant behaviour based on placing individual interests above group interests and racism."[30]

There is ample evidence to prove that racism is a by-product of capitalism. Walter Rodney refuses the myth that racism was the initial cause of the enslavement of African people and, by doing so, effectively negates the argument of those nationalists who say that the racism and sexism are the primary causes of their oppression today. According to Rodney, Africans were enslaved "for economic reasons, so that their labour power could be exploited."[31] Thus resulted racism, the doctrine based on the assumption that psychological traits and capacities are determined by biological race. In his words, "[After] having been utterly dependent on African labour, Europeans at home and abroad found it necessary to rationalise that exploitation in racist terms as well. Oppression follows logically from exploitation, so as to guarantee the latter."[32] The economic system of slavery, an early form of capitalism, was the cause of racism and sexism rather than the result of it. Kwame Nkrumah confirms Rodney's analysis when he writes: "It was only with capitalist economic penetration that the master-servant relationship emerged, and with it, racism, colour prejudice and apartheid."[33]

Eric Williams, an economist, offers indisputable facts to illustrate that racism was the result of the exploitation of the African's labour. He points out that the enslavement of the African had everything to do with the cheapness of labour, not the colour of the labourer's skin: "racial differences made it easier to justify and rationalize Negro slavery. . . . Finally, and this was the decisive factor, the Negro slave was cheaper. The money which procured a white man's service for ten years could buy a Negro for a life."[34] Williams substantiates this premise by examining the rise of capitalism. Offering convincing facts, he proves that the early European capitalists were willing to exploit the labour power of any group of people, even their own, to make a handsome profit. All these factors, according to Williams, confirm that racism stems from class exploitation.

However, to state that racism was the consequence of the European's quest for greater profits is not to imply that racism did not ultimately become a concomitant reason for oppressing African people. According to Rodney, "Oppression of African people on purely racial grounds accompanied, strengthened and became indistinguishable from oppression for economic reasons."[35] Nkrumah, too, believed that the African suffered from a nation-class oppression. In analyzing the African's plight in United States, he wrote: "Race is inextricably linked with class exploitation; in a racist-capitalist power structure, capitalist exploitation and race oppression are complementary, the removal of one ensures the removal of the other."[36] Rodney and Nkrumah agree, however, that while the African suffers equally from both—racism and sexism—racism cannot exist under a non-exploitative economic system.

Since race, sex and class have been so interrelated in the history of America, it is not surprising that when black women published novels, they necessarily reflected on that relationship, whether they intended to or not. From Harper's *Iola Leroy*, published in 1892, to Toni Morrison's *Beloved,* published in 1987, the tradition of African-American women novelists as an entirety is a stunning expression of various configurations of social definitions that have been inflicted on the black women. The novels of black women from 1892 to the present have had to react to the elements of race, gender, and class as the factors upon which the societal definition of the black woman is based.

IV

Black women have been victimized not only by racist, sexist, and classist assumptions but also by scholarly neglect. Yet they have tried down the ages to present their case through various media, especially through literature. Black women novelists of the twentieth century have openly portrayed in their works their experiences of exploitation—political, racial, sexual and emotional. Driven by an overriding impulse towards self-assertion, which can be traced back to the cultural ethos of the 1960s, they have later succeeded in turning their identity into a source of strength. Their works of fiction, published over the last two decades, reflect their version of American experience that was excluded from both black male and white female writings. They strive to present the black woman's quest for total freedom as a human being. A look at some of the novels of African-American women writers would take us through many a chapter in black woman's life in America and help see her rise gradually from passivity to consciousness.

Frances E.W. Harper's *Iola Leroy or Shadows Uplifted* is historically important as the first novel by a black woman to treat racism and sexism. It portrays a young Christian octoroon who, being totally unaware of the Negro blood in her veins, thinks herself white and behaves exactly like a racist. Deluded by her apparent skin colour, she feels proud of her parentage and justifies slavery as a necessity of plantation life. It is highly ironical that a person of her stock should advocate white values which shows the reversal of Iola's fortune. Because of her black ancestry, however remote it may be, she too is finally thrown into slavery. Her racist assumptions radically change as she herself faces racial polarity. She feels the pain of all blacks and looks on her own plight as a kind of penance for her past sins. Racism is then well-combined with sexism to focus on another facet of black suffering. Sex-crazed white men pursue Iola, although she successfully resists their advances. With her awareness, Iola wants to live and struggle as a black woman. She recreates herself in the light of her actual experience. The ending implies that American society cannot be transformed until white supremacy is understood and attacked by full-blooded whites.

Nella Larsen's *Quicksand* presents a mulatto's awareness of her true identity and her determination not to imitate white values. Helga knows that to embrace such values would simply mean falling into the white trap. She is equally aware of sexual polarity in the form of white, male dominance in American society. Helga's dignified appearance and bearing would easily qualify her as a true lady. She could surely marry a white man and enjoy great honor. But she rightly thinks that she would, in that case, disgrace her black blood and a chance revelation of her mixed parentage might also knock her off her pedestal. So, she marries a travelling minister instead, who takes her to rural Alabama. Yet, Helga cannot realize herself because there she sinks into the quicksand of poverty and continual childbearing. To her horror, she discovers that her gender, no less than her race, has left her vulnerable to exploitation. The novel, thus, records the simultaneity of racial and sexual discrimination faced by African-American women.

Zora Neale Hurston's *Their Eyes Were Watching God* articulates the black woman's plight in unambiguous terms. Remarkable is the following extract:

> de white man is de ruler of everything as fur as Ah been able tuh find out. So . . . (he) throw down de load and tell de nigger man tuh pick it up. He pick it up because he have to, but be don't tote it. He hand it to his women-folks. De nigger woman is de mule uh de world so far as Ah can see.[37]

Hurston was one of the foremost black thinkers to attack American capitalism for creating a tier of socio-economic classes that ranks the black woman at the bottom. At this point, it is interesting to note how Gloria Wade-Gayles later depicts the syndrome through the imagery of "circles":

> There are three major circles of reality in American society, which reflect degrees of power and powerlessness. There is a large circle in which white people, most of them men, experience influence and power. For away from it there is a smaller circle of sex, experience . . . exploitation and powerlessness. Hidden in this second circle is a third . . . in which black women experience pain, isolation and vulnerability.[38]

Janie, the protagonist of the novel, is a beautiful mulatto who is treated by the men around as a trophy to be fought over and won. Marriage jeopardizes her self-identity all the more and abandons her to anonymity. Her first husband, Logan, wants her to work like a mule for him and the second one, Jody, considers her an exotic possession. In either case, Janie has to live up to the irrational expectations of her man and suffer humiliation. Janie's sense of deprivation is coupled with a feeling of utter isolation as she is eventually cut off from the local black community. With Janie stepping out of her small, dark enclosure, Hurston's delineation of black womanhood takes a new turn. The woman shakes off her marital bonds and becomes free to choose the course of her own life. She meets another man, Teacake, who treats her as a human being and helps her realize her self-worth. His death leaves her sad, yet his fond memory gives her the strength to live on. Sexism plays a more important role than racism in this novel.

Ann Petry's *The Street* shows how racial discrimination renders blacks jobless and how poverty, in turn, exposes the African-American woman to sexual exploitation. Lutie Johnson, a lower class black woman, has been abandoned by her husband for her obsessive desire for 'a comfortable life.' Alone with a small child, she has to come out on the streets of a big city for her livelihood. Petry portrays with remarkable clarity the social and economic problems faced by black women in urban areas. With all her decency and moral integrity, Lutie is labelled a whore by her neighbours because they cannot accept a single black woman with trust or dignity. Deprived of the basic necessities of life, Lutie encounters overwhelming odds in rearing her child. Unable to find a job, she desperately tries to get established in the entertainment world by becoming a singing woman. This leaves her more vulnerable to the ugly demands of the urban society. Frustrated and lost in the sea of crowds, she painfully realises that if she cannot sell her talent she must sell her body. Petry points out that her people "were so damn poor they didn't have time to do anything but work and their bodies were the only source of relief from the pressure under which they lived."[39] However, Lutie still refuses to buy happiness at the cost of her moral values. She murders her prospective employer as he tries to rape her. In fact, the black woman experiences the threat of rape not only from the dominant group, but from within her own. Lutie's final action, which is a definite sign of rebellion, speaks of her resilience and her inviolable sense of self-dignity.

Paule Marshall's first novel, *Brown Girl, Brownstones*, as has already been pointed out, ushered in a new period of female characters in African-American literature. It prefigured the major themes of black woman's fiction in the 1970s: "the black woman's potential as a full person and necessarily a major actor on the social, cultural and political issues of our times."[40] Marshall gave new meaning to black womanhood by transforming abused creatures into self-conscious rebels who meet the challenges of the world and seek to define their identity within the context of their own culture.

Brown Girl, Brownstones centers around Selina, a girl child of first generation—Barbadian immigrant, who pass from a traumatic childhood to womanhood. With a psyche damaged by the moist and sexist ideology, she initially judges her self-worth by the white standards of feminine beauty. She suffers from a sense of inadequacy as she does not have blond hair, blue eyes and white skin. Selina's craving for white elegance and refinement, in fact, alienates her further from her native value system. Fostering a debased self-image and subordinating herself to the beautiful white people around, she only confirms her invisibility and worthlessness. Black psychiatrists analyse the crippling effects of such double-consciousness on the black woman: "[Her] blackness is the antithesis of a creamy white skin, her lips are thick, her hair is kinky and short. She is, in fact, the antithesis of American beauty. . . . There can be no doubt that she will develop a damaged self concept and an impairment of her feminine narcissism which will have profound consequences for her character development."[41] We do find black women in fiction as well as in real life. We have incorporated a white ideology into the fabric of their consciousness and consequently failed to realize their authentic self. But Marshall believes that it would be suicidal for the black woman to accept white values. Selina, who initially failed to grasp the truth, later becomes aware of her misconceptions and revolts against the distorted image of the black woman which white America carefully keeps alive in order to hold her in perpetual enslavement. Selina also disabuses herself of her false belief in male supremacy which she inherited from her black father. The girl who was once proud of being called 'Deighton's Selina,' now identifies herself with her long-suffering mother. She tells her, "Everybody used to call me Deighton's Selina but they were wrong. Because you see I'm truly 'your child. Remember how you used to talk about, how you left home and came here alone as a girl of eighteen . . . ? I love hearing that. And that's what I want."[42] She takes her mother, Silla, as the symbol of black womanhood and becomes her daughter.

Consequently, Selina discovers her close affinities with all the oppressed black women in their struggle for human rights. Moreover, she realises that they cannot change the present without a search for roots. Selina finally decides to go back to Barbados, the centre of her life. It is no escape but rather a conscious choice to restore the self and the community, a spiritual return back over history in order to have a sense of total experience. Selina's tossing of her bangle high into air before departure is symbolic of her ultimate emergence as a black woman determined to seek out a more truthful identity.

Alice Walker's *Meridian*, one of the most celebrated novels, reflects her strong belief in the black womanist tenets. It tells the story of the black woman in a period of transition, the story of a coming to consciousness and a subsequent development of self and search for authenticity. The first part of the novel describes Meridian's initiation into adulthood and the beginning of her search for her black woman self. The second part focuses on her renunciation of her child and active participation in the Civil Rights Movement. The third and final part deals with her release from sexual bonds with an accent on her great preoccupation with the 'survival whole' of her people. Meridian's quest for black womanhood finally turns into a concern for the survival and wholeness of the entire black community. She finds the real meaning of her life in her very attempt to change the present social system for the benefit of all blacks, male and female. The transformation she insists on is possible not through violence but through a spiritual awakening. Meridian, thus emerges as a liberated black woman with a hard-won insight into the riddles of life. Evidently, the novel creates an image of the African-American woman with her complexity, diversity and depth.

Like other black woman novelists of the contemporary period, Toni Morrison analyses the relationship between race, gender and class assumptions. In each of her novels she explores some aspect of the oppression afflicting African people. Titled as a 'Black Woman Writer' committed to survival and wholeness of entire black people, male and female, Morrison has also been called a 'womanist' by Alice Walker. Though most of the stories of her novels are revealed through the eyes of black women, she does not adopt the kind of political feminism associated with women's movement of the 1970s. Rather, she writes in the tradition of black women writers like Hurston and Paule Marshall as a cultural feminist, celebrating the strengths of black women against the heavy odds of racism, sexism and classism by developing the necessary political, social and aesthetic consciousness.

V

A number of factors contributed to Toni Morrison's developing social, political and aesthetic consciousness—environment, familial background, community, African-American folklore, her educational background and early professional life, her Random House experience and literary works by great writers. These factors helped her become more conscious of the nature of the African's dilemma, the crisis of the African personality, the cause and effects of it, and her increasing commitment to help solve it in terms of fictional art, thereby combining her political consciousness with aesthetic sensibility.

Toni Morrison's personal landscape—the environment in which she was born and brought up—has been at once colourful and complex like that of many of her fictional characters. She was born on 18 February 1931 in Lorain, Ohio, a small Midwestern steel-mill town located twenty-five miles west of Cleveland. Situated far from the madding crowd—the hustle and bustle of New York's inner city, as well as from the noisy highways—the salubrious atmosphere of Morrison's home provided important insights into the life of this significant African-American woman writer. Wilfred Samuels and Clenora Hudson-Weems highlight the complexity and subtlety of life this pastoral setting offers, ensuring the privacy and gateway to the past, when they put it:

> Permanently docked off the Hudson River, it looks toward a horizon of infinite possibilities that seems oblivious to and unbound by the city's skyline or the wired mesh of a towering bridge in the foreground. The pier off the patio appears to serve as a runway, offering passage and passport to a world of known and unknown realities; fact, fiction, fantasy; mystical and magical realms that converge in the world that Morrison creates.[43]

Morrison's early years in the steel-mill town of Lorain, Ohio, during the Depression years created within her a sensitivity toward the struggling masses in general and the African people in particular. As a child, she experienced enough poverty, hatred and racism to last a lifetime. From her parents, George and Rahmah, Southern migrants who left the deep South in search of improved social, political, economic and educational opportunities for their family, whose profound and positive influence is still borne by her, Morrison learned many lasting lessons relevant to race, gender and class. They firmly believed that "black people were the humans of the globe."[44] Their diverse personalities gave Morrison, the second of their four children, wherewithal not only to live in America but to do so successfully.

From her father, a shipyard welder, who was a stickler for excellence, Morrison gained a garvy-like perspective on whites as he believed that all African people were morally superior to Europeans. She admits: "My father was a racist. As a child in Georgia, he received shocking impressions of adult white people, and for the rest of his life felt he was justified in despising all whites, and that they were not justified in despising him."[45] Her father, thus, impressed upon her a positive self-image while instilling in her the tools for combating what Carolyn Gerald calls "the zero image."[46] Her mother, who was ever optimistic in her belief that the future would bring better race relations, unyieldingly handled offensive landlords and insidious social workers. Though on relief during Great Depression, she was self-assured enough to belong to a Black woman's club and was bold enough to write to President Roosevelt when the meal received during the Great Depression as dole was bugridden. Furthermore, the hair-raising ghost tales told by her parents particularly her father who told her the scariest folktales "would become the genesis of the mysticism and magic that permeates Morrison's fiction."[47] Her father told such thrilling terrifying ghost stories that Morrison confesses, "We were always begging him to repeat the stories that terrified us most."[48] Small wonder if Morrison said, "we were intimate with the supernatural."[49]

Morrison's grandparents also made their impact on her. Her grandmother Ardelia, made her greatest impact during Morrison's childhood, by acquainting her with the blacklore that now permeates her fiction. Similarly, her grandfather Solomon, influenced her as a writer with his skilled craftsmanship as a carpenter and his superb artistry as violinist. Thus, all her early life Morrison absorbed the black lore, music, language and rituals that give her prose its special favour and tone. And, as Jean Strouse observes: "Morrison's world, like the world of her novels, was filled with signs, visitation, and ways of knowing that reached beyond the five senses."[50]

Morrison's foundation and sense of self were also strengthened by the cohesiveness of the small black Lorain community which parented and nurtured her for seven years. Morrison considers this community a 'neighbourhood'—a life-giving and sustaining compound, where myth abounds as a "concept of truth or reality a whole people has arrived at over years of observation."[51] Like the community in which Pecola of *The Bluest Eye* finds herself, it was a place that cared if someone was in difficulty. This is made clear when Morrison, in her interview, tells Robert Stepto how people were taken care of: "If they were sick, other people took care of them; if they were old, other people took care of them; if they were mad, other people provided a small place for them, or related to their madness or tried to find out the limits of their madness."[52] It is this family background that convinced Morrison that there are no boring black people and, what is more, interested her in 'scratching the surface' to discover the complexity and subtlety in their lives as clearly revealed in her novels.

African-American folklore is arguably the basis for Morrison's fiction as for most Black American literature. As Trudier Harris observes, "The link to orality is one of the keys to unlocking African-American literary history."[53] In a country where, as late as the 1830s, there were laws prohibiting the teaching of slaves, it was necessary for the oral tradition to carry the values which the group considered significant. Transmission by word of mouth took the place of pamphlets, poems and novels. Themes such as the quest for freedom, the nature of evil and the powerful verses of the powerless became themes of African-American literature. For instance, William Wells Brown's slaves in his

Clotel (1853) verbalize the disparity in riches and their exploitation:

> The big bee flies high,
> The little bee makes the honey;
> The black folk makes the cotton
> And the white folk gets the money.[54]

This folk rhyme encapsulates the history of black and white interaction in the United States and, what is more, it epitomizes the sentiments expressed in protest literature.

The African-American folklore has wielded a tremendous influence upon the characters and worlds that Morrison creates, as well as upon the very shape of her novels. Her awareness of the inseparability of oral forms and effects from written media in African-American culture informs her writing throughout her career. In her use of folklore, Morrison is fascinated by the magic of fairy tales and intrigued with the horrors to be found in monsters or at least in monstrous behaviour. Her familiarity with African-American folk communities and with other oral traditions enables her to develop her themes, shape the structure of her novels and delineate the characters. Furthermore, like Zora Neale Hurston, Morrison exhibits a fascination for patterns of black folk speech and uses folk metaphors so authentically engaging that they compete with theme and character in most of her novels. Perceiving herself as a cultural activist, Morrison writes from a folk aesthetic that is much like the one that informs Ralph Ellison's theoretical assertion that folklore is the basis of all great literature:

> For us [black Americans] the question should be, what are the specific forms of that humanity, and what in our background is worth preserving or abandoning. The clue to this can be found in folklore, which offers the first drawings of any group's character. It preserves mainly those situations which have repeated themselves again and again in the history of any given group. It describes those rites, manners, customs, and so forth, which insure the good life, or destroy it; and it describes those boundaries of feeling, thought, and action which that particular group has found to be limitation of the human condition. It projects this wisdom in sym-

> bols which express the group's will to survive. . . . These drawings may be crude but they are nonetheless profound in that they represent the group's attempt to humanize the world. It's no accident that great literature, the product of individual artists, is erected upon his humble base.[55]

Morrison's educational background and early professional life has helped her a good deal in moulding herself into a creative writer with social and political consciousness. Her precocity was detected very early when she was in the first grade as she was "the only black in the class and the only child who could read."[56] Eventually, literature became her favourite subject and reading her fondest pastime. Moreover, she studied Latin for four years before graduating with honours from Lorain High in 1949. After receiving a Bachelor of Arts degree in English from Cornell University in 1955, she embarked on a teaching career as a member of the English faculty at Texas Southern University in Houston. Her fascination for books especially the classics, continued though she showed no real interest in writing fiction.

Morrison's years at Random House, where she served as an editor, went a long way in stimulating her developing consciousness. By editing some of the significant works written by Africans, she was exposed to the thoughts of those who were more conscious than she was of the nature of the plight confronting her people. One such African, Chinweizu, must have had a considerable impact on her. After the edition of his book, *The West and the Rest of Us*, which is one of the most insightful works that explore the nature of African oppression, expounding the theory that economics precedes racism, Morrison's own works would reflect a qualitative leap in the author's consciousness, not only of the race and gender oppression of Africans but also of the primacy of class exploitation. The major premises of *The West and the Rest of Us* that the primary problem confronting Africans is capitalism and that the solution lies in the unity of African people would become major themes in works such as *Tar Baby* and *Beloved.* Morrison has also been influenced by a pictorial she edited—The *Black Book* (1974), a compendium of news clippings and advertisements chronicling the life of African people in the United States from slavery through the Civil Rights Movement, in her concern about the significance of place, history and myth, and especially in writing *Beloved.* She got here the kernel of her novel—the ex-slave mother so devastated by her own oppression and exploitation in slavery that she murders one of her children to prevent it from experiencing that life.

Morrison gained social consciousness not only by reading and editing historical works of pan-African writers such as Chinweizu, and *The Black Book*, but also by reading literary works by such writers as Ralph Ellison, Alex Haley, Toni Cade Bambara, Henry Dumas and Jean-Paul Sartre. The bits and pieces that she borrowed from the monumental works of art of these writers have a significant impact on her. Ellison, who burst the seams of traditional fiction in context and form, and synthesized myth and reality, folklore and history, in his effort to recreate the world from the perspective of the crisis-ridden African, served as a strong role model for her. Morrison was greatly impressed by Ellison's world in which Africans can live a life of visibility underground and invisibility above ground.

As regards Alex Haley, Morrison learned from his *Roots* the dialectical relationship between discovering one's ancestral roots and discovering one's self. Morrison seems to have greatly liked Haley's pertinent remark: "The memories of the mouths of the ancient elders was the only way that early histories of mankind got passed along . . . for all of us today to know who we are."[57] This idea of the interconnectedness between past and present impressed Morrison, and it forms the theme of *Song of Solomon.* Clearly, the underlying premise of both books—*Roots* and *Song of Solomon—is* that discovering one's roots is a precursor to discovering oneself.

Morrison is indebted to Toni Cade Bambara for the concept of the 'African Spirit.' Evidently, this concept of a haunting collective of African women who offer advice to the female protagonist, Velma Henry, in Bambara's work, had a tremendous impact on Morrison. She uses it in *Tar Baby* in which a group of African women direct the female protagonist, Jadine, toward her African, woman self, in their effort to prevent her from becoming the model of a European female. And, like Bambara's Velma Henry, Jadine rejects the sister-women's advice to be what she is—African and woman.

Morrison has been influenced by Henry Dumas in developing her commitment to write about African people in ways that would capture the positive essence of their lives and thereby help them to reclaim the African personality. She seems to have readily joined Dumas when he says: "I am very much concerned about what is happening to my people and what we are doing with our precious tradition."[58] Morrison has such a great admiration for the brilliant works of Dumas that she extracted several key concepts and names like 'sweet Home,' 'Heyboy' (the dog in one of Dumas' most impressive stories, "Ark of Bones") which figure prominently in *Beloved.* Sweet Home, Dumas' hometown, becomes Sweet Home plantation in *Beloved.* Similarly Heyboy in Dumas' "Ark of Bones" becomes Here Boy in *Beloved.*

Morrison also seems to have been considerably influenced by Jean-Paul Sartre, the French existentialist, who professes that "man is nothing but what he makes of himself" but that in his freedom he "carries the weight of the world on his shoulders."[59] This is evident when Toni Morrison tells Gloria Naylor: "The point is that freedom is choosing your responsibility. It's not having no responsibilities, it's choosing the ones you want."[60] Morrison's protagonists who express either the 'effort of will' or a 'freedom of will' live richer, although their lives may be said to be dangerously free. The danger emerges from the nature of what is an existential perspective. For, it is freedom that is not without responsibility for the neighbourhood, involving angst.

Thus, Toni Morrison's familial, educational, cultural and literary background with an ambience of historical and social consciousness, mysticism, master craftsmanship and a love of excellence and work must have gone a long way in shaping and moulding her as a committed novelist. The various factors of influence further provide us with the subtle and profound insights into the human condition in general, and black life in particular, that Morrison has carefully woven into the landscape of her fictional world. In other words, Morrison's fiction emerges from within the universe of her mind which has been shaped by the African-American culture of her childhood, expanded by a formal education in English and the classics at Harvard and Cornell Universities, and forged by her own experiences as an African-American woman.

VI

Although Toni Morrison is among the foremost African-American women novelists today, it is interesting to note that she never wanted to become a writer in her lifetime. As a studious adolescent, Morrison read Jane Austen and the great Russian novels like Dostoevsky's *Crime and Punishment* and Tolstoy's *War and Peace*, and remarked:

> Those books were not written for a little black girl in Lorain, Ohio, but they were so magnificently done that I got them anyway—they spoke directly to me out of their own specificity. I was not thinking of writing then—I wanted to be a dancer like Maria Tallchief.[61]

Not intending to became a writer, Morrison started writing as a therapeutic means of dealing with loneliness when she lived in Syracuse. Although at the point of going to Syracuse, Morrison had no real interest in writing as a vocation, she was still haunted by a need for greater fulfillment of her own creative talents and better direction of her creative energies.[62] In Syracuse, she decided to return to her short story about a little black girl who longed for blue eyes which she had jotted down when she was thirty. She was soon encouraged by Allen Rancler, then an editor at Macmillan, to expand it into a full-length novel. This is how Morrison became a writer. She says: "I realised in the process of *The Bluest Eye* that writing had became a compulsion so I became a writer. I will always be a writer."[63] Although Morrison confesses to writing both *The Bluest Eye* and the next novel, *Sula* because they were books she was interested in reading but had not been able to find, writing for her became 'the most extraordinary way of thinking and feeling—it became one thing that I was doing that I had no intention of living without."[64] In short, as

Morrison told Thomas LeClair, "writing became a way to become coherent in the world."[65]

Black writing did not come into being as a result of some black persons' desire to exercise the "inspirational muse." What motivated blacks to write was the condition of the oppression, and what they desired of their writing was to ameliorate their condition. By virtue of its origin, nature and function, black writing is mission-conscious. From the beginning, black writers have written a literature of social protest and human enlightenment. Being a black writer is an ennobling exigency in black literature and it constitutes one of the supreme enrichments of black life and black culture. This has been and is the burden as well as the heritage and the legacy of every black writer in white America. Toni Morrison has not only participated in the evolving canon of Black American literature but has done much to influence, expand and solidify the place created by its vanguard, including Phillis Wheatly, Fredrick Douglass, Langston Hughes, Richard Wright, Zora Neale Hurston, James Baldwin and Ralph Ellison.

Toni Morrison made her debut as a novelist in 1970 with *The Bluest Eye* and soon gained attention for her epic power, poetic imagery, fabulistic quality, richly expressive depiction of black America and the wonderful richness and vitality of her language. Set in a small Midwestern town in Lorain, Ohio, during the Depression, *The Bluest Eye* tells the story of Pecola Breedlove who, hating her black self, yearns for blue eyes which she believes will make her white, extinguish her position as pariah and give her the love and security that are desperately missing from her life.

By 1973 Morrison's career as a novelist soared as the publication of *Sula*, her second novel, clearly marked her as a significant literary voice in America. This seminal work reflected the shift in the mood of society at large where the emphasis had veered from the mass struggle for black consciousness, to the personal struggle for self-realization and affirmation. Just after the publication of *Sula*, Morrison in 1974 stated: "What we [blacks] have to do is to reintroduce ourselves to ourselves. We have to know the past so that we can use it for now."[66] This statement foreshadows the theme of *Song of Solomon* (1977)—truth compels one to get in touch with his or her heritage in order to comprehend and appreciate one's true self and establish a higher quality of existence. *Song of Solomon*, which would receive both the 'National Book Critics Circle Award' and the 'Friends of American Writers Award' established Morrison as a major American writer.

Morrison's fourth novel, *Tar Baby* (1981), mirrors the Eighties in which "individuals increasingly sought to tap their sixth sense to unravel the mysteries of the universe."[67] It is a truly public novel about the condition of society, examining the relationships between blacks and whites, men and women and civilization and nature. Filled with allusion to African-American folklore and mythology, *Tar Baby* won accolades and recognition from all critical corners, putting the author on the cover of *Newsweek* magazine. Toni Morrison had entered the mainstream of American literature and her name had become a household word.

With her fifth novel, *Beloved* (1987), Morrison's place in American literature has been expanded as it won the Pulitzer Prize for fiction. Six years in the making, *Beloved* artistically dramatizes a haunting amalgam of the past and present experiences of an escaped female slave, tracing the heroine's quest for meaning and wholeness in slavery and in freedom. Critics have been nearly unanimous in acclaiming *Beloved* as Morrison's finest work to date. Meeting the criteria for greatness in many arenas, *Beloved* was considered by one reviewer "a milestone in the chronicling of the black experience in America,"[68] and by another "a stunning and lasting achievement (which) transforms the sorrows of history into the luminous truth of art."[69] Such spectacular praise represents not just a hallmark in Toni Morrison's career, but quite possibly in the history of African-American writers in American literature.

Before readers had caught their breath from *Beloved*, Morrison launched *Jazz* (1992), her sixth novel, which met with generally positive reviews and solidified her prominence as "one of the finest contemporary writers in America."[70] For instance, David Gates, in a review of *Jazz*, calls Morrison "the last classic American writer, squarely in the tradition of Poe, Melville, Mark Twain and Faulkner."[71] A luminously literary rendering of an art of composition that Duke Ellington perfected sometime in the summer of 1926, *Jazz* represents an advance in her work. While many black writers have used musicians and music as theme and metaphor for their writing, none have attempted to drop on jazz as the structuring principle for an entire work until Toni Morrison's new novel, *Jazz.* Morrison has wed the mode of jazz to depict the experience of black community in the city of New York during the 1920s, a decade itself known as the Jazz Age. Through a meticulous use of the jazz idiom, Morrison relates the story of Joe Trace and his wife Violet, both of whom had train-danced to the City, leaving behind all the traumas of their childhood. With Jazz, Morrison has established herself as one of the truly original novelists at work in the world today.

Released simultaneously with *Jazz* was Morrison's *Playing in the Dark: Whiteness and Literary Imagination* (1992), a scholarly work based on a lecture series she delivered at Harvard University. It reveals Morrison's deeper analytical talents as she diagrams the presence of the Africanist personae in the works of white writers, while probing the problem of living in a rationalised society with its democratic egalitarianism, on one hand, and its ideological dependence on racialism, on the other.[72] Morrison argues that the African presence in America, which shaped the entire nation, has had no significant place in the country's literature. She feels that a contemplation of the black presence is essential to any understanding of the nation's literature. Morrison writes with a clarity and simplicity which can attract a general audience Her discerning discussion on Africanism in major works of white American fiction enlivens debates on the function of literary criticism and alternative constructions of the Africanist character in African, African-American and related interdisciplinary studies. It is bound to alter our reading of the so-called classics in white American literature. The very fact that Harvard University Press decided to run twenty five thousand initial copies of *Playing in the Dark*, instead of the traditional number of fifteen hundred, is clearly indicative of Morrison's stature as a great American novelist. Morrison has also written several essays which have a bearing on her fictional art. They include "What the Black Woman Thinks about Women's Lib" (1971), "Behind the Making of the Black Book" (1974), "City Limits," "Village Values: Concepts of Neighbourhood in Black Fiction" (1981), "Recitalif" (1983), "Rootedness: The Ancestors as Foundation" (1984), "Memory Creation and Writing" (1984), "A Knowing so Deep" (1985), "The Site of Memory" (1987), "Unspeakable Things Unspoken" (1989), and a collection of essays which include "Racing Justice," "En-gendering Power," essays on Anita Hill, Clarence Thomas and "The Contribution of Social Reality" (1993).

Morrison has also to her credit a play, *Dreaming Emmett* (1986), which is based on the life of the young boy, Emmett Till, who was killed by a lynch mob in Mississippi in 1954. The play was written in honour of the first national observance of the birthday of Dr. Martin Luther King Jr. It was performed by the Capital Repertory Theatre of Albany, New York, on January 4, 1986. The play reveals that Morrison has many literary gifts—her instinct for storytelling, her free-standing characters and her astute ear for language and observation of human gesture—to offer the theatre. Even more important, however, is her focus on the historical and psychological complexities in the lives of ordinary black women and men. And, as Margaret Wilkerson in her brilliant critical essay, "The Dramatic Voice in Toni Morrison's Novels," points out the richness of language and perception that Morrison brings to her subject matter "should be brought to the stage so that there itself many learn from her dramatic voice."[73] The dramatic voice is strong in Morrison's novels. Her characters are complex and well-developed. Conflict is sharply defined as in any powerful play. Above all, her dialogue is crisp, concise and revealing.

VII

It seems appropriate to end this excursion into the world of Toni Morrison by having her speak for herself so as to know of her views regarding her function and goal as a writer. In an interview with Steve Cannon and Ntozake Shange, Toni Morrison offers a candid insight into her goal as a writer. She says: "My attempt, although I never say any of this, until I'm done . . . is to deal with something that is nagging me, but, when I think about it in a large sense, I use the phrase 'bear witness' to expiain what my work is for."[74] Here, Morrison refers to the act of rememory, of tapping into the deepest recesses of consciousness and of ripping the veil so that one's interior life and history can surface. She defines the role of the writer as witness bearer—an idea that will be repeated throughout her career. The ability to bear witness is closely tied to her concept of prophecy that has sacred undertones. This prophecy, or bearing witness, in her fiction is essential to her belief that the future is inextricably linked up with the past.

In her conversation with LeClair, Morrison envisions herself writing what is called village literature. She glories in writing peasant literature for her people. She declares: "I write what I recently began to call village literature, fiction that is really for the village, for the tribe. Peasant literature for my people, which is necessary and legitimate but which also allows me to get in touch with all sorts of people."[75] The function of novels in village literature is to clarify the roles that have become obscure and to identify those elements from the past that are useful and give nourishment to the people in the present. Morrison believes in the need to bring forth the meanings and lessons of the past into the present. She takes up this mission as a writer as a challenge against forgetfulness: "I think long and hard about what my novels should do. They should clarify the roles that have become obscured, they ought to identify those things in the past that are not and they ought to give nourishment."[76] She does not seek a historical rendering of facts, but endeavors to incorporate into the action, values, feelings and emotion that accompanied events in black life which she believes contains the lesson for survival.

In a 1984 interview, Toni Morrison comments that she tries to incorporate into her fiction one of the major characteristics of Black art; that is,

> the ability to be both print and oral literature; to combine those two aspects so that the stories can be read in silence, of course but one should be able to hear them as well. It should try deliberately to make you stand up and make you feel something profoundly in the same way that a Black preacher requires his congregation to speak, to join him in the sermon to behave in a certain way, to stand up and to be and to cry and to accede or to change and modify—to expand on the sermon that is being delivered.[77]

These functions were once culturally performed by black music, but are no longer. This is made clear when Morrison states: "For a long time, the art form that was healing for black people was music. That music is no longer exclusively ours. . . . So another form has to take that place."[78] What she suggests here is that the African-American novel is that form. She believes that the black writer can bring something unique—approximating the profound depths of black music—to fiction, "an ineffable quality that is curiously black."[79] As a black woman writer, this is what Toni Morrison seeks to do in her fiction. This is driven home to us when Morrison herself proclaims: "lam not like James Joyce; I am not like Thomas Hardy; I am not like Faulkner. I am not like that in that sense. . . . My effort is to be like something that has probably only been fully expressed in black music. . . . Writing novels is a way to encompass this—this something."[80] Morrison's explanation of the affinity between her writing and black music defines her strong sense of tradition. From the foregoing statements of Morrison it is clear that what she seeks to do in her fiction is what others in the past have done in black music.

To accomplish this, Morrison offers a solution to restore the power of African-American language to the people—the 'nommo' or power that exists in language and has the potential to reshape reality. She says: "I don't like to have someone call my books 'poetic,' because it has the connotation of luxuriating richness. I wanted to restore the language that black people spoke to its original power. That calls for a language that is rich but not ornate."[81] Morrison succeeds brilliantly in restoring the language of black people to its original power by turning it into "a musical instrument that trumpets the desires, disappointments, and triumphs of African-Americans."[82] As Dannile Taylor-Guthrie points out, "she writes and rewrites and rewrites, and, if necessary rewrites again and again until the language achieves a high level of exactness."[83] It is this labour that she enjoys most. Morrison says: "It must appear effortless! No matter what the style, it must have that. I mean the seams can't show!"[84] Morrison's novels, constituting as they do village literature, portray an exotic, fantastic world in which even the everyday black life of ordinary Midwestern towns comes alive in folklore, magic, superstition, fable, poetry, song and myth.

In her interview with Mel Watkins, Morrison discusses two related major concepts regarding her writing. First, for her, writing is a "way of thinking" and a process. She says: "It [writing] stretches you, makes you think the unthinkable, project yourself into people you even dislike, people I couldn't stay in a room with for 20 minutes. It makes you stay in touch with yourself; I guess it's like going under water for me, the danger, yet I'm certain I'm going to come up."[85] Secondly, she is a writer who works from images. She must have an image of a scene in her mind before she can write it. She is fascinated by the techniques of painters—their ability to re-create interpreted images to usual forms. As a writer she seeks to transform the visual to the aural via language, so that readers can create pictures in their own mind.

Morrison proudly presents herself as a branch on ancient tree of black assertiveness and self-definition that is richly and deeply rooted in the folk culture. As a Black Cultural Nationalist, she "validates black culture, and reaffirms its adaptive survival power, its creativity amidst oppression, life-affirming qualities, as well as its ancient wisdom and humanity and its capacity for survival."[86] She unapologetically declares herself to be a 'black woman writer.' Like Faulkner, she wants to write regional literature which is at once specific and universal, and have it published all over the world. In other words, she delves deep into the particular in order to reach the universal. This is made clear when she says:

> If I tried to write a universal novel, it would be water. Behind this question is the suggestion that to write for black people is somehow to diminish the writing. From my perspective, there are only black people. When I say "people," that's what I mean. Lots of books written by black people about black people have had this "universality" as a burden. They were writing for some readers other than me.[87]

Much of what Morrison writes individually as a black woman writer eventually leads back to the universal condition of being human. Morrison's ability to transform the individual into universal forces and idiosyncrasies into inevitabilities has led some critics to call her the "D.H. Lawrence of the black psyche."

Unlike other black artists—Gwendolyn Brooks, Clarence Major, and Albert Yound—who use art for strictly political purposes, Morrison realizes that strict adherence to political dogma would be insufficient to promote the aesthetic qualities of art. She, therefore, chooses to subordinate the political in order to "establish a positive black identity and to reorder racial consciousness through serious exploration and rediscovery of the black community's unique cultural heritage: its own particular beauty, its rich and varied oral tradition, its private joys and agonies, as well as its communal trials and tribulations."[88] Though she validates the aesthetic qualities of the black community, Morrison is anything but apolitical. She unequivocally declares: "The work must be political. It must have that as its thrust. . . . The best art is political and you ought to be able to make it unquestionably political and irrevocably beautiful at the same time."[89] There is no contradiction in Morrison's belief that art is political, that it must have aesthetic qualities and that ideally it must be committed to its people. For, by combining political consciousness with aesthetic sensibility, she achieves a very delicate balance. Without directly denouncing white society, she illustrates the demise of blacks who have adopted the corrupting influence of the white community. While valorizing the black community and igniting both blacks and whites into political action, she wishes to elevate, through art, the beautiful in the human condition.

It is but natural that Toni Morrison, with her political commitment to her people and her aesthetic responsibility to her art of fiction, is sensitively concerned with race, gender and class as three major forms of oppression of blacks in America. Morrison's novels document the author's awareness and concern for the historical conditions that sparked the national struggle of African people against oppression and exploitation, thereby revealing her heightened consciousness of the interrelationship of race, gender and class.

Though all the three elements—race, gender and class—are present in all the novels of Toni Morrison, the emphasis on them varies from novel to novel. *The Bluest Eye*, her first novel, examines racism as a primary source oppression of the Africans. *Sula* lays emphasis on gender oppression and *Song of Solomon* on the importance of knowing one's history to determine one's identity. *Tar Baby* is about class contradictions that keep African people divided and *Beloved* is about the solution—collective class struggle—that will help solve the exploitation and oppression of African people. *Jazz* focuses on gender solidarity through women bonding. Certainly, no one could choose and develop such themes as racism, gender oppression, identity crisis, class contradictions and class exploitation within the African race, as well as collective class struggle and women bonding, without herself having a commitment to struggle for African people.

NOTES

1. Richard Wright, "Blueprint for Negro Literature," *Challenge*, 1937.
2. Barbara Smith, "Doing Research on Black American Women," *Women Studies Newsletter*, 4 (Spring 1976), 4, 5, 7.
3. Barbara Christian, "Trajectories of Self-definition: Placing Contemporary Afro-American Women's Fiction," *Conjuring: Black*

Women, Fiction and Literary Tradition, ed. Pryse Marjorie and Hortense J. Spillers (Bloomington: Indiana University Press, 1985), p. 234.

4. Alexis De Veau, *Black Women Writers at Work*, ed. Claudia Tate (New York: Continuum, 1983), p. 55.
5. Barbara Christian, "Trajectories of Self-definition," p. 234.
6. Frances Harper, *Iola Leroy, Shadows Uplifted* (3rd ed.; Boston: James H. Earle, 1895), p. 281.
7. Jessie Redmon Fauset, *The Chinaberry Tree* (New York: Fredrick A. Stokes, 1931), p. ix.
8. Mckay Nellie, "Ann Petry's *The Street and the Narrow*: A Study of the Influences of Race and Gender on African-American Women's Lives," *Diedrich and Fisher Horrnung*, p. 139.
9. Barbara Christian, "Trajectories of Self-definition," p. 236.
10. Barbara Christian, *Black Women Novelists: The Development of a Tradition 1892-1976* (West Port, Connecticut: Greenwood Press, 1980), pp. 70-71.
11. Selwyn R. Cudjoe, "Maya Angelou and the Autobiographical Statement," in *Evans*, p. 7.
12. Barbara Christian, "Trajectories of Self-definition," p. 239.
13. Brock Sabine, "Talk as a Form of Action," *Lenz*, 1984, p. 206.
14. Cluistel Helene, "Paule Marshall's Bajan Women in *Brown Girl, Brownstones*," *Diedrich and Fischer-Hormong*, p. 141.
15. Alice Walker, *In Search of Our Mother's Gardens: Womanist Prose* (New York: Harcourt, 1983), p. xi.
16. John O'Brien, *Interviews with Black Writers* (New York: Liveright, 1973), p. 192.
17. *Ibid.*
18. Barbara Christian, *Black Feminist Criticism: Perspectives on Black Women Writers* (New York: Pergamon Press, 1985), p. 79
19. *Ibid.*, p. 72.
20. Gloria Wade-Gayles, *No Crystal Stair: Visions of Race and Sex in Black Women's Fiction* (New York: The Pilgrim Press, 1984), pp. 3-4.
21. Hernton Calvin, *Sex and Racism in America* (New York: Grove Press, 1965), p. 175.
22. Joel Kovel, *White Racism: A Psychohistory* (New York: Columbia University Press, 1984), p. 18.
23. A.J. Plakkoottam, "Racial and Gender Discrimination in Fiction by Afro-American Women," *Indian Journal of American Studies*, 20, 1 (1990), p. 13.

24. Gloria Steiner, *Outrageous Acts and Everyday Rebellions* (London: Fontana, 1984), p. 7.
25. Heal Frances, "Double Jeopardy: To be Black and Female," *The Black Women: An Anthology* (New York: Signet, 1970), p. 90.
26. Paula Giddings, *When and Where I Enter: The Impact of Black Women on Race and Sex in America* (New York: Morrow, 1984), p. 6.
27. Gerda Lerner, *Black Women in White America* (New York: New American Library, 1969), p. xxiii.
28. Gloria Wade-Gayles, *No Crystal Stair*, p. 7.
29. Emile Bums, *An Introduction to Marxism* (New York: International Publishers, 1966), p. 54.
30. Walter Rodney, *How Europe Underdeveloped Africa* (Dar es Salaam: Tanzania Publishing House, 1972), p. 16.
31. *Ibid.*, pp. 99-100.
32. *Ibid.*, p. 100.
33. Kwame Nkrumah, *Class Struggle in Africa* (New York: International Publishers, 1970), p. 29.
34. Eric Williams, *Capitalism and Slavery* (New York: G.P. Putnam's, 1944), pp. 18-19.
35. Walter Rodney, p. 100.
36. Kwame Nkrumah, *Class Struggle in Africa*, p. 27.
37. Zora Neale Hurston, *Their Eyes were Watching God* (New York: Fawcett, 1937), p. 29.
38. Gloria Wade-Gayles, *No Crystal Stair*, p. 7.
39. Ann Petry, *The Street* (Boston: Houghton, 1946), p. 206.
40. Barbara Christian, *Black Feminist Criticism*, pp. 103-5.
41. William H. Crier and Price M. Cobbs, *Black Rage* (New York: Bantam, 1968), p. 33.
42. Paule Marshall, *Brown Girl, Brownstones* (New York: Avon, 1959), p. 252.
43. Wilfred D. Samuels and Clenora Hudson-Weems, *Toni Morrison* (Boston: Twayne, 1990), p. 3.
44. Toni Morrison, "Slow Walk of Trees," *New York Times Magazine*, 4 July 1976, p. 152.
45. Jean Strouse, "Toni Morrison: Black Magic," *Newsweek*, 30 March 1981, p. 52.
46. Carolyn F. Gerald, "The Black Writer and His Role," *The Black Aesthetic*, ed. Addison Gayle, Jr. (New York: Anchor Books, 1970), pp. 349-56.
47. Samuels and Hudson-Weems, *Toni Morrison*, p. 4.

48. Colette Dowling, "The Song of Toni Morrison," *New York Times*, 20 May 1971, p. 42.
49. Jean Strouse, "Toni Morrison: Black Magic," p. 54.
50. *Loc. cit.*
51. Toni Morrison, "Behind the Making of *The Black Book*," *Black World*, 23 (1974), p. 88.
52. Robert Stepto, "Intimate Things in Place: A Conversation with Toni Morrison," *Chant of Saints*, ed. Michael S. Harper and Robert Stepto (Urbana: University of Illinois Press, 1979), p. 214.
53. Trudier Harris, *Fiction and Folklore: The Novels of Toni Morrison* (Knoxville: The University of Tennessee Press, 1991), p. 1.
54. William Wells Brown, *Clotel or The President's Daughter* (1853; New York: Collier, 1970), p. 108.
55. Ralph Ellison, *Shadow and Act* (New York, 1953), p. 172.
56. Doreatha Drummond Mbalia, *Toni Morrison s Developing Class-Consciousness* (Selingrove: Susquehanna University Press, 1992), p. 105.
57. Alex Haley, *Roots: The Saga of an American Family* (New York: Dell, 1976), p. 10.
58. Henry Dumas, *Goodbye, Sweetwater* (New York: Thunder's Mouth Press, 1988), p. xiv.
59. Jean-Paul Sartre, *Existentialism and Human Emotions* (Secaucus, N.J.: Castle, n.d.), pp. 15, 52.
60. Gloria Naylor and Toni Morrison, "*A* Conversation," *Southern Quarterly*, 21 (1985), p. 573.
61. Jean Strouse, "Toni Morrison: Black Magic," p. 54.
62. Although kept busy by full-time teaching of English classics and Freshmen composition by her role as faculty advisor for the English Club at Harvard University, and by the obligations of familyhood, Toni Morrison remained somewhat unfulfilled.
63. Jessica Harris, "Interview with Toni Morrison," *Essence*, 7, 8 (1976), p. 54.
64. Mel Watkins, "Talk with Toni Morrison," New *York Times Book Review*, 11 September 1977, p. 50.
65. Thomas LeClair, "The Language Must Not Sweat: A Conversation with Toni Morrison," *New Republic*, 21 March 1981, p. 25.
66. Toni Morrison, "Behind the Making of *The Black Book*," p. 90.
67. Samuels and Hudson-Weems, *Toni Morrison*, p. 8.
68. Review of *Beloved*, *Publishers Weekly* (17 July 1987), p. 53.
69. Merle Rubin, "Review of *Beloved*," *Christian Science Monitor*, 5 October 1987, p. 20.

70. Faye Chadwell, "Review of *Jazz*," *Library Journal*, 15 (April 1992), p. 122.
71. David Gates, "Review of *Jazz*," *Newsweek* (27 April 1992), p. 66.
72. See Toni Morrison, *Playing in the Dark: Whiteness and Literary Imagination* (London: Harvard University Press, 1992), p. 64.
73. Margaret B. Wilkerson, "The Dramatic Voice in Toni Morrison's Novels," *Critical Essays on Toni Morrison* (Boston: Hall, 1988), p. 189.
74. Ntozake Shange, "Interview with Toni Morrison," *American Rage*, November 1978, p. 52.
75. Thomas LeClair, "The Language Must Not Sweat," p. 25.
76. Elaine Showalter, *Modern American Women Writers* (New York: Charles Scribner's, 1991), p. 334.
77. Toni Morrison, "Rootedness: The Ancestor as Foundation," *Black Women Writers (1950-1980)*, ed. Mari Evans (New York: Anchor Books, 1984), p. 340.
78. *Ibid.*, p. 341.
79. *Ibid.*, p. 342.
80. Nellie Mckay, "An Interview with Toni Morrison," *Contemporary Literature*, 24, No. 4 (Winter 1983), p. 426.
81. Thomas LeClair, "The Language Must Not Sweat," p. 27.
82. Nancy J. Peterson, "Introduction: Canonizing Toni Morrison," *Modern Fiction Studies*, 39, 3 and 4 (Fall/Winter 1993), p. 476.
83. Dannile Taylor-Guthrie, ed., *Conversation with Toni Morrison* (Jackson: University Press of Mississippi, 1994), p. xi.
84. Jane Bakerman, "The Seams Can't Show: An Interview with Toni Morrison," *Black American Literary Forum*, 12, 1978, pp. 56-60.
85. Mel Watkins, "Talk with Toni Morrison," *New York Times Book Review*, 7 (11 September 1977), p. 49.
86. Harry Read, "Toni Morrison, *Song of Solomon* and Black Cultural Nationalism," *Centennial Review*, 32 (Winter 1988), p. 50.
87. Thomas LeClair, "The Language Must Not Sweat," p. 28.
88. Norris Clark, "Gwendolyn Brooks and a Black Aesthetic," *A Life Distilled: Gwendolyn Brooks, Her Poetry and Fiction*, ed. Maria K. Mootry and Gary Smith (Urbana: University of Illinois Press, 1987), p. 82.
89. Toni Morrison, "Rootedness: The Ancestor as Foundation," p. 340.

Black Women Novelists: Development, Flowering and Fruition of a Tradition

BHARATI A. PARIKH

Bharati Parikh traces the development of black women's literature. Iola Leroy *by Frances Harper is the first novel by a black woman. The heroine has created a lasting impact on black literature for decades. Hurston in* Their Eyes were Watching God *moved the image of black woman beyond a stereotype. Petry's* Street *was the precursor of 20th century literature for black women. Another important black writer Gwendolyn Brooks, in* Maud Martha, *focuses with sensitivity the difficulties faced by black women in an urban community. Morrison's novels represent the lasting aspects of black creativity. They are rich in symbols, signs and omens set by nature.*

Editor

Tradition, in the context of Afro-American women novelists is indeed a complex issue. That is why it is equally interesting and challenging too. Speaking from a distance and differences of history, geography and race, an Indian woman can definitely derive much inspiration from the heroic struggle of Afro-American women in white America.

"Black women have been doubly victimized by scholarly neglect and racist assumptions." (Lerner, xvi) They belonged to two groups which were traditionally been "treated as inferiors by American society—Blacks and women—they have been doubly invisible." (Lerner, xvi) In their native African culture, women were treated equally with men. They not only were able stateswomen, warriors and tradewomen, but also on equal footing with men in all spheres of life. The Euro-centric white culture reduced these earth-mothers to most menial status during slavery in America. It is a long odyssey of Afro-American women writers who excel in various genre of writing. Their potential, genius and creativity are acclaimed when several Afro-American women writers won much coveted literary prizes. This includes Toni Morrison, one of the most appealing and popular writers of our times, who was awarded the Nobel Prize for Literature in 1993.

The two different racial groups, whites and blacks, in America, represent two separate cultures, with separate traditions and "diametrically opposed past experience." Likewise, Afro-American writers represent images of black women whose roles, history, experiences and contributions constitute separate culture.

There are umpteen number of novels where Afro-American women are portrayed as mammy, nurse, maid, conjure women, cook or you name it! Just to give some instances, in Morrison's *The Bluest Eye*, Pauline Breedlove works first as a maid in a white household and later on with Fishers as a housekeeper. So does Alice Walker's *The Third Life of Grange Copeland* depict Mem as a maid. Black women have struggled throughout in partnership with their men to keep the black family together and to allow the black community to survive and sustain. "Their dual and often conflicting role has imposed great tensions on black women and has given them unusual strength." (Lerner, xviii) It is noteworthy that through thick and thin, black women have shown "the pride and strength of people who have endured and survived great oppression." (Lerner, xviii)

It is indeed an illuminating journey through major novels by Afro-American women novelists, who reveal their major preoccupation, the 'black woman,' her various images. They are complex, diverse and have strength and depth of character.

Though the institutionalized slavery reigned for almost three hundred years in America, the woes of the black people reverberate till date.

Iola Leroy (1892) by Frances Harper is the first Afro-American novel written by a woman. Since then the Afro-American women have been writing under duress. This first novel depicts the tribulations of the beautiful mulatto protagonist, Iola Leroy. This eponymous novel should be viewed, "as a woman's novel" in words of Dandridge, "presenting the difficulties of the protagonist, Iola Leroy, as a black and as a woman." (Lerner, 5)

What interests a present-day reader is how Harper focuses Iola Leroy as a black woman and the strength of her character. It is particularly interesting that even though the heroine is a mulatto, she prides herself in being black. She overturns the offer of a white man Dr. Gresham to marry, when he becomes reticent after discovering that she is black. "By denying herself marriage to Dr. Gresham" as Dandridge remarks, "she affirms the morality of black motherhood and passes up her golden opportunity to overcome the stigma of her race." (5) The important issues like black pride and the quest motif are at the centre stage.

To Iola, being recognized as a black mother is just as important, if not more so, as being treated justly as a black. She supports her affirmation of black motherhood, by postponing her future happiness and engages herself in an arduous search for her own mother. This quest covers two-thirds of the novel. Thus, *Iola Leroy* (1892), the first published novel by a black woman, "sets the stage for this heroine as a lasting image in black literature for decades to come." (Christian, 3)

This is the sure beginning of Afro-American novelists' quest for their being recognized as writers, artists. Although the mainstream white, male literary tradition did not take notice of these women artists, they continued their long journey since 1892. The literary establishment already had labeled their work, and critics repeatedly opined: "for joining the literary mainstream that black women writers took special pleasure in ignoring the critics altogether. As a result, they directed their sights onto a frontier of their own choosing, proclaiming their freedom to select their own subjects." (59)

Right from the early days of slavery, black women were neglected, maltreated and had struggled against harrowing circumstances. The same is applicable to Afro-American women novelists in white America. As Naylor speaks out in her talk with Goldstein: "a rich vein of literature [was] left largely unexplored. . . . the belated recognition of writers like Zora Neale Hurston, (is a case in point) . . . [and] the discovery of Harriet Wilson's *Our Nig,* the recent acclaim for Alice Walker's work, are examples of the fact that "blacks have been writing in this country since this country has been writing and have a literary heritage of their own. Unfortunately, they haven't had encouragement or recognition for their efforts."

Zora Neale Hurston's name immediately recalls her contribution to the rich tradition of Afro-American women novelists. She was a writer and an anthropologist. She lived and grew up in an all black community town, Eatonville in Florida. Her novels exude "the wonderful richness and beauty of black folk culture." (Christian, 9) *Their Eyes Were Watching God* (1937) is her most acclaimed novel. It has "the Hurston blend of complexity of character within the frame of a good story." (Christian, 9)

Janie, the heroine of *Their Eyes* . . . fits the outlines of the conventional tragic mulatto. Janie's portraiture is unique. She marries twice. Her first marriage takes place with an old man, Logan Killicks. He is jealous of her youth and beauty. Second time she marries with Jody Stark. He is the black entrepreneur who creates a town partly to establish Janie as its queen, seated on the porch, aloof and apart from everyone, as it was customary for a mulatto to imitate the norms of the white society lady. But Janie cannot stand this isolation. She wants to know herself and her husband. Such a desire is perceived as a threat by Jody. There is a dramatic change in Janie's life when Jody dies. She falls in love with Tea Cake, who is younger to Janie. But he is interested not in her money or in her long black hair, but in her essence. Their love story forms the hard kernel of this novel, as Christian observes: "romantic in its abandon, but tingling with a poignancy borne of a dream, dream dreamt so long that it had to come true. That Janie must kill Tea Cake because he is mad with rabies leads us back to the stereotype of the tragic mulatto, except that to Janie, her life has not been tragic but rich." (9)

Hurston, through the character of Janie, not only probes Janie's nature but "the condition of all black women." This novelist also grasped in her works the theme of black Folklore, the delving into the nature of man, the nature of woman, and how these two natures blend or conflict. As Christian notes: "Woman, viewing and viewed, is part of the theme of *Their Eyes* . . ., as if the writer were illuminating one part of a canvass in order to give meaning to the entire painting." (10)

Zora Neale Hurston's voice is one of the richest in the black women novelists' orchestrating chords as she created the most memorable creation of black folks' life. She used black idiom in fiction and gave the special flavour of black life. Thus, Hurston, in her life and work "moved the image of the black woman beyond stereotype, as she sought the ever evolving ways of the folk. She grafted onto the nineteenth century mode, a new way of looking at the mulatto and the Southern black woman, preparing the way for different spice boxes in the twentieth century." (Christian, 11)

Alain Locke, the philosopher of Harlem Renaissance said that *Their Eyes Were Watching God* was "folklore fiction at its best." In spite of racism and sexism, there is a rich and powerful tradition of black women novelists who have "woven works of lasting beauty."

In the saga of black women novelists Ann Petry's *The Street* (1946) is a landmark. It functions, along with Hurston's work, "as a transition from the tragic mulatto pattern and/or the rural southern woman as heroine to a more contemporary view of the black novel." (Christian, 11)

During the Great Depression in the thirties in America, countless number of blacks migrated to the Northern urban centers from the Southern rural background. The impact of the hostile urban environment, where one felt dislocated and cut off and the inevitability of crime as the black person's only release from fear and alienation were two elements that Petry used in her first novel *The Street.* The novel is the poignant and unblinkingly honest story of Lutie Johnson, a young black woman, and her struggle to live and raise a son amid the violence, poverty and racial dissonance of Harlem in the late 1940s. This novel won the Houghton Mifflin Literary Fellowship Award.

Petry worked as a journalist, during the early forties, for *The Amsterdam News* and *The People's Voice.* Thus, she knew the social problems of Harlem. In 1944 she joined the New York Foundation to work on a sociological study of the effects of segregation on ghetto children. These experiences helped her in delineating the details of a Harlem street.

The Street assumes the role of a major character in the novel. Petry's major concern in the novel was the hostile environment of Harlem and its effects on the people who must endure it. Many notable writers/critics have noted similarities between Richard Wright's *Native Son* (1941) and Petry's *The Street* (1940). The hero of *Native Son* Bigger Thomas represents an alienated black male created partially by concrete plantations of the North. Similarly Lutie Johnson in *The Street* is the lost black female, alone and struggling. Thus, both these characters become literary types that are often used by writers in later years that they have become stereotypes.

The strength of the heroine Lutie is tried, out and out in a system which is hostile to black woman in forties in a big city like New York. Her struggle to survive and survive 'whole' leads her to commit the murder of her potential employer Boots. It is the most powerful novel depicting the woes of a heroic black woman who does not want to make amends with her moral values. She is a "brown, good-looking girl" plagued by the sexual advances of men, both black and white. The dominant male would use her identically as the black female slave was used. She works as a domestic working in the rich white folk's home, northern style. Petry also reveals how white society manipulates to break black family life in *The Street.* Here, the husbands leave their wives not because they are unable to be a man in their own eyes. They fail to find a job and protect their women and children. The struggle for survival "strangles friendship and family ties." Everyone suspects each other as slaves were expected to.

The Street is a novel that depicts sordid reality of life for blacks in general and black women in particular. The novel also focuses on situation, setting and environment. Metaphorically speaking, Lutie Johnson might be one of any husbands of thousands of black women, whose aspiration for a better life was the only thing that kept them going. Like the 116th Street of the novel, Lutie's plight is also the major character of the novel. Such a plight can only lead to crime and tragedy. Lutie—poor, helpless, without any support from community, or any warmth of companionship—struggles all by herself. Thus, Petry heightens the intensity of overwhelming odds that her heroine faces. Lutie never has any opportunity for choice in life.

Her beauty, finally, becomes the cause of her defeat. The reader is left helpless, gaping at the fate of such a fine character. But in creating a hostile environment persistently, Petry realized the stereotypes that were inflicted on black women. So all her characters intended to counteract them. Petry delineates her characters with particular physical characteristics that match specific stereotype and then proceeds to show how they are totally different. Thus, she both adheres to and deviates from the standard images. The impact left by the novel is so grim, and the novel so depressing, that some may not believe. Yet it is "horribly true as the treatment of black slaves in southern plantations." (Christian, 12)

This novel can be called the precursor of the twentieth century in the literature of the black women, as there is a marked change in setting and tone. Instead of the southern plantation, the concrete plantation becomes the dwelling place of more and more blacks in the 20th century. After the publication of *The Street,* "the black city woman could not be forgotten." (Christian, 12)

Another notable title is *Maud Martha* (1953) by Poet Laureate of Chicago, Gwendolyn Brooks, one of the finest poets. This is the only novel by Brooks apart from several volumes of poetry and an autobiography. *Maud Martha* is "a series of lyrical, autobiographical, vignettes about a black girl growing up in a closely knit family set in Chicago during the late 30s and 40s. The novel focuses on the sensitivity of the black girl—woman in an urban community." (*Ibid.*) In the novel one feels both, in the words of Christian, "the lyricism, a soul-singing that is found in Zora Neale Hurston's works, and the harsh cutting edges of Petry's *The Street* .

Maud Martha, the heroine is an intense perceiver. In the fabric of this novel Brooks has woven the impact of racism, either hidden or subtle. Maud Martha has been endowed with an imagination. She is not alone; she is loved by her family and nurtured by their communal rituals. The reader hears through her mind's voice the sounds of her family, her community, and the unknown outer white world. Her world is a cocoon in which she has sufficient protection and nourishment to find her own self. The novel unfolds thus:

> What she liked was candy buttons, and books, and painted music (deep blue or delicate silver) and the west sky, so altering, viewed from the steps of the back porch; and dandelions.
>
> She would have liked a lotus, or China asters or the Japanese, Irish, or meadow lilies—yes, she would have liked meadow lilies, because the very word meadow made her breathe more deeply, and either fling her arms or want to fling her arms, depending on who was by, rapturously up to whatever was watching in the sky. But dandelions was what she chiefly saw. Yellow jewels for everyday, studding the patched green dress of her back yard. She liked their demure prettiness second to their everydayness; for in that latter quality she thought she saw a picture of herself, and it was comforting to find that what was common could also be a flower. (1)

Thus, Maud Martha is no beautiful heroine but an ordinary person. Yet, Christian observes, "like all ordinary people, she is herself, a marvel. (69) Brooks heightens our awareness of the wonderfulness of the commonplace and created a new type of black woman character.

Margaret Walker's *Jubilee* (1966) is another awe-inspiring creation. It is a wonderful historical novel of mammoth scope; depicts the heroine Vyry as a slave before the Civil War and as a freedwoman after Emancipation. This is a unique novel, a work of giant proportions which Walker wrote after 20 years of research based on the stories about her great-grandmother. It is different from the usual Civil War romance. The novelist tells the story from a slave's perspective rather that from the master's. *Jubilee* is a story not only of "one slave's life, but of an entire culture." To achieve these two objectives, Walker used "folklore as her major structural element." Thus, at times, *Jubilee* is reminiscent of the novels of Zora Neale Hurston. It is "saturated with many of the various aspects of folk culture: the songs, sayings, customs, food, medicinal remedies, language, and of course the double-leveled styles of behaviour through which the slaves manage to survive." (Christian, 71)

Like Hurston's Janie, Vyry is a mulatto. Although she does not feel caught between two worlds she is a black woman, a slave who cooks for her master's household and must work long hard hours. Of course, the master is her father who hardly has much impact on her life. She has no pretensions about herself. Neither slaves move around her because of her mixed blood nor she performs extraordinary feats of heroism. Nonetheless she loves her children.

It is interesting to examine the story line of the novel. Vyry's mother, Sis Hettie, is the concubine of the master. Her life is a long struggle. She dies at the age of 28, due to constant childbearing. Ticey, the granny treats her on her deathbed. She is a herbalist and the closest thing to a medical doctor available to the slaves in Southern Plantation. There is Aunt Sally, the cook who precedes Vyry. She becomes young Vyry's substitute mother for a short spell, but is not a typical mammy: "She steals food, has little respect for mistress, and teaches Vyry the tricks of survival in Missy's Kitchen. Even the stereotypical view of the white mistress is somewhat revised. Big Missy is no pining alabaster lady. She is the thrifty manager of her husband's estate who is bitter at being cut off from the rest of the world."

Jubilee depicts the importance of the practical slave culture, which helped black people as an abused race to survive. Walker also emphasized that this culture helped the slave to retain some measure of his own self-respect. It is Walker's most important contribution to the development of black woman novelist's tradition that "when the negative images of Afro-American women took hold, she went to the root of the old stereotypes, making spaces for younger novelists to create character rather than type, and to explore many dimensions of their consciousness and craft." (Christian, 73)

In recent times Toni Morrison, Alice Walker, Gloria Naylor and several other Afro-American women novelists have caused "a dramatic shift in the American literary landscape." Henderson also remarks that "what has happened" in the past two decades or so "is a 'revolution within the Revolution,' one that was initiated by and has been sustained chiefly by Black women. . . . As Black women have come into new awareness of their powers, as they have struggled to liberate themselves, they have enriched and expanded the international corpus of Black literature."

It is especially a rewarding and enriching experience for Indian women to delve into the corpus of Morrison's 'narratives,' as she prefers to call her works of fiction. She struck a new chord in writing novels like *The Bluest Eye* (1970), *Sula* (1974), *Song of Solomon* (1978), *Tar Baby* (1981), *Beloved* (1991) and *Jazz* (1992).

Morrison explained about the genesis of her first two books: "I wrote *Sula* and *The Bluest Eye* because they were books I had wanted to read. No one had written them yet, so I wrote them. My audience is always the people in the book I'm writing at the time I don't think of an external audience."

Her fictional world is predominantly black. In her earlier novels, young black adolescent girls and black women, by and large, are at the centre stage. *The Bluest Eye* is a novel which is a testimony to Morrison's deep interest in black people and their lives, their culture, their love of music, racial and sexual injustice and poverty faced by black people. Morrison's creations represent "lasting expressions of the black woman's creativity." In her *Black Women Novelist: The Development of a Tradition, 1892-1976,* Christian remarks: "Toni Morrison's works are fantastic earthy realism. Deeply rooted in history and mythology, her work resonates with mixture of pleasure and pain, wonder and horror. Primal in their essence, her characters come at you with the force and beauty of gushing water, seemingly fantastic but as basic as the earth they stand on." (137)

Sula (1974) and *The Bluest Eye* (1970) depict the search for beauty amidst restrictions of life, both from within and without. In both these novels the black woman, as girl and grown woman, is the turning character, and "the friendship between two women or girls serves as the yardstick by which the overwhelming contradictions of life are measured" (*Ibid.*).

Pecola and Sula, Pauline and Nel, are double-faced. They look outward and search inward. They try to find some continuity between the seasons, the earth, other people, the cycles of life, and their own particular lives. They, more often than not, find that there is a conflict between their own nature and the society that man has made, to the extent that one seems to be an inversion of the other. Thus, Morrison's novels are rich, not only in human characterizations, but also "in the signs, symbols, omens, sent by nature. Wind and fire, robins as a plague in the spring, marigolds that won't sprout, are as much characterizations in her novels as the human beings who people them." (*Ibid.*)

The Bluest Eye depicts the story of two young sisters Claudia and Frieda Mac Teers growing up in a tiny provincial black community in Lorain, Ohio in 1940s. Their friendship with Pecola Breedlove, a homely outcast little girl, is the focus of the novel and how she has been mercilessly victimized by her parents and community that she retreats into insanity. Morrison described this novel as a book about "the absolute destruction of human life because of the most superficial thing in the world—physical beauty." (*Current Biography*, 265)

The theme of *The Bluest Eye* is simple, the desire of a black girl for blue eyes. But it is also a real and symbolic statement about the conflict between the good and beautiful of two cultures and how it affects the psyche of the people within these cultures. Thus the theme embraces "the conflict of artistic and societal values between the Anglo-American and Afro-American cultures, complicated by the psychopolitical dominance of one culture over another." In short this novel is "about mythic, political, and cultural mutilation as much as it is a book about race and sex hatred."

The nature image of marigolds not sprouting in spring of 1940-41, is the major structural element of the novel. There are ironic insights and intensely evocative imagery, which renders a great strength and lyrical charm to the narrative.

Sula is again an evocative, overpervading search for 'self' of the heroine. There are unforgettable characters of Eva, the grandmother and Sula the granddaughter. The household of Eva Peace is strange, where Eva, the matriarch manipulates the lives of all around her. Sula is a rebellious, unconventional woman, whose life becomes one of unlimited experiment. *Sula* depicts the intense, forty-year friendship between two women: Sula and Nel. Nel is the conventional woman who accepts the societal mores and rigid moral code of the insular black community of Bottom whereas Sula defies them. Sula is a complex woman who is "at once self-reliant, amoral, predatory, alluring and completely ruthless." (*Current Biography* 265) In her community of blacks, Sula is first thought to be simply unusual, then outrageous, and eventually evil. She becomes a pariah of her community, a measuring stick of what is evil, and, ironically, inspires goodness in those around her.

Morrison's use of spare, precise language, "economical, life-like dialogues and totally convincing characterizations" make *Sula* an unforgettable experience. Morrison wants the readers to feel and experience all the sensuousness of her descriptions, images, metaphors and similes, which she does successfully through all her novels. She wants that the language should be 'sweet' and 'seems should not be seen.' This is virtually achieved in *Song of Solomon* (1977)

The novel revolves around the central metaphor of flying. During slavery how the blacks survived with the help of wishful thinking is grandly portrayed in the flying myth of Solomon. The hero, Malcolm, known as Milkman because his mother Ruth nursed him well past infancy, leaves his middle-class Midwestern home for the South. He tries to search for a secret cache of gold, which turns out to be his successful awakening and search of his roots. The novel can be read at several levels. The women characters have a charm of their own. Among all of them, Pilate, Macon Dead Sr.'s lost sister, is a towering figure, one without a naval and a box hanging in her earlobe for the security of her name, which should not be forgotten. She loves her brother and becomes invariably a pilot for her nephew, Milkman. Thus, the woman plays a pivotal role in safeguarding the black values, heritage and steers clearly out of dominating white value system. She is a nurturing figure to her sister-in-law Ruth, who was dying of 'lovelessness' at the hands of her husband. The largesee of her heart is explicit while dying, when she says if "I had known more people, I would have loved them all." This reveals the nobility of spirit of black woman.

Tar Baby (1981) is based on Joel Chandler Harris's Brer Rabbit stories. The story is set in rich Caribbean Island Isle des Chevaliers, where nature is in its full bloom. The story has several layers of meaning. Valerian Street, the white millionaire tries to tame nature in his green house and control his much too younger wife. The old faithful black couple, Ondine and Sydney, who worked for the entire life with Valerian reared orphan niece Jadine. She is a successful black model who studied at France. What Morrison stresses here is that the black woman must retrain her natural properties, and 'heritage.'

The story depicts an intimate relationship between Jadine and a vagrant, Son, for a while, who finally does not succumb to Jadine's values. In *Tar Baby* Morrison suggests that reconciliation between the black man and the black woman can only occur when they mutually understand that they are both victims of racial exploitation. The language is sheer poetry and descriptions evocative of the sights, sounds and color of the locale.

Thus, one can conclude with Morrison in the forefront of Afro-American women novelists, the odyssey of this specific culture group is one of great triumph and celebration. Their journey has come full circle in the fruition of Black women novelists of rare courage, artistic merits and unforgettable portrayal of black women characters as vivid, distinct and lovable as life itself.

Works Cited

Brooks, Gwendolyn. *Maud Martha.* 1953. New York : Harper.

______. "Black Women Novelists: New Generation Raises Provocative Issues," *Ebony*, Nov. 1984, 59-63.

Christian, Barbara. *Black Women Novelists*: *The Development of a Tradition*, 1892-1972. Westport, Connectict: Greenwood Press, 1980.

______. *Black Feminist Criticism: Perspectives on Black Women Writers*. New York: Pergamon, 1985.

Dandridge, Rita B. "Male Critics/Black Women's Novels," *CLA Journal*, Vol. XXIII, 1 (Sept. 1979), 1-11.

Evans, Mari, ed. *Black Women Writers* (*1950-1980*). *A Critical Evaluation.* New York: Anchor/Doubleday, 1984.

Henderson, Stephen E. "Introduction" in Mari Evans, xxiii-xxviii.

Harper, Frances E.W. *Iola Leroy* or *Shadow Uplifted.* 1982; New York: AMS Press, 1971.

Hull, Gloria T. et al. *All the Women are White, All the Men are Black but Some of Us are Brave.* New York: Feminist Press, 1982.

Lerner, Gerda (ed.) *Black Women In White America: A Documentary History*. New York: Pantheon, 1972.

Toni Morrison, *The Bluest Eye*. New York: Pocket Books, 1970.

Toni Morrison, *Sula*. New York: New American Library, 1982.

Toni Morrison, *Song of Solomon*. New York: New American Library, 1978.

Toni Morrison, *Tar Baby*. New York: New American Library, 1981.

Toni Morrison, *Beloved*. New York: New American Library, 1987.

Contribution of African-American Women Writers in the Cause of Women with Special Reference to Toni Morrison and Alice Walker

R. GANDHI SUBRAMANIAN

The problem of inequality existing between nations and classes has preoccupied various committed writers and has been a part of their scholarly endeavours. African-Americans, though free, were deprived of every semblance of equality within the political system in America. Rightly does DuBois contend that the problem of African-American is the problem of colour line. R. Gandhi Subramaniam draws an analogy between women's rights movements and anti-slavery movement. He shows how Morrison's and Walker's works have championed the cause of African-American women, by bringing the readers' attention to day-to-day injustices faced by them.

Editor

Men and women all over the world irrespective of their differences of nationality, race, religion, colour or government are governed by more or less the same feelings and passions. Hence the inequality—existing between nations, between classes, between men and women, between the haves and have nots—has not remained just a matter of scholarly interest but over the years it has also become everyone's concern.

A literary work utilizing one's experiences—expectations, yearnings and dreams, doubts and dilemmas and hopes and despairs—to look at the world in a different light with the intention of creating a better, more prosperous and more peaceful world stands to be acknowledged as creative. Such a work not only draws the attention of the people but it attains their approval and appreciation too. The great legends, in whichever language they have been written, stand testimony to this with their deep concern for mankind and its betterment.

Though America is a free country, the urge, the demand of the African-American to be treated as an equal, still remains a distant dream. Though generations of Americans, right from the seventeenth century to the twentieth century, have "sought to create a social order" with "equity and justice, as they understood it," extending the benefits of equality and justice to the African-American has always been elusive.[1] It is a fact that various congresses right from the First through Sixteenth made certain that the African-Americans though free were deprived "every semblance of equality within and the political system . . . a man not only had to be free, but also white, in order to enjoy equality or even to aspire for it."[2]

The problem of the African-American is the problem of 'Color Line' as mentioned by William E.B. DuBois in 1902. In an environment vitiated by centuries of violent oppression, inequality and injustice, the reaction of the African-American is natural. His/Her anger against inequality and injustice is his/her righteous indignation.

The African-American problem has an impact on several writers like William DuBois, Claude McKay, Richard Wright and Ralph Ellison on the one hand and women writers like Toni Morrison and Alice Walker on the other. Their novels have been written with a specific social purpose. The trying circumstances make the novels of African-Americans like Richard Wright and Ralph Ellison especially relevant with their graphic details. The novels of Toni Morrison and Alice Walker written about three decades later become equally significant by representing the plight of African-American women. Shockingly for them, their tormentors are their own men who join those other external, traditional, non African-American oppressors. The pain and agony caused by the African-American oppressor make an integral part of their novels.

Mary Wollstonecraft, an English woman, in her pioneering essay "A Vindication of the Rights of Women" written in 1792, addressed the rightful place of women in society. Her "work was widely influential in America . . . and helped to spearhead the anti-slavery and the women's rights movements in America in the nineteenth century."[3]

Elizabeth Stanton was one of the best known advocates for equality of women during the nineteenth century and at the end of the century Charlotte Perkins Gilman championed the economic independence of women. Hence, even during the nineteenth century, many feminists fought for political freedom, the right to vote, equality before law, economic independence and reproductive freedom.

The early twentieth century had women's suffrage as its primary objective, resulting in the Nineteenth Amendment in 1920, the American constitution assuming the "right of citizens of the United States to vote shall not be denied or abridged by the United States or by any States on account of sex."

During the decade of the Great Depression, in the 1930s many states legally prohibited married women from working, and "the middle class woman who wished to work was an anomaly and was seen to be acting against her social status and the dominant cultural norms of her day."[4]

The contributions of writers like Toni Morrison and Alice Walker has to be seen in this background, though writers like Richard Wright have highlighted the oppressive plight of African-American women in his novella *Long Black Song* and has presented Sue, a female protagonist in *Bright and Morning Star*, as an exemplary woman, fighting for the downtrodden and sacrificing her life in the cause.

Toni Morrison, one of the most significant African-American writers and Nobel Laureates, was born almost a quarter of a century later than Richard Wright and Ralph Ellison. Her first novel, *The Bluest Eye*, was published in 1970, and it is to be realised that even a quarter of a century after Wright's and Ellison's works were published, not much has changed in the conditions of the exploited African-Americans. The less spoken about the conditions of women, the better.

Morrison's father was responsible for creating a positive self-image in his daughter, preventing her from acquiring "the zero image," a negative definition of self commonly associated with oppressed peoples and familiar to black children.[5] Her positive self-image makes Toni Morrison choose the novel form and in one of her interviews she has stated:

> In a novel . . . there's so much room and the possibilities are infinite. That's why I find it the most challenging form. . . . I'm overwhelmed by all the space in a novel, all the possibilities, all the ways in which characters can turn.

Morrison's concern is not racism, and she does not bother being called 'racist'; but her concern is the oppressive conditions thrust on her protagonists, and the traumatic effect caused by such oppression. As a woman in general and as an African-American in particular, Morrison "examines problems of race and gender oppression before exploring class contradictions within the race."[6]

The oppressive world portrayed by Morrison shows the loss of identity of the African-American and his/her quest for establishing his/her identity. Pain, horror, violence and crime are not uncommon but rather the order of the day in the life of the African-American. In this world of oppression, the African-American women remain more exploited, violated and oppressed. To survive in such a world, Morrison's "protagonist must somehow violate the rule of the oppressive system, reject the values it venerates, and recover the human potential denied to blacks."[7]

Morrison's words "I have never met yet a boring black person. All you have to do is scratch the surface and you will see. And that is because of the way they look at life," come alive in her novels.

A study of Morrison's novels reveals not only her evolution as a writer but also her growing concern for the African-American in general and the African-American women in particular. Mbalia's statement, "In each of her novels, Morrison explores some aspect of and/or solution to the oppression afflicting African people. *The Bluest Eye* examines racism; *Sula*, gender oppression; *Song of Solomon*, the necessity of knowing one's family, community and heritage; *Tar Baby*, the class contradictions that keep African people divided; and *Beloved*, the solution that will help solve the class exploitation and racial oppression of African people" (9-10) categorises some of the major concerns of Morrison's novels. Her concern for the African-American is carried further in her *Jazz* and *Paradise*.

Morrison's *The Bluest Eye* has its inspiration from an earlier attempted short story by her about a little African-American girl, who longed for blue eyes. This theme has been developed later into a highly thought-provoking novel, *The Bluest Eye*. The novel speaks at length on the problem of the forced imposition of the zero image on the African-American children, especially the girls. Mbalia has asserted, "The thesis of the novel is that racism devastates the self-image of the African female in general and the African female child in particular." (28)

Morrison identifies the emotional violence heaped upon the children by parents as a special concern, which she sets out to explore in *The Bluest Eye*. The lack of love that shatters a family, the misfortune of being born in a breed 'hate' family, a family which has thrown the mantle of ugliness on themselves without a question and the denial of self-love, all these contribute to make Pecola's tragedy the worst being, Pecola being raped by her incestuous, drunken father. Thus, *The Bluest Eye* also throws light on the problem of incest and child abuse afflicting the African-American female .

In *Sula*, her second novel, Morrison "turns her attention to securing individual's rights in general and women's rights in particular," (20) writes Mbalia. Mbalia considers *Sula* as a continuation of *The Bluest Eye* and she has stated that *Sula* in effect, has taken up from where *The Bluest Eye* has left off: "when *Sula* opens, the heroine is the twelve-year-old Pecola, isolated and oppressed." (25)

Sula Peace comes of a family who have learnt to live hard, in ways others cannot even imagine. The creator and sovereign of this family is Eva Peace, who according to somebody stuck one of her legs under a train and made them pay off! Sula rejects the traditional role ascribed to women, telling Eva, "I want to make myself." Probably here Morrison tries to infuse the idea of individual or gender freedom as the African's solution.

Sula is different from the others from the very beginning in that she will not tolerate harassment or oppression. She grows up as a tough girl. Her rebellious nature makes her unpopular and she is unforgivable in the opinion of the people of Medallion, and Sula becomes an outcast and untouchable. By developing two female characters, Sula and Nel, neither of whom is complete in herself, "Morrison chooses to explore the nature of women's oppression" (40) in a unique way, according to Mbalia. Sula remains independent till she breathes her last. Sula's last, final moment on this earth is touching: "Then she realized or rather sensed, that there was not going to be any pain. She was not breathing because she didn't have to. Her body did not need oxygen. She was dead."

"She was not breathing because she didn't have to," seems to suggest that the total freedom, the freedom even from breathing is available to the African-American woman, only when she ceases to be, only when she is clinically dead! Barbara Christian remarks: "The *Bluest Eye* and *Sula* teach us a lesson about the integral relationship between the destructive limits imposed on the Black woman and the inversions of truth in this society."[8]

Tar Baby is a novel revealing that Morrison has reached a well-marked stage in her evolution as a writer. The novel shows the whites and the African-Americans in a different light. The novel differs from the previous ones by its setting also. Jadine, an African-American's repulsion for another, whom she calls a "nigger," surrogates the role of the white tormentor. Son, the hero of this novel "is from the beginning a wanderer in search of self," (77) states Otten.

Thus, Morrison's novels reveal that oppression is not confined just to one race, age group or sex, resulting in violence, hatred and the blindness to recognise truth and the practical realities. Her novels reveal the plight of the women from Pecola to Sula and Jadine's inability to give up her ancestry leaving her in an unenviable plight. In other words, Morrison portrays a transition of her women—from zero image to independent individuality—a portrayal showing her deep concern for women.

Alice Walker is another African-American, occupying an eminent place among women writers. She feels though "the twentieth century black women writers all seem to be much more interested in black community . . . there just has not been enough examination or enough applications of findings to real problems in our day-to-day living." She has "a commitment to write the 'authentic' lives of 'real' Black people . . . with an urgency to tell the specific stories of Black women."[9] Alice Walker has stated in one of her interviews:

> I am preoccupied with the spiritual survival, the *whole* of my people. . . . I am committed to exploring the oppressions, the insanities, the loyalties, the triumphs of the black women . . . for me, black women are the most fascinating creations of the world.

Walker feels that a commitment to writing—to be significant—must be combined with social and political activism, and that the artist must stay close enough to his/her people and "to be there wherever they need "such a presence. To fulfill her commitment, Walker uses her narrative, grounded in racial history and focuses on the histories of women of African ancestry. Butler-Evans writes: "These historical narratives of women while contained within the framework of racial historical narratives, becomes signifiers of sexual difference." (126)

Walker traces the history of African-American women's creativity in her essay *In Search of Our Mothers' Gardens*. Though she wrote of the Civil Rights Movement with unreserved approval in 1967, she contended later that the movement continued to oppress women and hence failed in its mission of human liberation. These positions taken by Walker clearly reveal that she is more committed to her people than to her earlier statements.

Walker's collections of short stories such as *You Can't Keep a Good Woman Down* and *In Love & Trouble: Stories of Black Women* show her concern for women. The titles have been thoughtfully chosen to indicate Walker's viewpoint that women remain exploited and oppressed.

"Really, Doesn't Crime Pay?," one of the short stories in *In Love & Trouble*, shows how a woman gets exploited so easily. The woman cheated, seduced and exploited can only have the satisfaction of telling her husband some day that she had relied on the security of the pill, to deny carrying his child, the unnoticed female character very much revealing the plight of the woman tortured with an incompatible married life and how such a woman can become an easy prey to be exploited by another man.

The other collection of short stories by Walker, *You Can't Keep a Good Woman Down*, also contains stories about women, child abuse and exploitation. "How Did I Get Away with Killing one of the Biggest Lawyers in the State? It was Easy" and "The Abortion" are two such stories.

The short story "How Did I Get Away" begins by revealing the terrible psychological scar left in the mind of the narrator: "My mother and father were not married. I never knew him." The narrator's statement, "It was nothing for a girl or woman to be raped," reveals the terrible environment. At twelve, she was raped and her mother never knew and she never told anybody: "It was just a boy, passing through."

At fourteen she looks "like a grown woman." Her mother's employer, a lawyer, rapes her 'legally' in his law office, and adds insult to injury by threatening and blackmailing her.

> he began to touch me, and I pulled away. But he kept touching me and I was scared . . . he raped me. But afterward he told me he hadn't forced me, that I felt something for him, and he gave me some money. I was crying, going down the stairs. I wanted to kill him.

A lawyer raping a fourteen year young girl, threatening, "he hadn't forced her" and blackmailing the victim speak volumes about child abuse and oppression of the female.

The affair continues, the hatred remains latent, but her body does "what it was being paid to do." When her mother dies, she kills Bubba, her tormentor:

> How did I get away with killing one of the biggest lawyers in the state? It was easy. He kept a gun in his desk drawer at the office and one night I took it out and shot him. . . . No one came after me and I read in the paper the next day that he'd been killed by burglars. I guess they thought 'burglars' had stolen all that money Bubba kept in his safe—but I had it. One of the carrots Bubba always dangled before me was that he was going to send me to college: I didn't see why he shouldn't do it.

This short story reveals not only the exploitation of the African-American woman, but also reveals the least expected, extreme reaction of the victim. The exploited, oppressed victim has turned the tables on the oppressor for a change.

The theme of unwanted pregnancy leading to abortion occupies the centrestage in "The Abortion." It reveals through the narrator the pathetic and irrefutable fact: "There was no way to explain abortion to a man." The short story reveals the psychological scar left on womanhood by unwanted pregnancy. When pregnancy becomes unnatural and fearful, the legal recourse to terminate unwanted pregnancy—abortion—becomes all the more painful, physically and emotionally leaving a scar and shattering the psyche of the woman forever.

Alice Walker has distinguished the chronicle of an African-American family and the tale concerned primarily with racial confrontation as the two major strains of African-American fiction.

Walker's *The Third Life of Grange Copeland* focusses on the family of Copelands and makes a record of its history covering three generations—Grange, Brownfield and Ruth. Her next novel *Meridian* reveals her conviction that oral expression is basic to building both personal and communal identity. Walker's *The Color Purple* reveals through "Celie's letters to God and Nettie, . . . her growing self-awareness and confidence as a sexual and capable woman"[10] It shows a "complex redemptive artistry that encompasses saving gestures of various types."[11]

The Third Life reveals Walker's conviction that even at one's death one can preserve what he values in life. Walker seems to say that through the phenomenon of willingness to die, one can continue to live through someone else. This conviction continues and is carried further in *Meridian* with Meridian Hill's only reason for self-sacrifice being her intention of preserving another life.

Walker's *The Third Life* unfolds the history, the trials, deaths, defeats, oppressions and finally the hope of three generations—Grange, Brownfield and Ruth. While Grange's and Brownfield's lives represent oppression and injustice, Ruth remains a symbol of hope and life. In a way *The Third Life* may be considered as a novel which states unequivocally that hope and life still flourish in spite of oppressions.

Meridian shows how Truman Held, a Northern African-American goes to the South and leaves Meridian, a local girl, behind "physically, psychically and emotionally violated."[12] The novel also reveals that the violator must owe the responsibility for his violation and oppression. Truman is haunted by thoughts of his aggressive exploitations. By being stricken by his conscience, by being haunted by thoughts of his criminal exploitations, Truman makes himself accountable and thereby owns responsibility to a certain extent. He cannot "just walk away" from his crimes.

Meridian is made rebellious by her oppressive environment in particular and the oppression let loose on the African-American women in general. The college where she studies—Saxon College—remains a monument of oppression. By refusing motherhood, by saying "no", Meridian offends and loses her mother, her family and her community.

At the end, Meridian becomes more mellowed and sympathetic. She realises that she is responsible for her rebirth, by embracing the art form and making herself reborn through her artistic expressions.

Walker's *The Color Purple* has elicited a wide range of both praise and censure. The novel explores the exploitation of the oppressed woman, the exploitation, abuse and harassment commencing from childhood, leading to traumatic experiences and leaving psychic scars in the victim.

In one of her essays, "Living by the Word," Walker has remarked, "there is no story more moving to me personally than one in which one woman saves the life of another and saves herself," a feat that "black women wish they were able to do all the time." *The Color Purple* reveals saving gestures of various types.

Alice Walker's intention to champion the cause of the African-Americans, especially African-American women is revealed by a study of her novels. It is a classic example of an intention assuming the shape of determination. Walker's own words stand testimony to her determination:

> I am preoccupied with the spiritual survival, the survival *whole*, of my people. But beyond that, I am committed to exploring the oppressions, the insanities, the loyalties and the triumphs of black women.

The novels of Toni Morrison and Alice Walker emphasise that the deliverance for the oppressed must come from within. Even though it is a fact that oppression exists even today, the silver line is that there is a positive attitudinal change in the American mindset and the attitude of the world community as a whole, giving one hope that inequality, injustice and oppression will vanish one day and a peaceful world will be created by means of non-violence.

NOTES

1. John Hope Franklyn, *Racial Equality in America* (Chicago: The University of Chicago Press, 1976), pp. 3-4.
2. *Ibid.*, pp. 26 and 35.
3. Judith H. Livingston, "The American Feminist Movement: Its Impact upon Academia and upon the Study of American Literature," *Indian Journal of American Studies*, Vol. 22, Number 2 (Summer 1992), pp. 29-39.

4. *Loc. cit.*
5. Wilfred D. Samuels and Hudson-Weens Clenora, *Toni Morrison* (Boston: Twayne, 1990), pp. ix-xii.
6. Dorothea Drummond Mbalia, *Toni Morrison's Developing Class Consciousness* (Selinsgrove: Susquehanna University Press, 1991), pp. 9-10.
7. Terry Otten, *The Crime of Innocence in the Fiction of Toni Morrison* (Columbia: University of Missouri Press, 1989), pp. 1-7.
8. Barbara Christian, *Black Women Novelists: The Development of Tradition* (Westport: Greenwood Press, 1980), p. 179.
9. Elliott Butler-Evans, *Race, Gender and Desire: Narrative Strategies in the Fiction of Toni Cade Bambara, Toni Morrison and Alice Walker* (Philadelphia: Temple University Press, 1989), pp. 3-17.
10. Harold Hellenbrand, "Speech after Silence: Alice Walker's *The Third Life of Grange Copeland*," *Black American Literature Forum*, Vol. 20, Number 4 (Winter 1986), pp. 113-28.
11. Felipe Smith, "Alice Walker's Redemptive Art," *African-American Review*, Vol. 26, Number 3, 1992, pp. 437-51.
12. *Loc. cit.*

Re-Organizing the Lives of Women: Toni Morrison's *Beloved* and Alice Walker's *The Color Purple*

MADHUMALATI ADHIKARI

Madhumalati Adhikari focuses on the central protagonists' quest for identity and self-empowerment in Toni Morrison's Beloved *and Alice Walker's* The Color Purple. *In* The Color Purple, *Celie is oppressed by society, patriarchy and her stepfather. It is Shug Avery who rescues her and teaches her to be psychologically and financially independent. In* Beloved, *Sethe finds that the prevailing definitions of women, mother and wife are challenged by her racist masters. The voice of patriarchy on the other hand condemns her act of infanticide. Both Morrison and Walker insist on the role of community in the development of character.*

Editor

Traditionally, women's lives have been organized and manipulated by patriarchy in all ages, all cultures, all countries by establishing values, norms, roles, gender perceptions, and idealism that prescribes unequal means, methods and routes to achieve the so called 'wholeness' for women. It is uniformly believed that motherhood and wifehood are the dual crowns of womanhood and man has defined it in unequivocal terms. The images based on social conditions of woman drawn by male writers are either idealized versions close to angels or monsters in their essence permitting no moderate pictures real but different from the extreme. What patriarchy demands of woman is very different from what women demand of women. The history gives his story and not her story. Adrienne Rich emphasizes the absurdity of the situation by pointing out that though motherhood is the experience of women, the institution of motherhood is under male control and the physical situation of becoming a mother is disciplined by males(!). This glorious motherhood imposed on woman conditions her entire life.[1] Ironically, the experience unique to women is interpreted for them through male authorities and structures, through religions, myths, science, politics, and economics.[2] And when women begin to interpret and articulate their experience, they are condemned as reactionaries out to destabilize society. This revolt of women never goes unpunished.

Initially, women writers realising that they must narrate their stories or others would do it incorrectly, were interested in determining and picturizing the lives of women "as they have been living, as they live and as they are led to imagine themselves' but now they seem to be concentrating on 'how women can live afresh.'"[3] This revised version of woman's world through a fictional text, I term as a re-organization of woman's life. The defeat of a spirited woman, by 'a return to the fold' or release through 'self-slaughter' is no longer the point of reflection, distillation, organization or imagination. In extreme conditions, her death is turned into an act of victory as we find in Jean Rhys's *Sargasso Sea* or Toni Morrison's *Sula.* Often it is a progressively winning situation wherein the female protagonist in her search for wholeness, identity, fulfillment recreates her world on novel terms. Toni Morrison in *Beloved* and Alice Walker in *The Color Purple* design the life style of their protagonist as initially fragmented, disorganized but ultimately whole and organized. Different and significant and apparently insignificant situations are created to establish the process of self-encounter that finally brings about the metamorphosis. The analysis of the entire exercise is interesting.

I

The Color Purple is the story of a girl Celie, who ultimately manages to overturn the conventional definition of good and evil in relation to women by emphasizing that she exists primarily as and for herself and not merely, to be a mother or the lover of man. Celie begins her life as a physically and psychologically oppressed young girl raped by her step-father and later, becomes the wife of Mr. A, a widower with three children and a beautiful mistress Shug Avery who also continues to exploit her in different ways. In short, she is born to be the 'mule' of the family. From near complete degeneration, she fights against sexist and racist definitions of herself and enables the other women to realize that the entire black community's attitude towards women needs to be revised and revealed. The interesting point of the novel is Celie's process of regeneration that begins with an overt exploration of sexual relationships with Shug Avery, friendly and at times not so friendly, but definitely constructive.

Celie as a woman 'muted and silenced' by society/patriarchy/stepfather can write to God only and speak to none else. She can no longer consider herself to be a "good girl."[4] She is forced to become a 'girl-woman.' Her experiences as a daughter are not happy. The dying mother had died "screaming and cursing" (3) her because she is 'big' with the child in her womb. Soon after she is married to the grudging Mr. A who ultimately marries her because she is a good worker, he can do anything with her and she has a cow to take as a part of the dowry. (12) She is turned into a slave. Her stepchildren bully her, her husband beats her because 'she my wife. Plus she stubborn. All women good for." (23) Her sister advises her to fight, "You got to fight" (18) but "I don't know how to fight. All I know how to do is stay alive," (18) says Celie. Alice Walker through an intricate design of the plot reveals repeatedly Celie's desperate condition. It is also the traditional picture of woman performing the roles of daughter, wife and mother. In fact, a woman is equated more with animals than with humans. She is crippled by a sense of "inferiorization,"[5] "non-entity" and "guilt." Celie considers herself to be useless in everyway because she is "ugly." (48) A woman's appraisal in terms of physical beauty is an ancient tradition accepted and followed till today. Walker picturises the inadequacies of women, viewed by men, from different angles. Celie is unable to fight the world and reorganizes her life because her personal experience has not yet translated itself into self-conscious self-encounter. Being unaware of the inherent creative power of women, she is made to act as a stereotyped female. She had suffered in life and thus is happy when her husband asks

Harpo, to let Sophie know their daughter-in-law "who got the upper hand. Nothing can do that better than good sound beating." (37)

Celie's process of rehabilitation begins with the arrival of Shug Avery, her arch-rival, and Mr. A's mistress. Walker gives an interesting twist to the story by indicating that the 'other' woman, can never really be the enemy of the wife as is traditionally portrayed in the fiction of male writers. A woman of that class does not fragment but recreates from the decimated element. In *The Color Purple* Celie's liberation begins with the help of three strong women of the community: Shug, Nettie (Celie's Sister) and Sophie. The motif of liberation through one's sisters is to be found in Shange's *Sassafras,* Morrison's *Beloved,* Andre Lorde's *Zami* and many other novels written by Afro-American female writers. Walker insists on the possibility of black woman's empowerment through a community of sisters.

Sophie acts as a catalyst for Celie's transformation. Despite all odds, she refuses to succumb before Harpo's beating. In fact, she stands alone to pay him back. Celie the weak woman cannot but admire her and it is from her daughter-in-law, she learns the language of revolt and successful resistance. Later, Sophie comes to know about her plight and advises her, "You ought to bash Mr—." (44) If Sophie provides the atmosphere for the restructuring of Celie's life, it is Shug Avery who finally teaches her to become psychologically and financially independent. Shug's gracious act of dedicating one of her songs to Celie as 'Miss Celie's Song' enables Celie to appreciate her own worth. "First time somebody made something and named it after me." (77) Shug continues with the process of mending Celie by making her love herself. Walker suggests clearly that a woman should learn to respect the "self" before she can demand respect from others. Shug teaches her to sew pants and wear them too and finally comes a stage when Celie convincingly asserts before Mr. A—: "I'm poor. I'm black. I may be ugly and can't cook, a voice say to everything listening. *But I'm here.*" (214, emphasis added) She, at this point, has reorganized her life, achieved economic liberty, gathered the knowledge of meaningful things and relationships to create a new Celie. Walker takes us through different stages of Celie's life to pinpoint the various factors that finally recreates Celie as a whole, confident, self-aware woman with an identity.

It is also interesting to note that Walker's protagonist in *The Color Purple* has an uncommon attitude towards religion. She begins with confiding in God. He appears to be a friend but when her repeated requests go unheard she explodes: "anyhow, I say, the God I been praying and writing to is a man. And act just like all the other mens I know. Trifling, forgitful and lowdown." (199) The rigidity of religion is very casually eliminated. Further in the novel, Shug enlightens Celie by commenting "God love all them feeling," (203) meaning the uncommon sexual love between women. But God cannot be limited in erotic emotions only. He is annoyed if "you walk by the color purple in a field somewhere and don't notice it." (203) This broadening of religious attitude, not sanctioned by theological categories, includes new religious dimensions. Religion preached by male priests to limit women is negated. Thus Walker introduces new spiritual connotations in the novel to order women's life. It is a progress from ignorance to knowledge and in the process the roles of the wife and mother are considerably modified.

II

The planning of *The Color Purple* being very straightforward, it is not difficult to perceive the manipulation that has been carried out by Alice Walker to organize her protagonist's life. But in Toni Morrison's *Beloved* the design of personal growth and development directed toward creating a whole self is neither simple nor direct because of the complexities of the narrative technique.

Sethe, the protagonist of Morrison's *Beloved*, despite the double enclosures of racism and sexism, begins her life quite normally in Sweet Home, a plantation, as a slave worker. The master being very kind and considerate, she is neither raped nor tortured by anyone. Though through her memory we come to know about her mother, a slave who had been branded, raped repeatedly and ultimately hanged. This shattering experience has negative impact on her. It makes her more protective towards her children which ultimately culminates in the murder of her own daughter whom, by this act, she had tried to save from the terrible experience of being a 'chattel,' a slave. Paul D, the voice of patriarchy, condemns her by stating "You got two feet, Sethe, not four"[6] but her confident reply is: "It's my job to know what is and to keep them away from what I know is terrible. I did that." (202) Fragmentation of Sethe's personality begins with the coming of the schoolteacher and his nephews as masters. They make a "chokecherry tree on her back by a cowhide whip" (2l), "steal her milk meant for the baby daughters." (20) Celie had experienced the dark side of the Black men but not Sethe. Sethe had also not grown down with marriage and family life. She did not experience any dwarfing or maiming, after marriage. Marriage did not become an 'enclosure of patriarchy'[7] for her as it did for Celie. She is not made to feel inferior as a woman. Things change when the prevailing definition of woman, of mother and wife is challenged by the racist masters. The schoolteacher asks his nephews to "put her human characteristics on the left; her animal ones on the right." (237)

Sethe is no ordinary woman. Her decision to escape to the free zone of America is doggedly carried out. She leaves her husband Halle behind and considers him to be dead because he had failed to protect her milk and a husband who fails to protect his wife is no husband. Morrison through Sethe challenges the concept of a traditional husband; she consciously questions the ideological code of married life and investigates the sensibilities of her protagonist against the rigid interpretation of marital codes. For twenty-eight days, after the shattering experience of escape, Sethe remains fragmented and gradually begins to mend thereafter. But she faces another setback when she kills her child to protect her from the slave master. She is jailed. On her release, she is not broken but emerges as a determined woman who feels no guilt for her act. She believes "I took and put my babies where they'd be safe." (201) On her return from the jail, she takes up a job and continues with the act of living. Later when

Paul D questions her conduct, her confident statement is: "No more running—from nothing. I took one journey and I paid for the ticket, but let me tell you something Paul D Garner it cost too much." (18)

Deciding to go alone, all the way, is a wrong decision taken by Sethe and when her ghost-daughter Beloved manipulates to kill her it is Denver, the other daughter, who seeks the help of the community to liberate her mother. Morrison with the fictional situation insists that the role of the community sisters in developing a character is pertinent. Sethe was abandoned by the community because of her pride to go all alone. As the women of the community comment "she [was] trying to do it all alone with her nose in the air." (312) It is with Denver's effort that Sethe is brought back to the fold; she regains her peace and stability. Morrison's view is: a woman should not stand apart from the community and be an outsider while battling with the problems of life. The protagonist's life in the novel is fully and finally organized by this awareness. Sethe is made aware that as an outsider, with a destiny in isolation, she cannot succeed in solving her problems. Though she has to move through a process of intensive introspection yet she finally has to establish a meaningful relationship with other people. Sethe's journey is an internal as well as an external one. Her external journey remains chaotic in the absence of self-realisation. In this pursuit, she is assisted by her 'uncalled, unrobed, unanointed' mother-in-law Baby Suggs (106) who repeatedly advises Sethe to "lay 'em [terrible memories of the past] down; Sethe, sword and shield." (105) She preaches to all black men and women to love their flesh "hard because it is flesh that weeps; flesh that dances." (108) This vision of religion or rather the re-vision of religion is thought to be an essential ingredient of the self. Morrison too, like Walker, presents a new version of religion wherein the mother has the right to love the 'self.' In fact, deprived of this self-love, women cannot attain selfhood. Thus women are not envisioned only as the sacrificial goats, the mule of the world, the symbol of chastity and nobility but as human beings who have a right to organize their lives.

In both the novels it is interesting to note that the protagonists rise from the condition of nothingness to the position of self-empowerment. It is not a miraculous change coming suddenly but a gradual reorganization of the broken threads. It brings out a pattern that is meaningful and worthwhile. Woman's quest for self-identity, self-awareness, self-empowerment is made possible by their creator's intense desire to construct organized lives of women free from all forms of liminality—physical, material, spiritual, emotional and social. The difference between these two writers is; one suffers from over-enthusiasm and the other enjoys to record the facts of life. In *The Color Purple*, all women triumph in the battle but in *Beloved* the victory is limited to the protagonist and her living daughter. Morrison seems to stress that if Baby Suggs has been defeated, others have won the war. This is the pattern of life. Women need to reorganize their lives to develop and promote new systems, new attitudes towards the 'woman's question.'

NOTES

1. Adrienne Rich, *Of Women Born* (New York: Bantam Books, 1967), p. 65.
2. Barbara Christian, *Black Feminist Criticism: Perspective on Black Women Writers* (New York: Pergamon Press, 1985), p. 212.
3. Adrienne Rich, "When the Dead Awaken: Writing as Revision," *Lies Secrets and Silence* (New York: W.W. Norton, 1979), p. 35.
4. Alice Walker, *The Color Purple* (New York: Pocket Books, 1985), p. 1.
5. Sandra M. Gilbert and Susan Gubar, *The Madwoman in the Attic: The Woman and Nineteenth Century Literary Imagination* (New Haven Conn: Yale University Press, 1979), p. 7.
6. Toni Morrison, *Beloved* (New York: Signet Books, 1991). p. 202.
7. Annis Pratt, *Archetypal Patterns in Women's Fiction* (Bloomington: Indiana University Press, 1981), p. 14.

Black Magic:
The Works of Toni Morrison

ASHA S. KANWAR

Asha Kanwar gives an overview of Morrison's oeuvre, making the reader aware of the link between context and content in her novels.
Editor

When Toni Morrison won the Pulitzer Prize for fiction in 1988, the response, as she herself puts it, "in many quarters white, black, male, female, young and old was 'we.' We did it!" and with the announcement of the Nobel Prize for literature in 1993, this response became more global. While Toni Morrison is considered one of the most significant writers of the twentieth century America, and her works compared with those of James Joyce and William Faulkner, closer home, it is perhaps Alice Walker, another African-American Pulitzer-prize winning writer, who is more widely known. Thanks perhaps to the film *The Color Purple* based on her novel of the same name.

Toni Morrison's winning of the Nobel Prize is a significant event on many counts. The fact that an African-American woman should get a prestigious international award is the culmination of what started in the eighteenth century with the writings of Black literary foremothers like Lucy Terry and Phyllis Wheatley. More recently, it is a befitting endorsement and justifiable triumph of the struggle of the 1960s that we're familiar with as the Civil Rights, Black Power and Women's Liberation movements.

These gave rise to what we could broadly term the New Black Renaissance of which the chief protagonists were women—Maya Angelou, Terry Macmillan, Alice Walker, Sonia

Sanchez, Nikki Giovanni, Angela Davis, Gloria Naylor—the names are legion. This was quite different from the Harlem Renaissance of the 1930s. For while the earlier one was more bourgeois in character and dominated by men, this is more revolutionary and female. And for the African-American woman, it has been 'a long and winding road' from the cotton fields of the American South to the chandeliered halls in Stockholm as Toni Morrison steps forward to accept her award.

Traditionally assigned service positions as social workers, teachers, nurses, Black women writers have had to struggle far in excess of 'having a room of one's own and five hundred guineas a year.' In a recent interview, celebrated African-American poet Sonia Sanchez recounted that when she told her counsellor in college (in the 1950s) that she wanted to be a writer, the response was a curt 'you people don't write.' How then did Black women negotiate the ideological and material barriers that conspire in subtle ways to keep them in the position of 'de mule uh de world?' Their endless capacity for hard work gave them the confidence to fight against pernicious social and economic pressures. Their triple oppression in terms of their being women, black and poor gave them a special consciousness so that when they wrote, writing in itself became a political act, an act of transgression, a 'talking back' in their own voices, of their own experiences.

It is against this background that Toni Morrison's writing must be viewed. As she herself put it, "If anything I do, in the way of writing novels or whatever I write, isn't about the village or the community or about you, then it isn't anything. I am not interested in indulging myself in some private exercise of my imagination, which is to say yes, the work must be political."

Apart from being political, the distinguishing characteristic of Black women's writing is that their work is primarily about other black women. *The Bluest Eye* (1970), Morrison's first novel is the story of Pecola Breedlove, who unsuccessfully prays to God for a pair of blue eyes, which for her are the ultimate symbol of beauty. Raped by her father, and unfulfilled in her dream of a pair of blue eyes, Pecola degenerates into insanity.

And in telling her story, Claudia, her friend, understands how it could survive whereas Pecola could not. The stories of Pecola and Claudia unfold the different dimensions of being black and female in white patriarchal America. This story is based on a real-life conversation that the young Chloe Anthony Wofford (who changed her name to 'Toni' while an undergraduate at Howard University in the early fifties; 'Morrison' came from her marriage to Jamaican architect Harold Morrison in 1957 whom she divorced in 1964 and from whom she has two sons) had with a black girl who had prayed unsuccessfully for two years for a pair of blue eyes. This was first written as a short story and Morrison read it out to a group of ten black writers who met every month in Washington DC to read each other's works (in the late 1950s).

Morrison's second novel *Sula* (1973) was not much more acclaimed than was her first. This too is about the extraordinary relationship of two girls in the 1920s and 1930s—Sula and Nel—complete opposites. Sula a rebel, is somewhat evil whereas Nel is the good conformist. Morrison wants to show that nothing is simply good or evil but both are aspects of a human condition. Their friendship is special and critics have read a kind of 'lesbian' attachment between the two, though Toni Morrison denies that this was her intention. However, within the black community, a strong bond does exist between women who often nurture and support each other. Morrison herself as senior editor at Random House (1965-1984) helped launch and support the writing careers of several black women: Gloria Naylor, Angela Davis, Gayl Jones, Toni Cade Bambara.

It was with her third novel, *Song of Solomon* (1977), that Morrison won widespread recognition as a fiction writer. At the centre of this narrative is the ancestor figure of Aunt Pilate, yet another recurring feature in Black women's writing, who guides "Milkman" Dead from his alienated existence in the North to a search for his roots in the South. This journey towards self-discovery becomes symbolic of the African-American's quest of their history and heritage which has generally been whitewashed in historical documents.

Tar Baby (1981), Morrison's fourth novel, a fusion of fantasy and realism was an instant bestseller. The title refers to a black American folktale in which a white farmer makes a tarbaby to trap a mischievous rabbit but is outwitted by this clever little animal. Set mainly on an exotic Caribbean island, the story in portraying the relationship of Jade and Son, touches upon the themes of relationship between black men and black women, between black folks and white people, between black people of the servant class with the black elite and between black Americans and their African counterparts.

Morrison's next novel *Beloved* (1987) won her the Pulitzer Prize in 1988. Like *The Bluest Eye*, this novel too is based on a real-life incident. In 1854, a black woman escaped from bondage with her four children. When cornered and faced with captivity, Margaret Garner killed one of her children and tried to kill the others rather than have them returned to slavery. Morrison builds on this story to create the unforgettable Sethe and the ghost of her daughter Beloved, who forces her mother to remember the past. This novel projects a community that is trying to come to terms with its slave heritage and its four hundred years of terrible oppression and humiliation.

The remembrance of things past is also the subject of Morrison's novel *Jazz* (1992), set in the Harlem of the 1920s. The climactic incident of the novel in which Joe Trace, a fifty-year-old salesman kills his eighteen-year-old lover Dorcas in a fit of jealousy with his wife Violet barging into the funeral home in an attempt to slash the dead girl's face, has already happened at the beginning of the novel. The rest of the book examines how history impinges upon human emotions, having a profound bearing on human relationships.

In addition to these novels, Morrison has written a play which has had a discrete performance, a short story entitled 'Recitatif,' a textbook, book reviews and several essays and articles. Her book of literary criticism, *Playing in the Dark* (1992), examines the ways in which race has shaped the classics of mainstream American literature. In addition, Morrison has also edited *Race-ing Justice, En-gendering Power: Essays on Anita Hill,*

Clarence Thomas and the Construction of Social Reality (1992). Like Alice Walker and several other black women, Toni Morrison is both artist and intellectual. Important though her critical interventions are, it is as a novelist that posterity will chiefly remember her.

A Professor at Princeton University since 1989, with a grounding in European literature from the great French and Russian classics to Jane Austen, Toni Morrison is deeply rooted in her own culture. And it is this rootedness that imparts a special quality to her work. She tries to capture the orality of black culture and render it in her exquisitely crafted dialogues so that the reader may not simply see the words on the page but also hear the changing tones and see the gestures specific to those who people her fictional world. The prose is deliciously poetic. Consider the images evoked by 'Nuns go by as quiet as lust'; 'Winter tightened our heads with a band of cold and melted our eyes'; 'Fog came to that place in wisps sometimes, like the hair of maiden aunts. . . . Jadine and Margaret touched their cheeks and temples to dry the places the maiden aunts were kissing.' Here is language to be savored, nuances to be perceived, images to be cherished.

And the creator, the formidable Toni Morrison, continues to write, regardless of critical praise or blame, setting standards that only meticulous work can measure up to!

The Female Protagonist's Search for Wholeness and Toni Morrison's Discourse in *Beloved*

MADHUMALATI ADHIKARI

Madhumalati Adhikari draws an analogy between the loss of language and loss of identity. Her focus is on Sethe's journey to wholeness, which is unravelled through the talk think process. Broken by the desertion of Paul D and Beloved's attempt to draw her to servitude, it is the black community that helps to restore her self to her.

Editor

It is not that Morrison writes about black people or for Black readers but they are closest to her heart. Although, she has a particular perspective yet she writes to reach all: 'I don't try to translate for white readers. . . . Dostoevsky wrote for Russian audience but we are able to read him. If I am specific and I don't over-explain, then anybody can overhear me." One must accept that Morrison tries to communicate all-inclusive human experiences and conditions through the metaphor of slave experience. Like Sartre, Morrison believes, 'Man is nothing but what he makes of himself' and in his search for freedom he 'carries the weight of the world on his shoulders.'[2] In the final analysis, Morrison's exigent theme in her novels is the unveiling of the sense of 'me-ness' through her fictional characters who attempt to make a sense of their lives by creating a satisfying pattern of the future with the help of 'rememory.' 'Me-ness,' a force in all human beings, constantly urges man to strive for the goal of authentic existence. Morrison has given body and shape to this quest through her complex and subtle discourse that she found always 'more interesting' than 'the little plot.'[3]

Despite the liberalization of conservative thoughts and the broadening of outlook, Morrison has been functioning under double pressures: the creative activity of woman all over the world has been a walk on a crystal stair and regardless of the humanization of beliefs, Morrison was aware of the inevitable risk of alienating a section of people and a system to whom the sordid details of slavery were very offending and embarrassing. She was able to overcome both the pressures by 'taking refuge in the literary conventions of the day' tempering her voice to "pull the narrative up short."[4] She never felt the restraint practised in narration could undermine the quality of her writing because she resonated with the conviction, 'Black peoples' grace has been what they do with language.'[5]

Morrison knowing well the limitations of the 'oppressor's languages in *Beloved* has manipulated successfully the medium that demands 'silence, euphemism and circumlocution' from women.[6] Her tunes despite the androcentric perspectives have been interpreted and evaluated on her terms. She has 'demaximized'[7] plots, characters and language to unearth the silenced voice of the black slave women whose journey to wholeness is as significant as the male serf's. To unravel history, Morrison has narrated the desperation of the slave woman's story through her dimmed voice.

Language, the key to all successful discourse, neither develops in isolation nor is born full-blown like Minerva from Jupiter's head. Culture, memory, context create and nourish language that produces discourse 'a conversation formal, orderly and usually encoded expression of thought on a subject.' Discourse, a communication, may begin in the realm of words but is extended to ideas, theme, myths, folk-lore, characters, symbols, images etc. Discourse is the very instrument to unravel the writer's intentions about anything and everything. The successful discovery, projection, reconstruction of 'the unsaid' is the primary obligation of discourse. Morrison has confessed that her work is to 'bear witness' to things that 'somebody forgot to tell somebody' and 'somebody has to tell somebody something.'[8] She felt that the slave narrator was forced to hide many things against his/her wishes. Thus, to interpret, evaluate and absorb Morrison's discourse on wholeness inherent in *Beloved*, one has to redefine experience that is never transparent, deconstruct myths, demystify intentions, decode silence, straighten circumlocution, conceive and perceive presence in absence, unlock the mysteries of euphemistic statements often worded to appease the general sentiments. Through women's language, often said to have the power of the weak, Morrison explores and exploits the natal wisdom of her characters, sprouting from the very roots of the African culture. Loaded with meaning, her apparently inoffensive statements exhume buried truths; she manipulates silence that speaks volumes and redefines the meaning of authentic existence. Her every move, situational or compositional, drives us towards the concept of wholeness.

The search of self-hood establishes the thematic bonding between the black women writers. Alice Walker's Meridian (*Meridian*), Celie (*The Color Purple*) fight their battles of self-identity; Paule Marshall's Silla (*Browngirl Brownstones*) destroys essential parts of herself to pass unto her daughter Selina the sense of the necessary struggle to define oneself; Ntozake Shange's heroine in *For Coloured Girls* realizes that despite the exploitative conditions, self-assurance must emanate from within. The search for wholeness is the fundamental and the most important trope also in Morrison's novels: Pecola's (*The Bluest Eye*) erroneous perceptions regarding the need of physical beauty, a condition of the perfect ten image, propels her towards shame, alienation, self-hatred and destruction; Milkman (*Song of Solomon*) aspiring for the same completeness chases material possessions and learns through sweat and blood that one can fly figuratively and physically if one is fulfilled spiritually; Sula (*Sula*) the 'salt taster,' revolts against the constricting values of her society but returns to the fold, fragmented spiritually and physically, for solace and peace; Jadine's (*Tar Baby)* misdirected search leads her to the quagmire of materialism and frustration; Sethe, Suggs, Paul D, Denver (*Beloved*) in search of their identity; journey through many vicissitudes to find either failure (Suggs) or success (Sethe, Paul D, Denver) on reaching the state of becoming. The concept of wholeness, completeness, fulfillment or the perfect ten image is concretized through many situations, characters and expressions by Morrison.

Around the speck of Margaret Garner's historically true story, Morrison weaves the fabric of *Beloved.* She did not intentionally investigate the details of the slave woman's life because she 'wanted to invent her life that might be pertinent today.'[9] The novel has a lot of questions for her and she has attempted to deal with those pressing questions.[10] Some of the questions are: 'How much is a nigger supposed to take?'[11] Can a mother kill her children? (314) Can a child kill her mother? Can a woman go in search of wholeness selfishly? Should the quest of self-affirmation be carried out inside one's self? What is the meaning of slavery? By answering these questions obliquely, Morrison reconstructs and redefines the meaning of wholeness.

Beloved revives the female and the male slave narrator's voice though the female voice is heard more dominantly than the male's. Among the females, Sethe the black heroine's quest for wholeness captures our attention. The novel begins in the middle. Gradually we come to know that her search initially was dormant, as she was launched into the journey of life *sans* roots. Born of a slave mother, Sethe was brought up by the surrogate mother, Nan. Consequently, she had forgotten 'the same language her mother spoke.' (79) Sethe was made familiar with her mother's mark of branding. 'I am the only one got this mark now. The rest is dead.' (76) Sethe innocently requests her mother to brand her also. As her reply, she gets a slap from her mother. Now, when she has her own mark, she grasps the meaning of the debasing sign: the mark had dehumanized her to the level of animals. Her loss of her mother-tongue is an oblique indication of her rootlessness and precarious existence that amounts to nothing. To save her this physical and psychological degradation, Sethe takes the drastic step and the ensuing tragic experience brings about her fragmentation. Sethe's act is an example of resistance to slavery and thus is not a senseless crime but a necessity born out of serious contemplation. Since she had analyzed her experiences well, she wanted to keep her children from 'what I know is terrible.' (202) She was quite unaware of her insufficiency when she first came to 'sweet Home' as a young slave. Here men were like 'paid labour' and there were 'no man bred slave.' (173) Morrison, by naming the plantation ironically, establishes the dark truth. In this semi-idyllic atmosphere, with a false sense of security, Sethe consciously obliterates the most painful memory of her childhood of having no meaningful relationship with her mother that affirms her forlorn condition. By burying her painful past, she consciously makes her first effort to claim wholeness. Unfortunately, she builds her castle on sand dunes. Her Eden is soon violated with Garner's death and schoolteacher's arrival who draws the limiting line by pronouncing, 'definitions belonged to the definers—not to the defined.' (234) With this aphoristic statement, Morrison rips the golden veil. Sethe attains her womanhood here and becomes the mother of three children. Foolishly she considers herself to be a human being and a mother but her euphoria lasts for a brief period. Ironically she considers schoolteacher to be a 'fool,' when it is she who had been denigrated to the level of an animal by him. He asks his nephews to 'put her human characteristics on the left; her animal ones on the right.' (237) She had been so far trying to imagine herself as the eternal nurturer (Eve, Eva, Pilate). Culmination of this role could have resulted in the satisfying feeling of totality but soon the growing realization of being of value as 'property that reproduced without cost,' (281) decimates her hopes of being an individual and a true mother. Her wings are clipped quite decisively as she offers resistance against the stealing of her milk and is rewarded with the 'chokecherry tree' etched on her back by the nephews. Forcefully milked like a cow and beaten up like an untamed animal, she refuses to give in because her 'too thick' love for her children defies the attempts to break her. She flees to Cincinnati. Morrison at once makes the reader conscious of the contrast between the mother's role in Sethe's mother and Sethe. Sethe has the conviction, 'I'll protect her [her children in general] while I'm live and I'll protect her when I ain't.' (56) This protective conviction, her mother never possessed. Clearly the implication is that a woman is more than a maker of children. Sethe too was a nurturer though a slave mother was always deprived of her righteous claim. The Demeter image is common in Morrison's novels. It articulates the idea of motherhood that leads to fulfillment and the recognition of the self. Having experienced the pangs of slavery, Sethe was determined to give freedom to her children that results in the killing of Beloved. Her reasoning is simple and clearly communicated to us, 'I couldn't let all that [the brief freedom] go back and I couldn't let her [Beloved] nor any of 'em live under schoolteacher.' (200) 'I took and put my babies where they'd be safe.' (201)

It is not uncommon to have the image of the 'Mother terrible' in Morrison's novels. The readers had met Eva (*Sula*) before and Sethe's image is not very positive yet she is a means of giving wholeness to the offspring. Stamp Paid rightly states, 'she loved those children. She was trying to outhurt the hurter.' (288) Sethe was convinced that death could provide a better existence to Beloved than a slave-life could. With the inborn wisdom of her race, Sethe knew that death was nothing but a continuation of life in a different form. It was 'anything but forgetfulness.' (3) The easy return of Beloved's ghost reveals the thin dividing line between life and death. She had often attempted to follow Baby Suggs' advice, 'Lay it all down, sword and shield' (213) but each time, the rising hope in her had dissolved into deeper loneliness and a feeling of inadequacy. She had never acted on 'bad faith' despite the instigations of the hostile world. Sethe's name definitely borrowed from the Egyptian god Seth, half-man half-bird, very clearly suggests her nature that wishes to roam in an unrestricted atmosphere. Unfortunately, her illusionary world fades into nothingness as her milk is stolen and she is given a 'chokecherry tree' that decorates her back. Sethe's act is disapproved by her community and thus she is alienated and segregated from all. In the absence of the nourishing energy flowing from her community, she begins to dry up and her daughter blames her for their isolation, 'Nobody comes by. . . . Its because of us. And its you.' (18) She has become so cold and dead that nothing can shock her any more. Despite the most revolting sights 'her [Denver's] mother had not looked away.' (15) Her emotions had died while she doggedly fought the battle of life, all by herself. Paul D's return and his symbolic act of putting 'his hands under her breast' (20) is an indication that henceforth he would take the responsibility of protecting her womanhood. It initiates the reconstructing process of Sethe's personality. But very soon, she is jolted out of her complacency when Paul D refusing to accept her act of mercy killing, accuses her indirectly, 'You got two feet Sethe, not four. . . . What you did was wrong' (202) and 'right then a forest sprang up between them; trackless and quiet.' (203) Through verbal compression and symbolic plus poetic expression, Morrison conveys the idea of the growing misunderstanding between the two. The more one ponders over its meaning the more one is overwhelmed by its expansiveness. The trackless forest of misunderstanding parts them. Her action may be incomprehensible to Paul D but to Sethe it is an affirmation of her genuine love for Beloved. To Sethe love can never be 'too thick.' 'Love is or it ain't. Thin love is ain't at all.' (203) With one stroke Sethe (Morrison) lets all know that Paul D had failed her. Her hopes of a fuller life is ruined again. She feels sorry to have been 'so trusting so quick to surrender.' (212) Yet again, she is left companionless. Her loss is clearly worded, 'Every eighteen or twenty years her unlivable life would be interrupted by a short lived glory.' (213) Sethe had been 'junk-heaped' twice before: the first time by her mother and the second time by her community that had rejected her because she was 'trying to do it all alone with her nose in the air.' (312) Her implicit attempt to claim independence is misjudged and when she loses her strength due to the temporary support offered by Paul D, he deserts her. Morrison artistically and metaphorically describes Sethe's attempt to rebuild her broken life. Sethe had always looked forward to 'us three' (Sethe, Paul D, Denver) and the spectacle of 'all three of them gliding over the dust holding hands' (58), in their shadows, is taken to be 'a good sign.' She had expected Paul D to stay to fill up the vacuum of her life but he had behaved like any other man. Rebuffed by him, she tries to pick up the threads of her life by forming a fresh trio comprising of Beloved, Denver and herself. Mistakenly believing 'the world is in this room. This here's all there is and there needs to be,' (224) she dreams of giving support and a feeling of completeness to each other. By turning towards her children, Sethe makes an age-old bid to reconstruct her life with the participation of the other two. The scene of skating on the 'frozen creek' is a beautiful example of Morrison's capacity to capture the meaning and nuance of the moment. It is made metaphorically rich by the refrain, 'Nobody saw them falling.' (213) Morrison uses the frozen creek as a symbol of infertility and incompleteness. The process of reconstructing the self through the emblematic uncontrolled act of skating is projected beautifully. While 'making a circle or a line, the three of them (214) could not stay upright, for one whole minute' but 'nobody saw them falling' is a figurative projection of their futile struggle to stay afloat amidst the destructive and disintegrating currents of this world. Since Sethe makes sure to find the skates and takes the girls out for the rejuvenating process hoping that her 'two shoes would hold and anchor her,' (213) the reader is convinced of her constructive role that Morrison is trying to convey. Though 'each seemed to be helping the other to stay upright yet every tumble' (214) makes it sure for us that Morrison is interested in painting a picture of failure and not of triumph. Her discourse highlights the concept of failure by way of contrast. The images of unity, wholeness like women holding hands, trying to protect each other, skating in circles, laughing etc. cannot dissolve the powerful images of death like the vast frozen creek, their repeated falls, their attempts to skate with a single shoe etc. This happy interlude comes to an abrupt end echoing the experience of the past when Beloved had tried to strangle her mother to death. It clearly signifies the incomplete and dangerous nature of their relationship. On return, both the girls are offered warm milk by the mother but it brings no satisfaction to her as it is not her milk. The episode excavates the memory of Sethe's stolen milk and conjures up the picture of her helplessness and her continuous debasement.

Humiliated and rejected by Paul D, Sethe's quest is temporarily misdirected as she gives up her job signifying her further loss of identity that leads to more rigid circumscription and isolation, always self-destroying. As a result, it shames Denver to see her mother 'serving a girl not much older than herself.' (297) Sethe often becomes apologetic. 'Beloved said "do it" and Sethe complied.' (296) It is ironic that it is Sethe's daughter who tries to revert her back to slavehood. She had paid a high price to free herself from its crippling effect. In fact, there has not been any improvement in Sethe's condition; the downward slide continues. The more she segregates herself, the more she loses control over the 'diminishing' circumstances. Beloved had returned 'to fix her mother.' (313) She was helped out of this abyss by her other daughter Denver. Interestingly enough, Sethe's identity and wholeness is regained by the assistance of others though she repeatedly attempts to reclaim it. If one of the daughters brings about her deterioration, the other becomes instrumental in her resurrection. Morrison clearly demonstrates that the mother-daughter relationship can be destructive or constructive. Similar roles can be played by the community as is illustrated in *Beloved.* In contrast, Pecola's (*The Bluest Eye*) and Sula's (*Sula*) me-ness is constantly undermined by those who matter. Sethe's torn body is 'draped' in 'two palmfuls of webs' (98) and the newborn child is wrapped in Amy's torn skirt. Amy, herself in search of freedom and sanctuary, not only restores her physically and emotionally but also by challenging her survival instinct with the question, 'What you going to do, just lay there and foal?' (42), draws her out of the self-annihilating stupor. A similar act of healing, physical and psychological, as a friend, nurse, midwife is performed by Baby Suggs when Sethe arrives in 124 'all mashed up and slit open.' For the first time, Sethe is able to claim herself with Suggs' help. She 'bathed her in section' her 'feet [she] wiped them lightly' (reminiscent of Christ's washing of feet), 'greased her back,' (113) gave her the message of love and on the whole brought her back on the path of life. This idyllic situation lasts for twenty-eight days and then the arrival of schoolteacher brings about doom. Suggs, unable to bear the consequences, fades out and Sethe isolates herself and turns herself into an island. Paul D's return and kissing of the chokecherry tree symbolizes the support that he gives temporarily. His incapacity to forgive her, destroys her world of happiness and she decides to cling to Beloved to protect herself against loneliness. In the absence of Denver, Sethe could never have been complete. She had reached a stage when her complete fragmentation was a foregone conclusion. She is so much enmeshed in her guilty feelings that she forgets about her previous attempts to free herself from the dehumanizing conditions. She becomes entirely passive and irresponsive to everything that is life. Fortunately, Beloved's final departure and Paul D's reappearance with the statement, 'Sethe you, and me we got more yesterday than anybody. We need some kind of tomorrow,' (335) brings her back from the threshold of death-in-life. Sethe is definitely more fortunate than Beloved who 'although has claim, is not claimed.' (336) Sethe is claimed by Paul D, Denver and her community as a result of which she is able to reclaim her wholeness. This realization of the intimate relationship with her near and dear ones finally tears off the veil that had been keeping her away from herself.

Morrison states, 'The language has to be quiet: it has to engage your participation. . . . The reader supplies the emotions. . . . My language has to have holes and spaces so the reader can come into it.'[12] Throughout the novel, the gaps and spaces are intentionally left for the reader's participation. As a result, they feel the dread and awfulness of Sethe's experience that is ever darkened by her perennial sense of guilt. Very rarely we come to know directly if Sethe is happy or sad through the use of symbols and images. Truly the reader supplies the emotions. The systematic annihilation of Sethe's personality through racist and sexist oppression and exploitation is very evident. Sethe's psychological and physical deprivation that leads to her loss of personal identity is deeply felt by all. It is obvious that Morrison does not even remotely favour a 'me-ness' that is ultimately selfish like Sula's who refuses to assume any responsibility for her fellow human beings. Her motto: 'I don't want to make somebody else. I want to make my self,'[13] is decried by Morrison that is exemplified through her tragic end. Since her search has been perverted, she dies unfulfilled. It is not that Morrison sets such ideals for women only (the traditional ones) but for men too wholeness lies in sharing, giving, loving and not in isolation, selfishness or meanness to preserve oneself. Morrison resists the idea that an individual's selfish pursuit is ever justifiable enough for fulfillment. One needs the right reason and the right context to grow. Neither a selfish self-affirmation is acceptable nor a life meant completely for others. The desire for me-ness and the consideration for others must be combined to attain wholeness. Morrison never judges her characters but this prickly problem is resolved by the readers' involvement. Each reader is left free to interpret the motives and conflicts that haunt the *dramatis personae* of Morrison's fictional world, in their search for wholeness. Her criticism of the entire social order is impossible to pass over. The contrast presented between the black and other cultures is implicit in her discourse. What is emphasized through merging of images and events, is the universal value system. Images borrowed from the physical and the psychological world mingle to create their own structures, parables and myths captured through the magic of words. Morrison, through 'rememory' and 'talk-think,' reconstructs the world that has been left behind and in the process not only highlights the protagonist's journey to wholeness but also reconstructs the myth of mother as the eternal nurturer, demystifies the longings of a baby ghost that has been searching for a face, interprets Sethe's destructive act in the light of her tragic and ghastly experiences. Her silence through the long period of eighteen years speaks volumes about her hopes and aspirations. Sethe's story is satisfactorily articulated because Morrison recognizes the unlimited possibilities of discourse. Her ultimate message through her beautiful but complex mode of expression reaches us: human behaviour is open to innumerable interpretations and if human beings are to achieve wholeness, they should learn to pass it on and also learn 'to lay it all down, sword and shield.'

NOTES

1. Walker Clemens, "The Ghost of Sixty Millions and More," *Newsweek*, 28 Sept. (1987), p. 75.
2. Jean-Paul Sartre, *Existentialism and Human Emotions* (Seconcus, New Jersey: Castle), p. 52.
3. Clenora Hudson-Weems and Wilfred D Samuels, Interview with Toni Morrison, New York, 17 June 1985 (unpublished).
4. Barbara Christian, "Community and Nature: The Novels of Toni Morrison," *The Journal of Ethnic Studies*, 7 (1980), p. 72
5. Mel Watkins, "The Talk with Toni Morrison," *The New York Times Book Review*, 11 Sept. 1977, p. 48.
6. Rich, qtd. in Elaine Showalter, "Feminist Criticism in the Wilderness," *The New Feminist Criticism* (New York: Pantheon, 1985), pp. 253, 255.
7. Nancy K. Miller, "Emphasis Added: Plots and Possibilities in Women's Fiction," in Showalter, 341.
8. Shange Ntozake, "Interview with Toni Morrison," *American Rag*, Nov. 1978, p. 52.
9. Marsha Darling, "In the Realm of Responsibility, A Conversation with Toni Morrison," *The Woman's Review of Books*, 5 March 1988, 19, p.5.
10. Sandy Russell, "It is Ok to say Ok," ed. Nellie Y. McKay, *Critical Essays on Morrison* (Boston: G.K. Hall, 1988), p. 43.
11. Toni Morrison, *Beloved* (New York: Signet, 1991), p. 289.
12. Claudia Tate, "Toni Morrison," *Black Women Writers at Work* (New York: Continuum, 1983), p. 125.
13. Toni Morrison, *Sula* (New York: Bantam, 1975), pp. 79-80.

"This is Where I am": Topos as Trophe for Self and Society in *Beloved*

URBASHI BARAT

Urbashi Barat points out that the idea of place in Toni Morrison's novels has symbolic significance—it is linked to cultural rootedness. The black community in Cincinnati plays an important role in moulding Baby Suggs or Sethe's life. The epigraph of the novel from Roman 9:25 reinforces the significance of the title of the novel. St. Paul's epistle to Christians in Rome extends a plan of salvation of the whole community. Similarly the character Beloved in the novel does not stand for an individual but for the whole black community.

Editor

The novel, observes Michel Zeraffa, "confronts us openly with the issue of the meaning and value of our ineluctable historical and social condition. . . . The novel is the first art to represent man explicitly as defined historically and socially."[1] Setting is thus of great significance in any novel; it provides not only a local habitation and a name to the action but also the history and the society against which the individual is defined and measured. If the major concern of the novel is to describe "the career of an individual in search of some totality, some coherence, some identity, whose image he carries deep within himself,"[2] it is location that helps to visualize this image, which is the product of historical and social forces. Without location neither individual nor society has existence; place is a favourite metaphor in fiction for the social and moral values it explores, especially through its analysis of the relationship between self and community, the perennial theme of all literature. In English poetry, for example, as W.H. Auden has pointed out, the garden and the city are used by Pope to express the community, as contrasted with the Romantic preference for the desert and the sea to project the self.[3] In almost every work in which the search for selfhood is set against the demands of society, in fact, place tends to act symbolically, whether it is *Tom Jones*, *Wuthering Heights*, *Great Expectations*, *Jude the Obscure*, *The Guide*, *Surfacing* or *Where Shall We Go This Summer?* This paper suggests that *topos* is trophe for this relationship in Toni Morrison's *Beloved*, as it is, indeed, in all her novels, so that Beloved's announcement to her sister. "This is where I am,"[4] sums up the meaning of place throughout her creator's work.

In an interview in Claudia Tate's *Black Women Writers at Work*, Alexis DeVeau noted that this is the major theme in the fiction of contemporary African American women writers: "I see a greater and greater commitment among black women writers to understand self, multiplied in terms of the community, the community multiplied in terms of the nation, and the nation multiplied in terms of the world."[5] Such a commitment, central to all is of especial significance in women's writing, for "Women see themselves primarily in relation to the people around them and their sense of self comes from rootedness."[6] But it is of even greater importance in the work of African American women, who have long suffered the double yoke of racism and sexism and whose relationship to their community and the world outside it has always, accordingly, been an even more complex and ambiguous one than those of other women. Morrison herself has said that the search for self "informs a great deal of [her] work," and Andrea O'Reilly, who quotes this statement from a radio conversation, explains the novelist's views further: "The self must be known and loved and, in Morrison's words, honored and released . . . self-love depends upon the self's first being loved by another self."[7] Self, that is, is inextricably bound up with society and thus ultimately with place.

The theme makes its first notable appearance in African American women's fiction in Zora Neale Hurston's *Their Eyes Were Watching God*,[8] in which Janie's realization that selfhood for a woman in a patriarchal world can lead only to social ostracism and loneliness foreshadows those of Alice Walker's *Me-*

ridian and Morrison's *Sula.* In earlier novels (*The Third Life of Grange Copeland*[9] and *The Bluest Eye* respectively), Walker and Morrison had shown how their community's acceptance of racist and sexist stereotyping turn women into pariahs: in *Meridian*[10] and *Sula*[11] it is the woman who chooses to stand outside her community instead of being thrust outside it. Meridian is able to create a community of support, but Sula remains a rebel and outcaste till the end, preferring selfhood and a lonely and early death to society's prescriptions. Jadine in *Tar Baby* goes even further: in her search for self, she becomes selfish, and as she destroys her relationship with her community she also loses herself. In all her novels, that is, Morrison seems to suggest that the way to wholeness and integrity for the individual lies not through a defiant assertion to selfhood by rejection of society but through the working together of self and community, even if the community itself does not at first appear to nurture individual selfhood for its women.

African Americans have for generations been dispossessed, wanderers, outsiders in mainstream white society, and location acquires a special poignancy and meaning in their writing. Morrison even suggests that there is a difference between the white and the black writer's treatment of place because of historical circumstances. In the essay "City Limits, Village Values: Concepts of the Neighborhood in Black Fiction," she points out that where the white writer appears to believe that society is inimical to selfhood, and so tends to reject communal space, the black sees self in terms of community and lays especial emphasis on place. For her, in fact, the street and the house are the locus of life and self.[13] That is why Barbara Christian regards location as Morrison's particular trophe: "That is why we are first introduced in these novels [*The Bluest Eye*, *Sula*, *Song of Solomon*] to the place that the characters inhabit, the land of the community. Like the ancient tradition, place is as important as the human actors. . . . Setting, then, is organic to the characters' view of themselves."[14]

Thus *Sula*, which explores what Christian has elsewhere called "the destructive limits imposed on the Black woman and the inversions of truth in this society,"[15] begins and ends with the Bottom, the black section of Medallion. The Bottom may be a common name for the black ghetto (cf. Amiri Baraka's *The System of Dante's Hell)*, but as Morrison retells the history of guile and victimization behind its naming in Medallion, it becomes a metaphor for the historical relationships between blacks whites and between men and women, and for the inversion of social and moral values that the novel examines through Sula's quest for selfhood. Sula dies alone in Eva's house, a pariah because her society cannot accept her selfhood, though it may use her to define itself. The Bottom is thus not merely a geographical place; it is the topos through which the action and the characters of the novel may be understood. This is Morrison's technique in *Beloved* too.

The title of the novel, focussing as it does on different kinds of love, indicates the ironies and the ambiguities of Morrison's theme. Beloved is of course the daughter whom the runaway slave Sethe had killed because she had loved her too much to let her live under slavery, and who returns to haunt and destroy her mother; she is the daughter on whose gravestone Sethe could only afford to have engraved the single word "beloved" rather than the entire phrase "dearly beloved" traditionally used by Christ for his disciples and Christian clergyman for his congregation, a phrase that thus emphasizes the close bond between the individual and society—and which also obliquely projects Sethe as a kind of Christ-figure whose reunion with her community at the end of the novel marks the resurrection of both herself and her people. In St. Augustine's *City of God*, Sethe means "resurrection"; "Beloved," then, is also Sethe, for she redeems and is herself redeemed by love and by her own inner strength. At the end of the novel, Paul D realizes that it is her selfhood that has made him whole. (335) When therefore, she grieves that Beloved has left her, who was her "best thing," he comforts her, holding her hand as he does so, "You your best thing, Sethe. You are." This gesture or this reassurance does not mean that Sethe needs a man to go on living but that her selfhood can be nourished only through self-understanding and social interaction: hence her tentative self-exploratory questioning, "Me? Me?" (334-35)

The epigraph to the novel, from Romans 9:25, reinforces the significance of the title. For Paul's epistle to the Christians in Rome presents the plan of Christian salvation not as limited to individual souls but as extending to the whole community. Sethe's black neighbours, who had chosen not to warn her of schoolteacher's arrival, and who had ostracized her after she had killed her daughter, become a community, a "people" with a sense of self, only when they reach out to her and accept her as one of themselves. Barbara Schapiro notes, "The characters in the novel are all working out of a deep loss to the self, a profound narcissistic wound that results from a breakdown and distortion of the relations between self and other,"[16] whether it is Sethe, or Halle, or Paul D, or even Beloved herself; once this relationship is restored, the healing process begins for both self and other, and both are able to reach identity. That is why the story is narrated not in linear fashion but in a series of images that acquire meaning through association: the novel is not only Sethe's story but the "spiraling, unfinished, many-voiced story of a community."[17]

Moreover, like Peter after him (1 Peter 2:10), Paul quotes here from the Old Testament prophet Hosea (1:6-9) to emphasize the importance of both self-realization and God's love for the individual and the community. God had ordered Hosea to name his children "not beloved" and "not my people" to indicate the estrangement between Him and His chosen people: but just as Hosea was in the end reunited with his wife, God, too, restored the Jews to His love. Hosea's story has obvious parallels with Sethe's. Significantly, besides, Paul builds on this story by using the metaphor of place in the very next verse following Morrison's epigraph—repeating Hosea's "Yet the number of the children shall be as the sand of the sea, which cannot be measured nor numbered; and it shall come to pass, that in the place where it was said unto them, Ye are not my people, there it shall be said unto them, Ye are the sons of the living God" (1:10) in "And it shall come to pass, that in the place where it was said unto them,

Ye are not my people; there shall they be called the children of the living God" (Rom 9:26)—to show that God's people are not any one particular community but all those who are truly righteous, who are illuminated by the spirit of *caritas* (see especially Romans 14). The mark of what Erich Fromm calls a "sane society" is after all the extent to which it fosters both self and interpersonal relationships.[18] Evidently, then, the title of Morrison's novel has behind it the ideal of the "Beloved Community" which recurs through the sermons and speeches of Martin Luther King (who had himself derived it from the writings of the black theologian Josiah Royce) and which was the focus of a group of white intellectuals as well, such as Van Wyck Brooks and Lewis Mumford, who have projected a local urban context for the ideal community. *Topos* as trophe is thus implicit in the title itself of Morrison's *Beloved.*

The novel begins, unlike Morrison's previous ones, not with the neighbourhood or the street, for the neighbourhood in *Beloved* is not yet a community, but with the house, the house in which Sethe and her children live with Baby Suggs, her mother-in-law, a house that has no name and for a long time no number either, a house that represents, accordingly, Sethe's isolation and her need for identity. The house has always been a central image in Morrison's novels, for her belief in the importance of what she calls "intimacy"—"the courage to go as a stranger in the village and transform the distances between people into intimacy with the whole world" (77)—has led her to project it as the symbol for self, love, family and community. She has spoken to Speto of the "woman's strong sense of being in a room, a place, or . . . a house" (213) and to Charles Ruas of the ambivalent feelings black women show towards houses, because black slave women worked in the fields with the men rather than in the house as domestic servants, and were usually deprived, accordingly, of the opportunity of being householders.[19] Consequently, where for white women writers the house is usually an image of enclosure, Morrison's women find the promise of selfhood and belonging in their houses, to which they are deeply attached.

In *The Bluest Eye* the characters remain isolated in their houses; Pauline Breedlove identifies herself passionately with the "proud house"[20] of her white employers but neglects her own, while Claudia's house, in spite of its poverty, is a home. In *Sula*, Eva keeps on adding to her house as though she is trying to compensate for her lost leg: indeed, she had in effect sacrificed her leg for the sake of a house for herself and her children. Nel's childhood home sums up her mother's personality and her own upbringing, and foreshadows what happens to her life; and the mark of Sula's alienation, and her intense belief in her self, is the loneliness of the chaotically organized house in which she lives after she returns to the Bottom and from where she removes her grandmother because she feels selfhood is incompatible with the expectations of the community regarding family ties. Sula's rejection of Eva not only deprives the old woman of her home, it also reinforces Sula's own isolation and barrenness, her inability to connect and to create. Claudia's comments in *The Bluest Eye* might be of interest here:

> There is a difference between put *out* and being put out*doors*. If you are put out, you go somewhere else; if you are outdoors, there is no place to go. The distinction was subtle but final. Outdoors was the end of something, and irrevocable, physical fact, defining and complementing our metaphysical condition. (18)

Eva may be "put out," but Sula, indoors, is effectively "outdoors." In *Beloved*, Sethe always has a "home," whether it is at the Sweet Home plantation or at Bluestone Road in Cincinnati; but she is a pariah in both places, in the plantation because she is not a person but a piece of property, who cannot even have a proper wedding and must couple with her husband outdoors, while the black neighbourhood in Cincinnati has to exorcise the ghost of Beloved from Sethe's house and heart and from their own censoriousness before she can find herself and her community.

No wonder, then, that this neighbourhood, which had once loved Baby Suggs and had celebrated with her Sethe's escape from Sweet Home, and which was so proud of its traditions of hospitality, but which had nonetheless refused to warn Sethe of schoolteacher's approach and had ostracized her for killing her daughter, is as nameless as the house at No. 124, Bluestone Road. Indeed, for many years the house remained unnumbered as "Cincinnati didn't stretch that far" (3) then, that is, at first the house existed in a kind of no-man's land, owned by an abolitionist family who had moved to the city and used to rent it out to slaves escaping to freedom and selfhood in a free State. The house, then re-enacts, as it were, the slave's experience—and particularly the female slave's—moving from a nebulous undefined position to one defined not by its own needs but by outer society, the world of the "white people." When Baby Suggs gets to live in the house in exchange for her labour, it is not through her own efforts that she finds a home but through the help of Mr. Garner, her erstwhile owner, who has allowed her son to buy her freedom with his own labour. No wonder, then, that after Sethe's act, Baby Suggs sees to it that the house has only one door, the front one, leading in but no back door leading outside; the ex-slaves who live here are still prisoners, enslaved by their past, not yet whole. The number the house later acquires is reminiscent of the numbers branded on slaves; the identification by the number the house achieves suggests the disintegration of self-hood consequent to slavery. To Denver, the house is a "person" rather than a "structure," (36) her fancies about it pointing both to her loneliness and to the unnaturalness of her relationship with Beloved. She makes a "playroom" for herself not inside the house but out in the open among the trees, where, "closed off from the hurt of the hurt world . . . veiled and protected by the live green walls, she felt ripe and clear, and salvation was as easy as a wish." (36) Appropriately, at the end of the novel, Edward Bodwin, the white owner of the house, comes back to it to reclaim his memories of his childhood and the toys he had buried there, ignorant and uncaring of what has happened there to the free slaves to whom he had rented it; he does not recognize Denver, and remembers the abolitionist movement only for the excitement and sense of commitment it had generated. (319-20)

Topos in Morrison's novels generally reflects the conflict between the African American individual and communal search for self on the one hand and the prescriptions and restrictions of the dominant culture on the other, as in the threat to the identity of the black community in *The Bluest Eye* or *Sula.* There is an increasing sophistication in her use of place—and especially of the house—in this connection. In *Song of Solomon*, Ruth feels dwarfed by her father's house and in turn dwarfs her son's emotional development; Pilate's house may not have gas or electricity but it is open and sunny, while Macon's house consists of a series of isolated rooms in which his daughters make artificial flowers, as though it were some kind of prison or lunatic asylum. Aunt Rosa's bedroom in *Tar Baby* has no windows, suggesting that she is self-sufficient, but Valerian's enclosed house, more a lifeless museum than a home, points rather to his withdrawal from life. Jadine's love might dream of attractive houses with women welcoming him in,[22] but Jadine herself rejects this male fantasy, regarding it as a stifling of the female quest for selfhood.

A certain ambivalence enters Morrison's treatment of city spaces with *Tar Baby*, in which New York is on one level the place where black women like Jadine have been able to make their own place, but on the other is also where Jadine and others like her lose their cultural identity. This is the kind of ambiguity in the Cincinnati of *Beloved*, particularly in its contrast to the Sweet Home plantation. The garden has traditionally been identified with Eden and the city with selfishness, greed and corruption; yet Sweet Home, in spite of its name, is a paradise only for Garner (note the symbolic significance of his name), not for his slaves. The city of Cincinnati, on the other hand, is where slaves find refuge, for it is situated in Ohio, which had emancipated its slaves long ago. Mr. Garner tells Baby Suggs when she sees it for the first time, "A queen of a city, Jenny. Everything you ever dreamed of, they make it right here. . . . Oh, this is a city, all right." (175-76) Even with the kindness she had received at Sweet Home, Baby had always been a slave and so had "never had the map to discover what she was like" (172); it is in Cincinnati that she draws her first free breath and begins to discover the lost map as she sees her hands and realizes, in an epiphanic moment, "These hands belong to me. These *my* hands," and feels for the first time her heart beat. (174) Wherever she has lived before, "sadness was at her center, the desolated center where the self that was no self made its home." (172) Now, however, her house on Bluestone Road is "a cheerful buzzing house where Baby Suggs, holy, loved, cautioned, fed, chastised and soothed." (106) Putting her heart to work, she tries to reach out to all who can respond to her, preaching to them of love and wholeness, "the prize" for accepting their own humanity. (108) But—like all lay preachers, of course—she chooses not a building but a Clearing to pour out her message of love and of a "grace" (107) that can only be imagined and that incorporates all the parts that can now be recognized. But she cannot link the parts to make a whole; her dance, symbolizing the integrity of personal identity, is only short-lived and must come to an end. For the end of the dance returns them all to the present in which everyone lives fragmented lives, under the shadow of the imminent arrival of schoolteacher and others of his ilk. Indeed, after schoolteacher enters her yard, Baby can no longer continue her search for integrity nor her dance, and "indifference lodges where sadness should have been." (218) She cannot approve or disapprove of Sethe's action, and withdraws from life as the black community withdraws from Sethe, finally retiring to bed to "ponder" on colour, (4) the only harmless thing in the world, (219) colour especially on her quilt—the African American woman's symbol of womanhood and identity and continuity. The fence and the gate at the house on Bluestone have been "pulled down," "yanked up" and "smashed" by "white boys,' "leaving 124 desolate and exposed at the very hour when everybody it stopped dropping by," (201) summing up the meaning and the effect of what Sethe has done and what the black neighbourhood has done to her and to itself.

Evidently, then, Cincinnati is no city of God. It is, rather, the pig-slaughtering capital of the Midwest, (190) full of the "stench" of offal and of money that turns it into Cain's domain, with Stamp Paid acting as ferryman across the Stygian river—Stygian in more ways than one, as he realizes what he sees the red ribbon with the bit of scalp hanging from it in the water. (221-22) Located on the border of slave-owning territory, this "pig-port" (189) is a conservative city that refuses to interfere with slavery elsewhere because it is a paying business. Significantly, the conversation between Stamp Paid and Paul D about Sethe takes place in a slaughter-house. Paul D has been able to get work there easily because it is a low-paying job that requires only the ability to tolerate the stink and to stand for long hours. (190) The proof of Sethe's crime that Stamp Paid offers Paul D, there is, ironically, a clipping from a white newspaper that the tatter cannot read for himself and which has judged her only from the outside—which the black neighbourhood, too, has been doing so far, and in so doing has clearly failed both itself as a community and Sethe as a black and an individual, because it is part of an urban agglomeration that has no heart or sense of self. After all, if Ohio had passed a Proclamation of Emancipation, it also had a Fugitive Slave Law that empowered slave-owners from other States to take away their runaway slaves from its cities by force, the ambiguity of its laws denying its blacks the feeling of security that nurtures personal and social identity.

Thus it is that Baby Suggs' garden, which only a day before had seen Eden-like celebrations of black fellowship and of Sethe's escape and reunion with her family, becomes the execution-yard of a prison, in which Beloved and the bonds of community are destroyed simultaneously, and Baby Suggs is reduced to helpless victim from her newfound identity as wise ancestor. It is of course schoolteacher's entry, which Baby had felt was like Satan's, (181) that turns her yard into the unweeded garden so abhorred by the medieval emblemists, just as he had done to the Sweet Home plantation earlier. The serpent in the Eden of plantation and city has the law on his side; Sethe's act of defiance is not only unnatural, it is also illegal, for she has deprived him of his lawful property, the child of his slaves, to whom she herself as mother has no legal claim. Not for nothing is schoolteacher left unnamed, never referred to with the definite article or a capitalized 's'; he represents all those forces of an exploitative and insensitive society that for its own motives and purposes denies selfhood to the other. (Denver's schoolteacher, on the other hand, who reaches out to her, has a name: Lady Jones.) Schoolteacher sees himself as the repository of civilization, believing that slavery has liberated the benighted Africans from the law of the jungle; when he sees what Sethe has done to escape him, he thinks: "All testimony to the results of a little so-called freedom imposed on people who needed every care and guidance in the world to keep them from the cannibal life they preferred." (185-86) Yet it is he himself who creates this jungle of barbarism and cruelty, he tries to teach his nephews the differences between the human and the animal sides of blacks by sending them to milk the pregnant and lactating Sethe on Sweet Home plantation, and by leaving her no option in the yard of 124, Bluestone Road, to kill her child, so that the "shoulder weeds of Bluestone Road [are] all that [comes] towards the house" now (201) and Paul D can recoil from her in horror: "You got two feet, Sethe, not four." (202)

This is very different from what he had felt when he had reentered Sethe's life as the hero who would chase away the ghosts and leave the house free for her. (57) Paul D is naive: he thinks he has got rid of the past by rearranging Sethe's house, hoping only that "there was some space" for him there, (56) and believing that the place was different from the person: "I knew it wasn't the place I was heading toward; it was you." (57) But the place *is* Sethe. Only when it is accepted as such that she can be made whole, the place well and truly exorcised of the guilt and the sorrows of the past, and the neighbourhood become a community. Because Paul D tries to enter Sethe's world without taking her past into consideration, it forces him out of the house and into an intimate relationship with itself until he realizes the truth it embodies. Paul D's ignorance about himself and about society is indicated by his excited response to the carnival in the lumberyard, surrounded by the smell of dying roses, (59) and specially with his pleasure at seeing Wild African Savage, significantly, in a cage; when he "shook his bars and said wa wa,

Paul D told everybody he knew him back in Roanoke" (6l)—a joke that loses its humour in the light of schoolteacher's belief and Stamp Paid's understanding that this is a belief shared by all white people. (244) It is only at the end of the novel that he achieves a sense of personal and communal identity, when he returns to Sethe's house and finds her dying as Baby Suggs had done, alone under a brightly coloured quilt that should instead have knitted her to her society. He begins to bring her back to life and social health by rubbing her feet and bathing her, as Amy and Baby Suggs had done. Now he has understood the significance of her action; she has defeated the makers of a world which denies others their selfhood and prevents them from forming a community. She has paid the price for this, but selfhood and wholeness are hers, though she may need to be shown this. He remembers what Sixo at Sweet Home, another survivor like Sethe, had said about his Thirty-Mile woman, and knows that it applies even more clearly to Sethe: "She is a friend of my mind. She gather me, man. The pieces I am, she gather them and give them back to me in all the right order." (335) Neither Garner nor his Sweet Home had been able to do this for anyone, their names, his behaviour with his slaves and the beauty of the farm notwithstanding.

Indeed, Sweet Home is so beautiful that whenever Sethe looks back, she thinks of its "shameless beauty" more than its terror and horror: "it made her wonder if hell was a pretty place too. Fire and brimstone all right, but hidden in lacy groves. Boys hanging from the most beautiful sycamores in the world." (7) The fact the Garner insists on referring to Baby Suggs as Jenny Whitlow rather than the name she prefers is indication enough that all is not what it seems like at first at Sweet Home, Eden-like though it might appear. Halle knows this. That is why he buys his mother's freedom and couples with Sethe in the open. Garner likes to play God to his "men," but, as Paul D realizes much later, his slaves were allowed to be men only in Sweet Home and only with his permission, so that their selfhood is his creation rather than their own making. (271) The reality becomes painfully clear to his slaves when he dies and schoolteacher is brought in to manage the plantation: their humanity is dependent on place and lasts only as long as he does. At Sweet Home, even a rooster has more of a self than a slave does. (89) The cage Paul D and the others are put into as punishment only externalizes the cage into which their selfhood has been thrust; they can be free only when they know how to break open the cage and enter the world, and not just by running away from Sweet Home.

Paul D might manage to escape from the plantation, but because he has no sense of self he has no place, and must be on the move constantly; even in Sethe's house, Beloved moves him from room to room until he goes outdoors. When he leaves Sethe, no-one offers him a place to stay in, and he finds refuge only in a deserted church. It is when he returns to Sethe and holds out his hand of friendship and *caritas* to her does he have the hope of stability, for together they can form a community that can extend outward to the larger world as well. As long as he keeps his heart in a tobacco tin, then, he has neither self nor place.

Since the dominant culture, personified by schoolteacher, turns the civilized spaces of town and country, city and farm, into a jungle in which neither self nor society can grow, it is the wilderness that gives Sethe hope and companionship. When the heavily pregnant Sethe, raped, beaten, humiliated, runs away from Sweet Home, she finds herself in an apparently inhospitable terrain, but there she also meets another fugitive, the white servant-girl Amy Denver. (Is it only coincidental that Denver is the name of an American city or that the old meaning of *denuer*—from where the surname is derived—was "to restore"?) Amy may feel socially superior to Sethe, as indeed she is—most of all because her employer cannot pursue her the way schoolteacher will Sethe—and her cultural and social background may be very different, but she can feel for her. She rubs Sethe's sore feet back to life, helps her to give birth and reminds the black woman that indeed a community of fellow-feeling can and does exist; both are women, poor and exploited, sharing a common past of sorrow and deprivation and the hope of a future that is firmly rooted in social interaction and understanding. The lullaby

Amy Sings, moreover, of a "quiet cozy home" (100) foreshadows Sethe's fate: she will have only twenty-eight days of a 'cozy home' herself before schoolteacher arrives at the gates of 124, Bluestone Road.

Yet it is this house that in the end restores Sethe's selfhood and Sethe to the community, when Denver goes outside it and Stamp Paid comes inside. Stamp Paid is the man who warns Paul D about Sethe and who displaces him from where he had, though he had found security and stability. But when he sees what suffering he has caused the newcomer to his town, he is reminded of his own lack of sympathy towards Baby Suggs and his wife in their hour of need, and he tries to enter Sethe's house to help her once again. There he sees for himself how Beloved is destroying her mother, and decides to make amends for the past by explaining to Paul D that Sethe's crime was actually an act of love for her children, and by telling the neighbourhood of what has been happening in the house on Bluestone Road by affirming, that is, the bonds of kinship and asserting his self.

What Stamp tells his people is reinforced by what Denver does. For Denver suddenly sees what Beloved is doing to her mother and decides to take action. The girl who had once retreated to a make-believe green room and who had encouraged Beloved now steps out of the house and rejoins the community, going to her neighbours and her schoolteacher for help, not for herself but for Sethe. By doing so, she not only reconstructs her self and her life, she breaks free of her dependence on her mother and brings the community back to Baby Suggs' yard, the place where they had once gathered for comfort and belonging and which they had also turned away from. The communal prayers in the yard drive away the incubus of Beloved and reunite Sethe to Paul D and to her society. Though there is always a possibility that Beloved may return, (331) the selfhood and the sense of social bonding that they have all regained will remain; even in the fragmented world of a hostile dominant culture they will survive—together. The community and its people have found themselves. They have discovered and created for themselves the bonds of the Beloved Community and a place for themselves where they belong.

NOTES

1. Michel Zeraffa, *Fictions: The Novel and Social Reality*, trans. Catherine Burns and Tom Burns (Harmondsworth: Penguin, 1976), p. 11.
2. *Ibid.*, p. 90.
3. W.H. Auden, *The Enchafed Flood* (NY: Random House, 1950), p. 37.
4. Toni Morrison, *Beloved* (NY: Signet, 1991), p. 93.
5. Claudia Tate, ed., *Black Women Writers at Work* (NY: Continuum, 1983), p. 55.
6. John Gray, qtd. Cris Evatt, *He & She* (Berkeley: Conari Press, 1992), p. 14.
7. Andrea O'Reilly, "In Search of My Mother's Garden, I found My Own: Mother-Love, Healing, and Identity in Toni Morrison's *Jazz*," *African American Review*, Vol. 30, No. 3, 1996, p. 367.
8. Zora Neale Hurston, *Their Eyes Were Watching God* (NY: Negro Univ. Press, 1969).
9. Alice Walker, *The Third Life of Grange Copeland* (NY: Harcourt, 1981).
10. Alice Walker, *Meridian* (NY: Harcourt, 1976).
11. Toni Morrison, *Sula* (NY: Signet, 1993).
12. Toni Morrison, "City Limits, Village Values: Concepts of the Neighborhood in Black Fiction," *Literature and the Urban Experience: Essays on the City and Literature*, ed. Michael C. Jaye and Ann Chalmers Watts (New Brunswick: Rutgers Univ. Press, 1981), p. 39.
13. Robert Stepto, "'Intimate Things in Place': A Conversation with Toni Morrison," *The Third Woman*, ed. Dexter Fisher (Boston: Houghton Mifflin, 1979), p. 167.
14. Barbara Christian, *Black Feminist Criticism: Perspectives on Black Women Writers* (NY: Pergamon, 1985), p. 48.
15. Barbara Christian, *Black Women Novelists: The Development of a Tradition* (Westport: Greenwood Press, 1980), p. 179.
16. Barbara Schapiro, "The Bonds of Love and the Boundaries of Self in Toni Morrison's *Beloved*," *Contemporary Literature*, 32:2, p. 197.

17. Wendy Harding and Jacky Martin, *A World of Difference: An Intercultural Study of Toni Morrison's Novels* (Westport: Greenwood Press, 1994), p. 169.
18. Eric Fromm, *The Sane Society* (NY: Fawcett Premier, 1955), p. 2.
19. Charles Ruas, *Conversation with American Writers* (NY: Knopf, 1985), p. 239.
20. Toni Morrison, *The Bluest Eye* (NY: Washington Square Press, 1972), p. 84.
21. Toni Morrison, *Song of Solomon* (NY: Signet).
22. Toni Morrison, *Tar Baby* (NY: Knopf), p. 119.

Memory, Creativity and Writing: Semiotic Discourse in *Beloved*

JAYITA SENGUPTA

Jayita Sengupta correlates Morrison's idea of "unspeakable thoughts unspoken" to Kristeva's language of abjection." She compares the gaps and spaces in the narrative to bursting points of "Kristevan sublime." She demonstrates how history of slavery, its anguish and rage, are translated through the interior monologues of Sethe, Denver and Beloved.

Editor

Everybody knew what she was called, but nobody anywhere knew her name. Disremembered and unaccounted for, she cannot be lost, because no one is looking for her, and even if they were, how can they call her if they don't know her name?[1]

Memory is a form of willed creation. The cultural memory lives within us and as Wideman points out, racial memories "exist in the imagination." They are a record of "certain collective experiences . . . that have been repeated generation after generation."[2] To use Toni Morrison's own words in *Beloved*, they are "unspeakable thoughts unspoken." (199) From the Kristevian perspective, the text is a fine example of the 'language of abjection'[3] that has its source in the repressed unconscious. The effect of the abject language is aesthetic, and this aesthetic experience is therapeutic for the reader as well as the writer. This experience takes the reader and the writer back to a vision of a "pre-symbolic" existence, as it discharges the semiotic violence in language. To quote Kristeva: "While everything else—its archeology and its exhaustion—is only literature: the sublime point at which the abject collapses in a burst of beauty that overwhelms us—and that cancels our existence."[4] In the context of this statement, and the above analysis, reading and writing of *Beloved* is surely an aesthetic experience, but this experience does not cancel out the Black existence, rather it reconfigures the Black history in the "swift and slow of human doing."[5]

The idea of *Beloved* was inspired by "two or three little fragments of stories" that Toni Morrison had "heard from different places."[6] The first was the story of Margaret Garner, a slave who in January 1856 escaped from her owner Archibald K. Gaines of Kentucky, crossed the Ohio river and attempted to find refuge in Cincinnati. She was pursued by Gaines and a posse of officers. They surrounded the house where she, her husband Robert, and their four children were harboured. When the posse battered the door and rushed in, Margaret's husband shot at them and wounded one of the officers. According to Levi Coffin,

> at this moment, Margaret Garner, seeing that their hopes of freedom were vain, seized a butcher knife that lay on the table and with one stroke cut the throat of her little daughter, whom she probably loved the best. She then, attempted to take the life of the other children and to kill herself, but she was overpowered and hampered before she could complete her desperate work.[7]

This story of Margaret Garner was eventually to become the historical analogue of the plot of *Beloved*. It made Morrison realise that "the best thing that is in us is also the thing that makes us sabotage ourselves."[8] The story stayed with Toni Morrison as it represented unclearly something about feminine selflessness. However, it took another study to clarify more precisely what Margaret Garner and her story meant. Morrison found that story in Camille Billop's *The Harlem Book of the Dead*, an album featuring James Vander Zee's photographs of Harlem funerals. These photographs according to Morrison had a 'narrative quality.' One photograph and its attendant story in particular caught her attention:

> In one picture, there was a young girl lying in a coffin and he [Vander Zee] says that she was eighteen years old and she had gone to a party and that she was dancing and suddenly she slumped

> and they noticed there was blood on her and they said, 'what happened to you?' And she said, 'I'll tell you tomorrow. I'll tell you tomorrow.' That's all she would say. And apparently her ex-boyfriend or somebody who was jealous had come into the party with a gun and a silencer and shot her. And she kept saying, 'I'll tell you tomorrow' because she wanted him to get away. And he did, I guess; anyway, she died.[9]

The story and the photograph made Morrison see clearly what she'd glimpsed through a darker glass: "Now what made these stories connect, I can't explain, but I do know that, in both instances, something seemed clear to me. A woman loved something other than herself so much that she had placed all of the value of her life in something outside herself. That the woman who killed her children loved her children so much; they were the best part of her and she would not see them sullied."[10] As early as 1978, nine years before the publication of *Beloved* Morrison had attempted to formulate the terms of that tension between remembering and forgetting, burying and reviving. In the foreword to *The Harlem Book of the Dead* she writes: "the narrative quality, the intimacy, the humanity of his photographs are stunning."[11] One of Owen Dodson's 'living' poems is on the page facing the picture of the young girl as she lives in her coffin:

> They lean over me and say
> 'Who deathed you who,
> who, who, who, who. . .
> whisper 'tell you presently. . .
> Shortly . . . this evening. . .
> Tomorrow. . .'
> Tomorrow is here
> And you out there safe
> I'm safe in here, Tootsie.[12]

If Van Der Zee's photographs give renewed life to the dead, so does Dodson's poetry give renewed voice. Even in 1973, Morrison was concerned with making the dead articulate. In 1987, she goes even further in giving the dead voice. Beloved resurrects herself as Margaret Garner's unnamed child in the novel: "So I just imagined the life of a dead girl which was the girl that Margaret Garner killed, the baby that she killed. . . . And I call her Beloved so that I can filter all these confrontations and questions that she has in that situation."[13] However, Beloved is not merely a character in the novel. She embodies the historical imagination of the Black race. In the text, she appears as the ghost of the infant Sethe had killed. In other words, she symbolizes the power and the horror of racism, or the revolutionary semiotics of the generation demanding recognition and claim in the history of the Black race.

Morrison has on more than one occasion asserted that she writes from a double perspective of accusation and hope, of criticizing the past and caring for the future. She claims that the "Black woman writer" is "one who looks at things in an unforgiving/loving way . . . writing to repossess, rename, re-own."[14] In the text, this dual perspective is referred to as "the glare of an outside thing that embraces while it accuses." (271) *Beloved* testifies as an act of remembering which is both a resurrection and a pain. It echoes the traumatic imagination for 'anything dead coming back to life hurts.' The chapters (pp. 200-17) where the repressed memory of the race finds voice between the gaps and silences of the written word, form together the bursting point of the 'Kristevian sublime.' From the Kristevian perspective, the chapters achieve the climax or form the emotional nexus of the text, allowing for the maximum aesthetic pleasure to the reader.

The first section of the portion mentioned above (pp. 200-5) contains the interior monologue of Sethe. Five pages record her attempt to justify her homicide to her infant returned to her as Beloved. The pages exemplify the revolutionary effect of the repressed maternal in language. The style of narration here creates the vision of the pre-linguistic/pre-Oedipal stage in the mother-daughter relationship. As Kristeva claims that the real content of the language of abjection is 'style,' the narration here gives the impression of a closed world between the mother and the infant where the meaning is supposedly contained between the addressor and the addressee. Sethe's repetition "Because you mine" creates a vision of togetherness, a sense of mother's extreme possessiveness for the child or a romantic yearning for some pre-linguistic bodily experience. The history of slavery, the torture of the slave body in pain, acquires a mythical dimension as Sethe articulates her anguish and rage in this interior monologue. She goes back to her own past, when as an infant her mother was often compelled to nurse the babies of her white mistress, while hers pined away in hunger and neglect. The craving for security and mother's love and affection had left permanent scars in Sethe's mind. So when she became a mother, she felt the compelling force of love, fierce and 'thick' within her to cater to the needs of her young. But the history of slavery continued to repeat itself in spite of Sethe's fierceness to claim her milk for her infants. Her milk was stolen by the children of her master and she was left 'dehumanised' as a 'cow.' (200) Her grief and rage thus assumes horrific proportions when the white oppressors come to get her and her children. Sethe, in her frenzy to avoid the inevitable repetition of the tale of torture and slavery happening to her infants, attempts to put them away to what she considered was 'a safe place for them.' If securing a decent tomb for the infant whom she murdered with her own hands meant selling her dignity once again, Sethe bore with it. She did it all for her fierce obsessive mother love. The return of Beloved to her is the return of her repressed memory, of her repressed guilt, sorrow and shame, which she has to come to terms with, before she attains a catharsis of emotions and be accepted back in the world of the symbolic order/community.

Sethe's monologue is followed by Denver's (206-9), who claims to have swallowed Beloved's blood with her mother's milk. She too claims Beloved to be her own. From her childhood, ever since Beloved's death, she has come to accept Beloved's ghost as her "secret company." She is the one who had heard the sound of Beloved crawling upstairs. Life would have continued in much the same way, if Paul D did not come. It was he, one of those Sweet Home men who chased the ghost away and broke the bond between the mother and daughter, the dead and the living. But the traumatic imagination probably could not be chased away so easily and by such force. So Beloved returns not merely as a 'sound' crawling up the stairs but in flesh to challenge and interrogate the past and its relevance in the present. Denver, who can understand the fierceness of mother-love wishes to secure Beloved as her own, safe from her mother's hands. She suffers from an acute anxiety for her own self and for Beloved.

> All the time I'm afraid the thing that happened that made it all right for my mother to kill my sister could happen again. . . . Whatever it is it comes from outside this house, outside this yard, and it can come right on in the yard if it wants. So I never leave this house, . . . so it can't happen again and my mother won't have to kill me too. (205).

Such terror of the mother who can love as to kill is continued in Denver's intensity of feelings to protect Beloved.

> I thought she was trying to kill her that day in the Clearing. Kill her back. But then she kissed her neck. . . . Don't love her too much. Don't. May be it's still in her the thing that makes it all right to kill her children. I have to tell her. I have to protect her. (206)

Denver has to handle Beloved, her mother Sethe and the dream of a father who surely must have been an "Angel Man." She reconstructs her image of her father out of the memories of her grandmother. She would invent all sorts of stories which may have hindered the father's return: "Something was holding him up. He had a problem with the horse. The river flooded; the boat sank, and he had to make a new one." (207) The solitude and quiet gave ample space for Denver's imagination to grow and engulf her. Beloved's return allowed for more expansion of her imagination for "that just made the cheese more binding: my sister come to help me wait for my daddy."

Beloved's narration, which follows Denver's, plunges deeper into the semiotic realm till it becomes undecipherable language mingling the thoughts of the mother, daughters, of dead and the living into one. The linguistic units in the first section of Beloved's narration are separated by spaces and not by marks of punctuation.

> I AM BELOVED and she is mine. I see her take flowers away from leaves she puts them in a round basket the leaves are not for her she fills the basket she opens the grass I would help her but the clouds are in the way how can I say things that are pictures. (210)

Only the first person pronoun and the first letter in each paragraph are capitalised. This is to place all the moments of Beloved's sensation and recollection in a continuous and eternal present. From her grave, Beloved yearns to be reunited with Sethe. In addition to such desire, she appears to have become one in death with the black and angry dead who suffered through the middle passage: "storms rock us and mix the men into the women and the women into the men." (211) Beloved's consciousness extends into the historical consciousness. She narrates her story in the fragmented monologue which describes her abduction from Africa and transportation in a slave ship. The story expresses her vehement attachment to a woman on land and ship who as Jennifer Fitzgerald points out "plays the part of the mother or primary care giver."[15] To follow Jennifer Fitzgerald's Kleinian interpretation of the text, this woman fits into the notion of the 'internal mother.' She is a 'double' of the external person playing the role of affection giver. The 'double' is created by the infant's ambivalent attitude to the person, she depends on. Feelings of love and dependence are often mingled with a sense of fear of being abandoned. This pattern of love and hate is repeated in Beloved's relationship with Sethe. While she sucks in Sethe's love and grows on it, she also accuses Sethe "of leaving her behind. Of not being nice to her, not smiling at her." (241) She projects into Sethe the image of her eternal mother, the woman who was about to smile at her and then who left her behind. Sethe in Beloved's vision is both idealized and demonized, both all-loving and all-abandoning. The apparently twenty-year-old Beloved sometimes behaves like a two-years-old. She confronts the typically Oedipal primal scene when she witnesses Sethe and Paul D in the bath tub. Beloved does not enter into any direct confrontation with the issue but compels Paul D into a sexual relationship with herself to expel him from the mother-daughter binding. Towards the close of the novel when the mother and daughter change positions as Beloved gains more and more authority over her, Denver too is excluded from their relationship. The repressed hunger for love grows into horrific proportions till it enforces in Sethe and Beloved a sense of drowning.

> I am looking for the join I am loving my face so much I reach for her chewing and swallowing . . . she knows I want to join. . . . I see me swim away. (213)

The disjointed discourse of craving for recognition continues in the second section of Beloved's monologue "as a conflagration of hasty voices—loud, urgent, all speaking at once." (172)

> Beloved
> You are my sister
> You are my daughter
> You are my face; you are me
> I have found you again; you have come back to me
> You are my Beloved
> You are mine
> You are mine
> You are mine. (216)

At this juncture, the novel in Kristevian terms renders "the beauty of a gesture that, here, on the page compels language to come nearest to the human enigma, to the place where it kills, thinks and experiences jouissance all at the same time."[16] But a continuation in this state will surely lead to disaster. As Kristeva admits, the semiotic is "only a theoretical supposition justified by the need for description."[17] This means that the semiotic is a symbolic construction that is needed in order to perpetuate symbolic description. So the cultural space/symbolic order is reconstructed through Denver who holds within herself the psychic power to heal Sethe and the community. Toni Morrison too, in an article "Re-discovering Black History," writes of "complicated psychic power one had to exercise to revert devastation."[18] So at the end of the novel, it is Denver who helps to rescue her mother from the clutches of Beloved or her traumatic projection of the self, by uniting her with the community. Paul D too returns "to put his story" next to Sethe's. (273)

At the novel's close, Denver, Sethe and Paul D have all proceeded from repressive isolation to a developed sense of self, reflected back from the love they see in the eyes of the others in the community. No one claims Beloved or looks for her, for she is absorbed into the "semiotic chora" of the generation to become a myth undeniable and unforgettable. She becomes the sign of the ironic laughter of history,[19] which disintegrates and dissipates into the futuristic space to allow for swallowing "her all away." (274)

NOTES

1. Toni Morrison, *Beloved* (London: Chatto and Windus, 1987), p. 274.
2. John Edgar Wideman, *Sent for You Yesterday* (1983; New York, 1988), prefatory page.
3. Kristeva defines abjection as a kind of "narcissistic crisis." It is the "realization" that the primary identification with the mother is a "seeming," a fake. Abjection thus is the beginning of a separation prior to the "mirror stage." Kristeva maintained that the human life and society is founded on the abject separation of one body from another at birth. This separation, like subsequent ones is laboured but necessary and it pre-supposes the repression of the maternal authority.
4. Julia Kristeva, *Powers of Horror*, trans. Leon Roudiez (New York: Columbia University Press, 1980), p. 210.
5. DuBois, qtd. Homi K. Bhabha, *Location of Culture* (London: Routledge, 1994), p. 9
6. Gloria Naylor and Toni Morrison, "A Conversation," *Southern Review*, 21 (1985), pp. 567-93.
7. Levi Coffin, *Reminiscences of Levi Coffin* (Cincinnati, 1876), pp. 557-93.
8. *Conversations with Toni Morrison*, ed. Danielle Taylor Guthrie (Mississippi: Mississippi University Press,1994), p. 585.
9. *Ibid.*, p. 584.
10. *Ibid.*

11. Toni Morrison, Foreword, Camille Billops, *The Harlem Book of the Dead* (New York, 1978).
12. *Ibid.*
13. Conversations with Toni Morrison, p. 585.
14. Toni Morrison interviewed by Stepto in "Intimate Things in Place" in Michael S. Harper and Robert Stepto, ed., *Chant of Saints: A Gathering of Afro-American Literature, Art and Scholarshi*p (Urbana, I, 1979), p. 225.
15. Jennifer Fitzgerald, "Selfhood and Community: Psycho-analysis and Discourse in *Beloved*" in *Toni Morrison: Contemporary Critical Essays*, ed. Linden Peach (London: Macmillan, 1998), pp. 110-27.
16. *Powers of Horror*, p. 206.
17. Kristeva, *Revolution in Poetic Language*, trans. Margaret Waller (New York: Columbia University Press,1984), p. 68.
18. Toni Morrison, "Re-discovering Black History," *New York Times Magazine*, 11 Aug. 1974, p. 18.
19. Kristeva maintains that the Abject literature laughs at horror. She refers to it as "A Laughing Apocalypse." See *Powers of Horror*, p. 206.

A Study of *Beloved* as a Neo-Slave Narrative

MADHU MEHROTRA

Madhu Mehrotra evaluates the contribution of black literature to the national literature of America. She points out the significatnt contribution made to American history by works of ex-slaves Olauaah Equiano, Phyllis Wheatley, Harriet Ann Jacobs. She feels that Morrison's Beloved *is a continuum of the same tradition.*

Editor

Slavery is the central fact of black history in America which contributed enormously to economic growth and the creation of wealth in colonial and nineteenth century America. Toni Morrison in her revolutionary pamphlet "Playing in the Dark" emphasizes that what one recognizes as 'Americanness' today has been shaped by the 400 years' old presence, first of Africans and then African Americans in the United States and "the contemplation of this black presence is central to any understanding of our national literature and should not be permitted to hover at the margins of the literary imagination.[1]

The first Africans were brought as indentured servants to North America around the 1600s but by the 1640s a racial system developed which forced thousands of black servants into a lifetime of servitude. It is a widely known fact that these slaves were exposed to the worst indignities—physical, mental and psychological—under white hegemony. For a long time narratives about slave life were shaped and censored by white scholars with the help of diaries, ledgers and records of white southerners who had themselves kept slaves. Owing to strict anti-literacy laws the slaves themselves remained illiterate and the few that received some rudimentary education had neither experience in writing nor the leisure to write. Condemned to a life of invisibility and silence, oral expression became for them the fundamental means of communication. Sojourner Truth, an ex-slave who later became a social activist, fighting for the rights of women had dictated her autobiography to Olive Gilbert.

Hence the number of Afro-Americans who participated in the print-culture at the end of the eighteenth and the beginning of the nineteenth century were very few, and those who did, had to conform to the views of the dominant class or be ignored and dismissed. Olauaah Equiano an ex-slave who had bought his freedom published in 1789, "The Interesting Narrative of Olauaah Equiano, Gustavus Vassa, the African, written by Himself," but followed the spiritual autobiography tradition which became the prototype of a number of slave-narratives, for religion was considered to be a 'safe subject.'

Phyllis Wheatley, best known for her Christian verses received no subscribers to her advertisement for the publication of her short racially conscious poem, "Thoughts on Being Brought from Africa to America." Attempts to tell the truth were fraught with danger. Frederick Douglass's "Narrative of the Life of Frederick Douglass, an American Slave," published in 1845 exposed him to the risk of capture and re-enslavement forcing him to temporarily escape to England.

Harrier Ann Jacobs, an ex-slave and an unwed mother, had to invent an alter-ego for her "Incidents in the Life of a Slave Girl" published in 1861, in order to expose the sordid history of sexual exploitation of females slaves of which she herself had been a victim. In order to get first hand information about slavery, the U.S. Govt. between the years 1936 and 1938 funded a Federal Works project wherein writers and teachers were sent to interview black men and women who could still remember what life as a slave was. Over 2000 interviews from seventeen states were collected, transcribed and published and now form pact of America's treasured collection. So, for the first time the illiterate black man's voice was heard but unfortunately most of these narratives were fragmentary, marked by reticence, and repetition. Toni Morrison's *Beloved* is an attempt in the same direction "the scholarship that looks into the mind, imagination and behaviour of slaves is valuable," says Toni Morrison[2] and her Pulitzer prize winning novel published in 1987, long after Civil Rights had been achieved attempts to do this. Labouring under no constraints of either conforming to White beliefs or complying with standards of White decency, Morrison vocalizes a painfully compelling and brutally frank account of the atrocities of slavery. Basing her novel on the Margaret Garner case, in which a Black slave woman had in 1855 attempted to kill her children rather than condemn them to a life of slavery, Morrison explores the psychic damage inflicted on Afro-American women by sexual abuse, drawing on the tradition of the slave narrative and creates a neo-slave narrative.

In the novel, Sethe, the prototype of Garner, attempts to kill like her, three of her children but succeeds in killing only a daughter. This child, known only as Beloved, returns after eighteen years to reclaim the love and identity that belonged to her. Morrison uses 'magic realism' to present this unusual and improbable phenomena by a deliberate manipulation of reality. The narrative presents a mingling of the mundane with the fantastic, treating the magical as normal without evoking any sense of surprise or amazement or emotional chills. Hence the narrative is not linear but multi-linear, not univocal but dialogic, and an attempt is made not merely to tell a story but also to open up a number of provocative issues. Thus the novelist incorporates the themes of history, slavery, guilt, the effect of the past on the present, the nature of motherhood etc. in a series of memories and re-memories.

Having grown up in a story telling environment, for both sides of her family had migrated from the South, it was natural for Morrison "to use an oral/aural narrative voice and communal story telling techniques."[3] Consequently there is a shift from third person narration to omniscient narrator to interior monologue in the novel. There are also different levels of narrative ranging from the traditional to the modern, oral to multi-voiced.

Making an effective use of the device of memory, the story has been told through the consciousness of different characters who are conceived and developed as characters and not stereotypes or caricatures as in the case of narratives by White authors.

Sometimes one incident is filtered through the consciousness of nearly three characters, thereby presenting a multi-dimensional view. Thus *Beloved* is the story not only of Sethe, Baby Suggs, Stamp Paid, Paul D and Halle but also of the thousands of slaves who had died before them.

The re-memories of Sethe reveal aspects of her life at 124 and go back to Sweet Home where she was brought as a thirteen-year-old by the Garners who treated their slaves as 'men.' The death of Garner and the advent of schoolteacher, a symbol of white patriarchal authority who used coercion and violence to maintain discipline, make life unbearable at Sweet Home. A hard task master who believed that "definitions belonged to the definers and not to the defined,"[4] he forbids Sethe's husband Halle from renting out his labour, which he had been doing every Sunday the last five years in order to buy the freedom of his mother Baby Suggs. Slave life had "busted her legs, back, head, eyes, hands, kidneys, womb and tongue." (87) Convinced that slaves were sub-human, schoolteacher asks his pupils to list separately the human and animal characteristics of the 'subject.' Sethe stands watching when his boys hold down the heavily pregnant Sethe and forcibly steal her milk. Deeply shocked and grievously insulted at having been deprived of her nutrient, her very essence, she reports the matter to Mrs. Garner, consequent to which the infuriated schoolteacher inscribes the text of slavery on her back with a whip. Later Amy Denver, the White girl who helps deliver Sethe's baby, describes the wound as "a chokecherry tree." See here's the trunk—its red and split wide open, full of sap, and this here's the parting for the branches. Leaves too . . . and dern if these ain't blossoms. . . . I had me some whippings but I don't remember nothing like this." (79)

Each of Sethe's re-memories adds to the story of her life and the central incident, the killing of the children, is filtered through her own memory and that of Stamp Paid's in varying details. Later it is also revealed in Sethe's interior monologue, thus enabling Morrison to deeply penetrate the emotional and psychic consequences of the act.

Stamp Paid's and Paul D's re-memories throw further light on the dehumanising effects of the institution of slavery. Paul D remembers how after the failure of their attempt to escape, Sixo and Paul A were killed and he was made to wear an iron collar with three spokes so that he could neither turn nor lie down. Another reminiscence recounts how he was shackled and hitched to a wagon and sold off not once but twice and then chained with forty-six others, and each one was forced to live in a wooden box five feet deep and five feet wide, fitted into a ditch with a cage-like door. Five attempts to 'cut' were foiled, during which he saw runaway slaves "fighting owls for food, stealing from pigs, hiding in slop and jumping into wells to avoid Patrollers." (66)

Stamp Paid's thoughts go back to the day of Sethe's heinous act and the memory of his wife whom he had killed on account of having been used and 'dirtied' by his master.

Thus slavery was bad for men but worse for women and the novel truthfully exposes their vicious exploitation. Working both inside and outside the house, as farmhands, housemaids, nannies and wet nurses, they were hardly ever able to nurse or nurture their own offspring. Easy targets of frequent sexual abuse, they were looked upon as objects of instant or long-term sexual gratification with absolutely no commitment. Frequent pregnancies only ensured an unfailing supply of slaves that added to the labour force and increased their dollar value as breeders.

Ella rememories how her puberty was spent being shared by the master and his son. Thus slavery not only undermined self-worth but also destroyed families, "in all of Baby Suggs' life men and women were moved like checkers. Anybody Baby Suggs knew, let alone loved, who hadn't run off or been hanged, got rented out, loaned out, bought up, brought back, stored up, mortgaged, won, stolen or seized. So Baby Suggs' eight children had six fathers and each one had gone away from her." (23) Convinced that there was no bad luck worse than white folk, she turns into an unchurched preacher after being freed and exhorts the community to celebrate their black bodies and laugh and clap and sing. Though dead, her consciousness is revealed through that of Sethe's and in like manner Sethe's consciousness is revealed through Denver who steps into the 'told' story of her birth. Identifying herself completely with the story, she not only conveys each minute detail to Beloved but like a clairvoyant is also able to see what she is saying and not just to hear it. In the second section of the novel, the narrative goes much beyond Sethe's multitudinous thoughts to an African folk memory and with the aid of Surrealism, reveals through the consciousness of Beloved the sub-conscious memories of an African-American girl whose mother had died in the 'middle passage.'

Throughout the narrative, the past is constantly evoked. In fact, the novel is itself a kind of remembering and retelling of the past. This results in a repetition of incidents, words and phrases which becomes central to the narrative strategy. It not only concretizes certain scenes and issues in the memory but also obliquely connects certain situations and time spans for the narrative keeps flitting between the past and the present. According to Brooks, "repetition in narrative dramatizes the way in which the mind creates meaning and is itself a form of remembering . . . a series of returns to and returns of, confounding the movement back to origins."[5] Sethe is reconnected to the past when upon first setting eyes on Beloved she experiences the breaking of the waters, as she had done in the past at the time of Denver's birth. The past thus feeds the present and Beloved herself appears as a resurrection of the past.

Chronicling a non-linear account of almost five decades of the life of Sethe, the novel has epic dimensions. Beginning at 124, after the death of Baby Suggs, the year mentioned is 1873. The narrative then meanders intermittently through the consciousness of various characters to Sweet Home and the slaves' attempt to escape, Beloved's burial, the killing of the children etc. Swinging back and forth, the narrative creates a tangled web of near incomprehensibility, lacking both chronology and continuity. Time flows without the restriction of time and past and present intermingle.

This relation between the past and the present lends itself to the constant exploration of the hidden intersection between the two time spans, the subtle similarities—wanted or unwanted—the disjunctions and dislocations.[6]

Most slave narratives, actual or fictionalized, apart from expressing resentment at their condition, focus on the protagonist's need to achieve freedom. William Styron's *Confessions of Nat Turner*, based on the life of Nat Turner who led the slave insurrection in 1831, and Margaret Walker's "Jubilee," based on the life of her great grandmother Elvira Dozier Ware, express the same sentiments. However, Sethe does not aspire for personal freedom alone, leaving her babies, the "most precious and fine and beautiful parts of herself" (163) was unthinkable. "I did it," she informs Paul D, "I got us all out." Freedom to her meant not only putting a stop to endless hours of work, but also the right to call her children her own and love them 'proper,' for slaves were dispossessed of the legal right of either owning their children or even naming them. Beloved thus takes her name from the single word inscribed on her tombstone.

The concept of motherhood is of central importance in African-American cultures and Sethe's triumph turns to dismay when schoolteacher catches up with her, determined to take her, who had at least ten more breeding years and her pickaninnies back to slavery. Acting on the spur of the moment and refusing to be a victim anymore, she attacks them with a handsaw: "I stopped him," she tells Paul D. when he meets her after eighteen years. "I took and put my babies where they'd be safe." (164) Rejecting stereotypical passivity, seeking neither sympathy nor acceptance from the community, she leads the life of a social outcast. Apparently unrepentant, for she convinces herself that her action had been motivated by love, her suppressed guilt finally surfaces when Beloved comes to live with them. Believing that Beloved returned because her love was 'tough,' she interprets it as the triumph of her motherhood. "She came back to me of her own free will, and I don't have to explain a thing." (200) Extremely possessive about Sethe whom she almost devours with her eyes, Beloved appears to be an enigma and defies explanation. Is it a projection of Sethe's guilt, her resurrected daughter, the prisoner found locked in a white man's cottage or a re-incarnation of Sethe's murdered African slave mother? Even though she appears in flesh "no footfall announces her" and she is found standing where "before there was nobody," when Denver looked. (123) She has new unlined skin and a jagged cut mark, and Enquirer about the ear-rings that Sethe had received as a wedding present. On another occasion she points to the sunlit cracks and tells Denver: "I'm like this." (124) Though both Seth and Denver realize that she is the resurrected baby ghost that had haunted 124 and had made the house "pitch," they are not at all confused or surprised. On the contrary, they are fiercely attached to her and pamper her, afraid that she might go back. The fact that 124 was haunted is revealed at the very opening of the novel, "124 WAS SPITEFUL. Full of a baby's venom. The women in the house knew it and so did the children." (1) Denver describes it as a house "peopled by the living activity of the dead." (19) Uncanny and incredible as this might seem to Western eyes, it seems perfectly acceptable to people of cultures which believe in the presence of spirits. Baby Suggs feels: "Not a house in the country ain't packed to its rafters with some dead Negro's grief." (5) Morrison tides over this situation by using magic realism, and the unusual and improbable is described in a simple matter-of-fact tone. The unbelievable ceases to have its source in the unknown when Baby Suggs performs a near miracle by feeding the whole community even with insufficient provisions, upon the safe arrival of Sethe and her children. Yet she is able to smell the disapproval of the community and behind it another odor of "something dark and coming." She squeezes her eyes to see what it was in her mind's eye "but all she could make out was high topped shoes, she didn't like the look of." (138) This was probably an ominous premonition of the arrival of schoolteacher leading to the killing of the children.

Towards the end of the novel when the community learns about the presence of Beloved, some of the women arrive at the house, curious yet cautious to catch a glimpse of the "Devil Child." As the group of women sing in unison, Edward Bodwin appears. Denver and Sethe, threatened by his appearance, run towards him and Beloved disappears mysteriously right before everybody's eyes. Paul D and Here Boy (the dog) return to 124; the narrative comes to a close, but leaves behind a chain of painful memories for the story of Beloved as Morrison herself reiterates was "not a story to pass on." (275)

NOTES

1. Toni Morrison, *Playing in the Dark: Whiteness and the Literary Imagination* (New York: Vintage, 1993), p. 5.
2. *Ibid.*, pp. 11-12.
3. Deborah Guth, "A Blessing and a Burden: The Relation to the Past in *Sula, Song of Solomon* and *Beloved*," *Modern Fiction Studies*, 39, 3 &4, Fall/Winter 1993, p. 590
4. Toni Morrison, *Beloved* (New York: Vintage, 1997), p. 198.
5. Peter Brooks, *Reading for the Plot* (New York: Routledge, 1985), p. 98
6. Guth, p. 589.

Delineating the Apparition: The Mystery Streak in *Beloved*

MONIKA GUPTA

Monika Gupta analyses Morrison's use of the elements of supernatural in bringing out various psychological realities. She highlights the trauma of being abandoned that encapsulates the character of Beloved and her relationship with three central characters—Denver, Sethe and Paul D.

Editor

Despite the rapid and revitalizing growth in the realms of science and technology, no country or literature in the world is free from the mystery-pangs of spiritualism. Whether the folk feature dominates the literary highlights of a renowned writer or the literature of the national kind carries the myths pertaining to the mystery tales of the supernatural, the things are the same that man's relations to himself is not all rational. One of the pioneers of the African-American literature, Toni Morrison, has exercised fine skills in delineating the elements of the supernatural, partly on the exuberance of Shakespeare and, partly, the Greek rituals. In her writings, Morrison tries to acquaint her readers to African-American oral folk culture and, for this purpose, uses the elements of the supernatural, mystery, magic and the mythology in almost each novel.

Beloved, which appeared in 1987 in its post-modernist approach, is dedicated to "Sixty Million and More." About her Pulitzer Prize-winning novel, Morrison comments: "I don't want to give my readers something to swallow. I want to give them something to feel and think about, and I hope that I set it up in such a way that it is a legitimate thing and a valuable thing."[1]

Being a black woman writer, Morrison is conscious of the social, cultural, sexual, economic and political issues and, for this reason, all female characters of her novel discover the fact that "they must go back to their African heritage if they are to find themselves in the fullest sense."[2] *Beloved* touches the hearts of the readers because of a perfect pathetic story of 'slavery.' Toni Morrison, a prolific and renowned American writer, who won the Nobel Prize for literature in 1993, has herself undergone such oppressions. Black woman is oppressed not only by the Whites but also by the Black men. Slavery is "terrible for men, but it is far more terrible for women; super added to the burden common to all, they have sufferings and mortification peculiar to their own."[3]

In *Beloved,* Morrison presents the story in flashback and pieces with the help of traditional African folklore and mysticism. After reading the text, readers are reminded that the oral tradition is very strong in black culture so that it is still alive; but it was "not a story to pass on."[4] *Beloved* is a narrative of the humiliation of the 19th century slave, "a Media-like woman who murders her daughter to save her from a slave master."[5] Morrison's motive of writing this novel was to tell the physical and the psychological effects of slavery not only upon women but also the community as a whole.

Beloved is Morrison's excellent piece of art difficult to be classified whether to accept it as a mystery or reality. Not only Indian but also the European literature is full of stories of supernatural characters, such as vampires, trolls and other monsters. Brunvand writes in this regard: "supernatural legends, concerning the returning spirits of the dead, are just as common and as varied in the United States as they are abroad."[6]

Though the readers are not introduced to the title character, Beloved, in the early part of the story, she reflects her shadow in the lives of the characters with whom she makes contact. Through the stream-of-consciousness technique, Morrison justifies Beloved's appearance, her change in the physical and the emotional form, and also her disappearance.

Based on a real story, *Beloved* deals with the story of a woman, Sethe, who works as a slave with her husband, Halle, in Sweet Home plantation in Kentucky. Like other female and male characters, she, too, is a victim of sexist and racist oppression. The racial problem in America means an understanding of its "counterpart—the sexuality of American racism."[7] After the death of their good master, they were brutally treated by their new master and faced brutal and dehumanizing behaviour. Sethe tolerates everything but when she is forcefully milked like a cow, she decides to run away from Sweet Home. Her escape from Sweet Home is to provide freedom to her children. She decides that she will "protect her" while she is alive and she will "protect her" when she is not.[8] As a provider and protector, she kills her youngest daughter, and her two sons, Howard and Buglar, run away from Cincinnati. After a span of long eighteen years, mysteriously Sethe's daughter, Beloved, reappears to claim her love. Beloved appears from the water. Morrison describes:

> A fully dressed woman walked out of the water. . . . Nobody saw her emerge or come accidentally by. . . . She had new skin, lineless and smooth, including the knuckles of her hands. (62-63)

In America, the black man was not allowed to form or protect his family. As a result, the burden of the family had to be taken up by the black woman and, for this reason, this class becomes the matriarchally dominant society. Because the mother runs the family, the daughters learn everything from their mother. The effect of such a bond is very strong but in Morrison's world of fiction, this relationship can be destructive or constructive. Living in the classist, racist and sexist society, black woman, "sharing her godliness with her female children,"[9] faces different kinds of humiliation. Realizing the relation between the three pairs—Sethe and Beloved, Sethe and Denver, Denver and Beloved—one finds that these three characters are linked together to tell the readers how black people survive and keep their history alive.

Beloved's major aim to appear in a form of a sensuous woman can be considered as a reminder of Sethe's act. She enters in her mother's life and destroys her happiness. As soon as Sethe realizes that Beloved is her daughter whom she had killed eighteen years ago, her natural love for her emerges and, just out of guilt, provides everything to her in a very apologetic manner:

> The best chair, the biggest piece, the prettiest plate, the brightest ribbon for her hair, and the more she took. . . . Beloved was more important, meant more to her than her own life. (296)

Sethe's act of killing her daughter is not supported by Baby Suggs, her grandmother, who has given her every kind of help. This kind of emotional and psychological understanding between Baby Suggs and Sethe is a unique characteristic of black women. But, in order to provide freedom to her children, Sethe has no other choice:

> That she lived with 124 in helpless, apologetic resignation because she had no choice; that minus husband, sons, mother-in-law, she and her slow-witted daughter had to live there all alone making do. (201)

If a mother is not able to love, protect and provide a good and free life to her children, it would be most horrifying black experience under slavery. Beloved captures Sethe, Denver and Paul D. Sethe spends most of her time taking care of Beloved, who becomes "a greedy ghost and needs a lot of love." (258) As a result, she distances herself from Denver and Paul D. Beloved starts sucking the life of Sethe:

> Dressed in Sethe's dresses, she stroked her skin with the palm of her hand. She imitated Sethe, talked the way she did, laughed her laugh and used her body the same way down to the walk, the way Sethe moved her hands, signed through her nose, held her head. Sometimes coming upon them making men and women cookies or tacking scraps of cloth on Baby Suggs's old quilt, it was difficult for Denver to tell who was who. (295-96)

As far as mother-daughter relationship is concerned, Sethe and the daughter, Denver, play a very important role in the novel. While living with Sethe, Denver, feels alienated because nobody from the community speaks to them. She wants to relate herself with her grandmother, Baby Suggs, who taught her many things, which are important in life. She also misses her brothers, Howard and Buglar. She is happy to know that her sister is back, with whom she can share everything. Denver enjoys playing and talking with Beloved. She asks Beloved:

> "What did you come back for?"
> Beloved smiled. "To see her face."
> "Ma'am's? Sethe?"
> "Yes, Sethe." (93)

As soon as she comes to know that this new guest at 124 Bluestone is nothing but her dead sister who has appeared to destroy her mother, she decides to protect her mother from this ghost:

> The job she started out with, protecting Beloved from Sethe changed to protecting her mother from Beloved. Now it was obvious that her mother could die and leave them both and what would Beloved do then? (298)

This caring and sharing feeling is a unique phenomenon in Morrison's works. Not only is Denver protective towards her mother but Sethe is also aware of her psychological state of mind:

> Sethe understood Denver. Solitude had made her secretive-self manipulated. Years of haunting had dulled her in ways you wouldn't believe and sharpened her in ways you wouldn't believe either. (121)

Paul D and Sethe were slaves together at Sweet Home. When he enters in the life of Sethe, she recalls atrocities and exploitation faced by her. She says: "I don't want to know or have to remember that." (86) He wants to take Sethe's responsibility. But Sethe, who is leading her life under the guilt of infanticide, is not ready to start a new relationship. She is in utter confusion. Paul D speaks: "Sethe, if I'm here with you, with Denver you can go anywhere you want. . . . Go as far inside as you need to. . . . We can make a life, girl. A life." And Sethe replies: "I don't know. I don't know." (57)

Beloved's aim is to divide 124 Bluestone and separate Paul D, Sethe and Denver. Her efforts of throwing away Paul D from her mother's life completes:

> SHE MOVED HIM. . . . Paul D didn't know how to stop it because it looked like he was moving himself. Imperceptibly, downright reasonably, he was moving out of 124. (140)

Beloved deliberately forces Paul D to touch her and call her name. Even Paul D could not hold himself and, in this way, Beloved's aim is completed. Though her attempt is not purely sexual but she traps Paul D to throw him out of her mother's life. Paul D becomes the victim of the apparition and leaves Sethe once again. In fact Paul D can make Sethe's life stable and happy both emotionally and sexually. For more than eighteen years, her feminine urges are suppressed and in order to fulfil her desire, she allows Paul D to enter in her life. Though Morrison's male characters are weaker to female characters but, in a vast cannon, Paul D is an exception. Throughout the novel, Sethe and Paul D share their past and remember the horrible days. In search of good days, he wants to complete his dream of a family whereas Sethe wants to lead her life under his shelter and protection.

> He held her breasts in the palms of his hands. He rubbed his cheek on her back and learned that way her sorrow, the root of it; its wide trunk and intricate branches. (21)

The intention of Paul D's act may be emotional or purely sexual but symbolically their union promises to bring real love in their lives. But Sethe is aware of this reality that life with Paul D cannot be successful unless she has a guilt of infanticide. When Paul D comes to know about her crime, he goes back from her life criticizing her act:

> "What you did was wrong, Sethe."
>
> "I should have gone on back there? Taken my babies back there?"
>
> "You got two feet, Sethe, not four," he said and right then a forest sprang up between them; trackless and quiet. (202-3)

Sethe realizes that Paul D has offered only temporary peace and company to her. She is hurt, and starts her life in which Denver, Beloved and she can live happily. At the end of the novel, he once more enters Sethe's life with a new hope: "Sethe, me and you we got more yesterday than anybody. We need some kind of tomorrow." (335) Actually, Sethe's act of infanticide, which was considered the worst crime, is discarded not only by Baby Suggs and Paul D but also by the community. She almost loses everything—sons, husband and, most importantly, her 'self.' Her lost 'self' does not permit her to lead a happy life with Paul D. Though her sexual relations with Paul D can be seen as biological need, her psychological trauma haunts her and also her family throughout the novel. In the end, Paul D helps her to re-establish her realization of the 'self' when he speaks: "You your best thing, Sethe." (335)

Morrison's *Beloved*, which is "a milestone in the chronicling of black experience in America,"[10] and mixture of mystery and horror, projects repressed collective memory of black people. After a careful reading of the novel, the reader feels presence of Beloved as a human being whereas she is in a state of transition. Denise Heinz describes that for Sethe "Beloved represents more of a psychological than a supernatural phenomenon."[11] Based on a real story, Morrison's motive of writing *Beloved* is not only to unveil that "peculiar phase of slavery," which "has generally been kept veiled."[12] Though Morrison's motive is clear, every reader asks the question whether Beloved is a person or a spirit. The answer could be anything. Beloved's story has to be considered at two levels, one from Sethe's point of view, another from the community's point of view.

From Sethe's point of view, Beloved always relates to herself from mother, so does Sethe. Out of guilt, terror and fear, she asks Beloved:

> "Tell me the truth. Didn't you come from the other side?"
> "Yes, I was on the other side."
> "You came back because of me?"
> "Yes."
> "You rememory me?"
> "Yes, I remember you."
> "You never forgot me?"
> "Your face is mine."

> "Do you forgive me? Will you stay? You safe here now." (265)

Sethe has her own right to protect her children from slavery and the "murder becomes Sethe's act of mother love."[13] In this case, both mother and daughter play different roles. Sethe is protector whereas Beloved is destroyer. Through stream-of-consciousness, readers can easily understand that Beloved does not differentiate herself from her mother; this is evident in three different thoughts: "I am Beloved and she [Sethe] is mine" (259); "I want to be the two of us I want to join" (263); and finally, "You are my face; you are me. . . .You are mine." (266)

At the end of the novel, Beloved leaves 124 only by the collective efforts of community. Here Morrison makes Beloved real and visible as a human being who is returning to the river from which she had first emerged. Thirty black women, who come to exorcise Beloved from 124, speak about her thus:

> The devil-child was clever, they thought. And beautiful. It had taken the shape of a pregnant woman, naked and smiling. . . . she stood on long straight legs, her belly big and tight. . . . Her smile was dazzling. (321-22)

Morrison's success depends in depicting the aspect of mystery vis-a-vis reality. Once Beloved is accepted as a ghost, her idea of the play of the supernatural not only succeeds but also exemplifies the existence of the para-psychological in the psychological being. The question of the fulfillment of the supernatural, both as a psychological fear and the metaphysical terror, is accomplished in Beloved's appearance from the water and creating an unpredictable and unforeseen force upon Sethe and her life. The story presents a consistent theme that the past has its appearance in the present and, in fact, there can't be a present at all without a past. Any guilt is committed in the present and its terrifying claws are felt in the past-ness of the conscious mind at a moment. The implication of the past in the present is that the real future is built with the presence of the past-ness in the present. No mind can avoid the effects of the past in the consciousness of the being of any type. It is a question of debate whether a past or the present of a being should be real and meaningful. Some past we inherit and some we create out of our actions. Morrison presents the ghost and witches as an almost mimetic impulse evincing the idea that the real present is not the emotional and the physical but the philosophical and the psychological past, which makes the being a philosophical as well as a psychological existence. Morrison innovates a fresh approach to show that the juxtaposing change between the entities of the philosophical and the psychological is the supernatural. It is on account of this convention that Morrison deals with the philosophical and psychological realities and nets out the supernatural, such that the reality of Beloved comes altogether a living and a dead figure.

NOTES

1. Nellie McKay, An Interview with Toni Morrison, *Contemporary Literature*, 1983, p. 421.
2. Karen Carmean, *Toni Morrison's World of Fiction* (New York: The White Stone Publishing Company Troy, 1993), p. 15.
3. Linda Brent, "Incidents in the Life of a Slave Girl," *The Classic Slave Narrative*, ed. Henry L. Gates Jr. (New York: American Library: A Mentor Book, 1987), p. 405.
4. Toni Morrison, "The Site of Memory," *Zinssar*, 1987, p. 336.
5. Charles Johnson, "Novelists of Memory," *The American Review*, 1989), 33: 1, p. 37.
6. Jan Harold Brunvand, *The Study of American Folklore* (New York: W.W. Norton, 1978), p. 109.
7. Toni Morrison, *Beloved* (New York: Signet 1987), p. 56.
8. K. Holloway and D. Stephanie, *New Dimensions of Spirituality: A Biracial & Bicultural Reading of Novels of Toni Morrison* (New York: Greenwood Press, 1987), p. 26
9. *Loc. cit.*, p. 26.
10. Toni Morrison, Review of *Beloved*, *Publishers' Weekly*, 17 July 1987, p. 53.
11. Denise Heinz, *The Dilemma of Double Consciousness: Toni Morrison's Novels* (Athens & London: The University of Georgia Press, 1993), p. 176.
12. Zinssar, p. 110.
13. Marcia Ann Gillespie, "Toni Morrison," *MS*, 17, January 1988, p. 60.

Memory, Text and Subtext in *Beloved*

SATISH C. AIKANT

In Beloved, *Toni Morrison uses the technique of inversion to alter the subject-object positions. The system of slavery forces a slave to deny and even suppress her maternal instincts; her act of infanticide follows a different order of morality. By asserting her position as a mother, Sethe asserts her subject position in the discourse of slavery. Satish Aikant characterizes Beloved's and Denver's excessive dependence on their mother as pre-Oedipal. At the same time, Beloved is a symbolic being whose position parallels "sixty million or more" of the epigraph of the novel. Beloved presents an alternative model to classical psychoanalysis which stressed individualism. The novel shows that an individual bears an organic relationship to community. It explores the therapeutic possibilities of a community which acts as a buffer to protect individuals from the harsh realities of slavery.*

Editor

The American Dream, a stimulus to work for the future, and nurtured on success stories, has not been without its nightmares for the multicultural spectrum of America. If the dream propelled a section of the population to hope, for others it has been a frustration and reason to despair. It has not been possible to reduce the dream to an essentially American concept, and it has, therefore, conveyed different signification for different people. Despite Martin Luther King Jr.'s much-publicized egalitarian exhortation of his "I Have a Dream" speech, the present has provided a paradox to the African-American, who has felt betrayed by cultural assimilation, which he finds a function of the discourse of power. The problem gets aggravated, for, as Toni Morrison remarks,

> There seems to be a more or less tacit agreement among literary scholars that, because American literature has been clearly the preserve of white male views, genius and power are without relationship to and removed from the overwhelming presence of black people in the United States.[1]

Unfortunately, not only the discourse of the dominant culture but also the Black Power movement of the 1960s and 1970s was instrumental in the historical erasures of those aspects of the past that could not be assimilated into a hegemonic rhetorical discourse. It is against this background that the fictional narratives of the African-American writers ought to be seen as interventions for recuperation of the past. Morrison revealed, in an interview with Christina Davis, "There is a *great* deal of obfuscation and distortion and erasure, so that the presence and the heartbeat of black people has been systematically annihilated in many, many ways, and the job of recovery is ours."[2] The trope of memory is used to foreground the part of experience ignored or suppressed and to make it accessible to contemporary readers. The author uses memory as "the metaphorical sign of the interior life to explore and represent dimensions of slave life that the classic slave narrative omitted."[3] She uses memory not in a mechanical, monologic sense to recount and record facts and experiences but in an active, dialogic, and imaginative way for a construction or reconstruction of the past. Challenging the Western notion of linear time, she makes her narrative meander through time and space, thus circling back and forth and bringing out the various psychic levels of meaning. Commenting on the course that language takes, Lacan finds that "the logos is circular; what begins with language always comes back to language."[4] The narrative thus produced engages the reader on the psychical level of the consequences of slavery and also on the psychological wounds inflicted on the individuals and community.

Beginning with nineteenth-century slave narrative (1830-1861), African-American texts established themselves as "a medium of propaganda."[5] During Reconstruction the texts projected stereotypes, and their overwhelming acceptance by white readers indicated that the ruling ideology was able to appropriate it.

Henry Louis Gates, Jr. sees the problem as rooted (since the very beginning of Western discourse) in a condition in which ethnocentrism and logocentrism are interrelated, so that there is an irony implicit in the attempt to posit a "black self" in the very Western languages in which blackness itself is a figure of absence, a negation.[6]

Memory, then, expands the historical sense by incorporating not only the ways of knowing but also the ways of feeling, and the narrative expands on several levels. "Reconstruction" is seen by Morrison as an act of survival, whereas the dominant culture uses reconstruction to sustain its supremacy. It is in this context that *Beloved* (1987) marks a significant intervention in disrupting the dominant discourse by expressions of black individuality and solidarity. The text uses the technique of inversion to alter subject-object positions. Even within the discourse of slavery the denial of the basic values of humanity and autonomy privileges humanity. Although each of the characters in *Beloved* has been damaged by slavery, they are seen not only as victims but also as agents. This is made possible since they can adopt subject positions to their advantage and thus mitigate their racial humiliation and psychic damage. They subvert, consciously or inadvertently, what the schoolteacher propounds as the maxim of the dominant culture, "to *show* . . . that definitions belonged to the definers—not the defined."[7] Sethe, the central figure in the novel, internalises the maternal discourse of good mother to adopt a subject position against the discourse of slavery. The system of slavery gives anonymity to the slave, denying him the parental role or rights, so that by asserting her position as mother, Sethe asserts her subject position in the discourse of slavery. Of course, her memory of her own childhood brings to her psychic traumas of infant abandonment that had severed her bond with her mother. Slavery positioned her as object and denied her the experience of a normal childhood. But it also helped in the formation of an identity for herself with separate subjectivity. By refusing the negative inscription provided to her, she assigns to herself a role that transcends racial and cultural differentials. The slave mother succeeds in creating a personal and familial identity by dispersing the idea of motherhood not only upon her children but on all those who "stole her milk." Her body thus creates new meanings for herself and her community. "The recurring images of water, milk, and blood combine in the novel to suggest some of the material conditions in which one creates the conscience of the race—for the race needs to survive—both physically and in our imaginations."[8] The nurturing power of Sethe is emphasized as she reports to Paul D, "I was big, Paul D, and deep and wide and when I stretched out my arms all my children could get in between. I was *that* wide." (162) "She had milk enough for all." This maternal body gives her a distinct identity and creates meanings for her and her community in defiance of the constricting impositions of the dominant culture.

As Sethe has the power to summon her resources and call up all the memories of motherhood, her memories soften the edge of her sorrow. When Paul D arrives at 124 Bluestone Road, where Sethe is living now, it is a reunion of sorts, as they are friends from Mr. Garner's Sweet Home plantation. While they admit that "It wasn't sweet and it sure wasn't home" and have an ambivalent attitude to it, Sethe warns against a total dismissal of it by saying, "But it's where we were" and it "comes back whether we want it to or not." (14) Desirous of all the attention of her mother. Denver finds Paul D a rather unwanted guest and tries to frighten him away by telling him that they have a ghost on the premises: and even when the ghost is expelled, Beloved, the reincarnation, seeks to undermine and exasperate Paul D by moving him from room to room and then having sex with her against his will. Like Sethe, Paul D is also a victim of slavery. In order to counteract his dehumanizing position as object in the discourse of slavery, he decides to assert his male ego and adopt the dominating subject position in the discourse of masculinity and its signifying practices of free will and self-control:

> Because he was a man and a man could do what he would: be still for six hours in a dry well while night dropped; fight raccoon with his hands and win; watch another man, whom he loved better than his brothers, roast without a tear just so the roasters would know what a man was like. And it was he, that man, who had walked

> from Georgia to Delaware, who could not go or stay put where he wanted to in 124—shame. (126)

Whereas Beloved tries to have control over him, affecting his self-image, he reinforces his self-image in relation to Sethe. Sethe, ironically, becomes a text upon which not only her white masters have inscribed the discourse of slavery but also becomes a text upon which patriarchy registers its signature. When Paul D declares his intention to have Sethe bear him a child, she suspects that he wants to use her body as a marker for establishing a legacy for himself: he will use her to have a child and thus exercise control as paternal authority. Indeed, Paul D becomes so assertive and can so gratify his masculine image of himself that he is surprised to discover self-sufficiency and autonomy in Sethe. He wants to circumscribe her in the stereotypical relationships of patriarchy by measuring her in relation to her husband Halle, rather than like herself. Thus he defines her identity when he learns that this Sweet Home girl can so effectively tear down the walls of social conventions and prescriptions by taking a decision as crucial as killing her own child.

The act of infanticide may be shocking and unpardonable and anathema to common moral sensibilities, but for Sethe again, it is a matter of putting her in the subject position by following her own code. She learns from Nan not the linguistic code of the African past but another code of absence, of silence. If she was unable to resist the oppression of the Blacks by the white masters, she will at least deny the authoritative history another victim of oppression. Sethe's language, thus, is one of denial and rejection. Born of desperation, she translates her code to say no to what is not acceptable to her individually and communally. Alone, and in control of herself, she practises this discourse in a woodshed, using the instrument of a handsaw. Her text is her beloved baby, her sign is a mark of a great refusal: "And if she thought anything, it was No. No. Nono. Nonono. Simple." (163) Her act of infanticide follows a different order of morality that implicates her role of motherhood under the dispensation of slavery. Against the demand of abstract moral law

("Be human"), her conscience is awakened to the potential risk of stark racial humiliation and the rape of her children. She decides to kill her own child in an act of resistance. "If Paul speaks in terms of the abstraction we call 'the human,' Sethe's situation and that of other slave mothers reminds us that humanity is itself measured in terms of a moral personhood, a capacity for self-determination, and that the institution of slavery denied the slave."[9] Sethe says,

> Anybody white could take your whole self for anything that came to mind. Not just work, kill, or maim you, but dirty you. Dirty you so bad you couldn't like yourself anymore. Dirty you so bad you forgot who you were and couldn't think it up. And though she and others lived through and got over it, she could never let it happen to her own. The best thing she was, was her children. (251)

Sethe thus claims that her children were "her best thing." Paul D, conforming to the Western notions of morality, may not have agreed with her, but he eventually accepts her norms, setting her judgment have the victimizers' moral canon when he tells her, "You your best thing, Sethe. You are." Sethe, then, succeeds in coopting her community in the moral vindication of her action.

Sethe's action is also directly related to the absence of systems of power among the black community. The absence in art is not only suggestive but has compelling presence, which directs the course of the narrative. As Timothy Walsh suggests, "Within the general slip and slide of meaning that forms the mercurial foundation of language, there may suddenly come a moment where any pretence about the ability to communicate the full nature of certain experiences or states of mind is summarily abandoned, where the reader is forced to accept something on faith alone. Such a moment represents, figuratively speaking, a lapsing into silence, a transient pressure point where the limited resources of language have been exhausted and the only recourse is to allow the eloquence of silence to intercede on behalf of those states of awareness that can find no linguistic equivalent." (81)

In the beginning of the novel, several historical and geographical facts are given, but one can distinctly feel the empty spaces that evoke a sense of loss. There are missing ancestors and missing descendants, and readers are placed generationally in space that floats somewhere between an absent past and an absent, uncertain future; and into this static fictional present a ghostly past haunts, to rake up memories. Though dead, Baby Suggs is from beginning to end a felt and seen presence in the narrative. We are given her image: an old crippled woman, lying in bed, hovering between the memories of an uneasy life and the certainty of a restless death. Her son Halle, who had, at the old plantation, Sweet Home, hired himself out every Sunday for five years in order to buy her freedom, has not managed to make it north to be with his mother, wife, and children. Baby Suggs has had to become accustomed to absences. And in this she is not alone. Sethe tries to replace the absent centre of power with her ingenuity, autonomy, and self-determination. As the story of slavery itself is premised on the absence of power, autonomy, and language, Sethe learns these lessons and refuses to turn her children over to the slave catchers who have come to take her family back to Sweet Home and eludes the captors by murdering her child. The presence of her baby's ghost (as well as its eventual reincarnation) serve as a constant reminder of the absence and longing that have led Sethe and Denver to take refuge in their isolated world at 124 Bluestone Road. As an disembodied spirit, Beloved says, "I need to find a place to be." Her insistence on a space for herself is not only a desire to be with Sethe, but also to activate the historical memories.

Sethe's body is a text upon which is inscribed the text of slavery. When the schoolteacher appears on the scene after the death of Mr. Garner, in order to help Mrs. Garner run Sweet Home, he becomes the speaking subject of slavery's discourse. Sethe recounts the Sweet Home experiences to Paul D:

> After I left you, those boys came in there and took my milk. That's what they came in there for. Held me down and took it. I told Mrs. Garner on 'em. She had that lump and couldn't speak but her eyes rolled out tears. Them boys found out I told on 'em. Schoolteacher

> made one open up my back, and when it closed it made a tree. It grows there still. (16-17)

As Rafael Perez-Torres says, "Sethe's body is violated: once when its nutrient is stolen, then again when torn open by a whip. Just like the page of schoolteacher's notebook, Sethe is divided and marked, inscribed with the discourse of slavery and violation." (696)

Yet in the discourse of power, the defined are not entirely powerless, for they reserve to themselves the power to decode and recode the appropriate signs to signify alternate possibilities so as to make the text appear in a different light. Both Sethe, as a back slave, and Amy, as a white indentured servant, know the evils of slavery and sexual violation. Paul D "reads" the story of savagery and slavery engraved on Sethe's back by the white master's whip; and, as the scar tissue is without sensation—"her back skin had been dead for years" (18)—Sethe's back, in a sense, is not her own: it has been appropriated by the white masters and it bears the marks of their cultural text. Amy, however, "reads" the same text in a different way: to give Sethe her dignity. While she affirms her solidarity with the battered, pregnant Sethe lying on the banks of the Ohio River, desperate to reunite with her children, she gives a different interpretation of the bloody marks on her back, as she tells her: "It's a tree, Lu. A chokecherry tree. . . . You got a mighty lot of branches. Leaves, too, look like, and darn if these ain't blossoms." (79) While this is not going to erase the marks of slavery, she teaches her a survival tactic. The marks of slavery inscribed on the one are transformed by the other into signs signifying an image of fruition, of fertility, instead of oppression and sterility. Amy, then, gives back to Sethe her identity as a nurturing source, reinforcing her self-image of motherhood, and she assigns her cherished position as a subject instead of as an object. There is also a suggestion of renewal as Amy massages Sethe's swollen feet and tells her, "Anything dead coming back to life hurts." (35)

Birth, death, and rebirth form a continuum in the narrative space of the novel. The ghost of Beloved and her later reincarnation occupy supplementary positions. Beloved's obsession with Sethe can be characterized psychologically as preoedipal. Morrison tries to incorporate the preoedipal into the racial discourse, although "trying to escape male linguistic and social dominance by basing a new discourse on the preoedipal raises the objection that the preoedipal is by definition proverbial and so always outside social discourse."[10] The author reinstates the discourse of the racially disenfranchised to incorporate it into a wider text. The Beloved-Sethe relation, then, can be read in two ways: Beloved as a psychically damaged real-life slave girl or as a ghost or fantasy object for the emotions of others.

Beloved's excessive dependence on Sethe corresponds to a symbiosis of mother and infant, a psychoanalytic state in which the child does not yet recognize its separateness from the world—and in particular from the primary care-giver. She charges Sethe with accusations of leaving her behind, of not being nice to her, of not smiling to her. The apparently twenty-year-old Beloved occasionally behaves like a two-year-old (as can been seen on page 98). This is the age not only at which the (crawling already?) baby was killed, but at which, according to classic psychoanalysis, children begin to undergo the oedipal crisis which should instigate their development into separate selfhood. Through the portrayal of Beloved, Morrison skilfully exploits the parallels between a spirit in search of a body and a preoedipal child who desires a merger with her mother. Sethe represses the knowledge for as long as possible; but Denver, in her isolation and loneliness, instantly recognises that Beloved is her sister, and she knows too that she is "more than that." Since Beloved brings the whole traumatic experiences of slavery with her, she not only knows more than she could otherwise have known in her previous short life, but she also contains the effects that slavery had: its profound fragmentation of the self and of the connections the self might have with others. She has, therefore, this tenuous dependence on Sethe; and she is dislocated in herself as well as dislocated in time, full of love and resentment born of desperation. As for Sethe, Beloved is above all a connection, the reconnection with and restoration of all that was lost when she was driven to kill her.

The generic name Beloved also suggests all the loved ones lost through slavery beginning with the Africans who died on the slave ships. In one sense, then, the pain that haunts Sethe's house is nothing special: "Not a house in the country ain't packed to its rafters with some dead Negro's grief." (5) The position of Beloved herself is outside any social discourse where she is "disremembered and unaccounted for." (274) Her position parallels or constitutes the "Sixty Million and more" of the novel's epigraph. Those souls perished on the slave ships midway between a place in African history and a place in the history of American slavery, and they never made it into any text. Their individual identities erased, they are merely referred as a quantified body in the similar anonymity which refers to them, while they are living, as property of the white masters. Morrison's "and more" indicates the residue left over and unaccounted for by any text like *Beloved* at the end. The author makes the historical parallel explicit by linking Beloved to the "Sixty Million and more" and by joining her spirit to the body of a woman who died on one of the slave ships. The author demands that readers confront the horrors of slavery "in the flesh" rather than obliquely as a metaphor: "I wanted that haunting not to be really a suggestion of being bedevilled by the past," she comments, "but to have it be incarnate."[11] What at first appears symbolic becomes actual in a characteristic collapse of metaphor into literal reality—a slippage that accompanies the central materialization of the novel, Beloved's embodiment.

Like Beloved, Denver mostly articulates herself in preoedipal discourse. She is noticeably dependent on her mother, whom she also fears. She feels imprisoned at 124, Bluestone Road. Her brothers have gone away. Her grandmother has died, and her mother is ostracized by the community. At the age of seven, after a year of taking lessons, Denver abandons language to avoid learning the truth about her mother's murder of her sister—as if to be in complicity with her mother's silence. She becomes deaf and mute for two years. And it is an option forced upon her, as her primal hunger is for words: it is her mother's wish that the story remain unspoken, the act unnamed, the memory repressed. Even after Denver returns to speech and hearing, she lacks the narrative context to deal with the baby's death on a conscious level, so she processes it unconsciously in monstrous dreams: "She cut my head off every night." (206) Her dreams keep her unconscious centred on the non-signifying marker "thing" to allude to the signifier of her conscious thought. The "thing" is a recurring image: "certain odd and terrifying feelings about her mother were collecting around the thing that leapt up inside her." (102) Sethe's inability to articulate her action and Denver's protection of her mother lead to their locking it in silence and the consequent burden on Denver's conscience.

Denver thus finds herself imprisoned within her mother's house and within her mother's time. She is afraid to step out of her mother's house, as she is constantly reminded of the pain and humiliation inflicted on her mother and her grandmother. Even when she goes out in search of food for her mother and Beloved, she moves from one maternal circle to the other nurturing circle of Lady Jones.

Beloved weaves together different strands and different levels of narratives—traditional and modern, oral and written—and draws together the voices remembered and filtered through the consciousness of various characters (Sethe, Paul D, Stamp Paid, Beloved, and Denver as well as the absent and dead Baby Suggs) and merges the different voices into a communal voice. What, then, emerges from the novel is the deference to and authority of the community, which is what constitutes black experience as well as is its distinguishing mark. The author indicates in several ways why historical memory might be available to human subjects only if we expand our notion of personal experience to refer to both ways of feeling and ways of knowing and to include not just individual selves but also collectives. As the narrative does not follow a linear, progressive chronology, the text is fragmented and charged with what Morrison calls "rememory"—the continual entry and re-entry of past into present. It is not that the larger historical context is forgotten; it is, rather, evoked through images and metaphors that connect and repeat themselves. "Rememory," then, creates fusion of a renewed, living memory where, as Denver comes to understand, 'nothing ever dies." Sethe has her story in her rememory; and in transmitting it to Denver, she allows her to create an imaginative self that extends the possibilities for personal and cultural regeneration. "By evoking a historically decentered narrative—the communal voice articulating African-American experiences, for example—and placing it within the same discursive space as a powerful narrative—an aesthetically decentered but culturally privileged modernism—*Beloved* takes quite literally the decentering impulse that is supposed to inform postmodern culture."[12]

Morrison herself talks about the centrality of community voice in her novels:

> I am simply trying to recreate something that defines what makes a hook "black." And that has nothing to do with whether the people in the books are black or not. The open-ended quality that is sometimes problematic in the novel form reminds me of the uses to which stories are put in the black community. The stories are constantly being imagined, constantly being retold within a framework.[13]

The narrative emerging from multicultural spaces contains interpretations from multiple voices and relies mainly on collective thinking and memory, and through the process of storytelling the storyteller also creates community, uniting the teller, the listener, and the wider world of experience from which the narratives are drawn and on which are inscribed the discourses of power and of language.

The suppressed voices are then called upon to exult in what others spurn in them. Baby Suggs makes an obvious invocation of black solidarity to counter the discourse of the dominant white culture, so that the ex-slaves are exhorted to regard their own colour, their looks: "This is flesh I'm talking about here. Flesh that needs to be loved." (88) For Baby Suggs, mother love extends beyond the bounds of nuclear family, which is the dominant cultural practice of the Western industrialized societies and which tends to corner the marginalised communities. She counters this marginalisation by a collective act of self-glorification in which all those damaged by dehumanization and hate can learn to love and nurture themselves in a manner that affirms their solidarity.

> "Here," she said, "in this here place, we flesh; flesh that weeps, laughs; flesh that dances on bare feet in grass. Love it. Love it hard. Yonder they do not love your flesh. They despise it. They don't love your eyes; they'd just as soon pick 'em out. No more do they love the skin on your back. Yonder they flay it. And O my people, they do not love your hands. Those they only use, tie, bind, chop off and leave empty. Love your hands! Love them. Raise them up and kiss them. Touch others with them, pat them together, stroke them on your face 'cause they don't love that either. You got to love it, you!" (88)

In privileging community, *Beloved* presents an exposition of communal solidarity and offers an alternative model to classical psychoanalysis, which stressed individualism and autonomy as self-sufficient modes for development. In the revised model identity formation and individual development bear an organic relationship to community as against the hegemonic nuclear-family concept. The communal voices also act as catharsis and therapy for the psychically deranged black subjects, victims of racial oppression. The scene in the clearing brings to mind an act of collective healing ritual presided over by Baby Suggs, so that the survivors of slavery can share the communal life. The fusion of voices leads to possibilities that could not have been created by the act or effort of an individual.

The text of *Beloved*, then, allows us to explore not only the psychic damage of slavery but also the therapeutic possibilities, the cooperative self-healing, of a community of survivors forging a "livable" life for themselves. Through communal interaction the individual proceeds from repressive isolation to a developed sense of self. Thus the facelessness and anonymity imposed by the dominant culture on the marginalised communities in America is resisted by a voice and ideology forged out of cultural and social absence. Morrison, however, does not give a resolution to the story, for every resolution has to refer to a historical specificity. It is in this sense that it is not a "story to pass on." (274) The triumph of *Beloved* is that it turns on the processes of reinscription and reinterpretation.

NOTES

1. Toni Morrison, *Playing in the Dark: Whiteness and the Literary Imagination* (Cambridge: Harvard University Press, 1992), p. 5.
2. Christina Davis, "Interview with Toni Morrison," *Toni Morrison: Critical Perspectives—Past and Present*, ed. Henry Louis Gates, Jr. and K A. Appiah (New York: Amistad, 1993), p. 413.
3. Marilyn Sanders Mobley, "A Different Remembering: Memory, History, and Meaning in *Beloved*," Gates, pp. 357-58.
4. Juliet Flower Maccannell, *Figuring Lacan: Criticism and the Cultural Unconscious* (Lincoln: University of Nebraska Press, 1986), p. 46.
5. Patrick Bryce Bjork, *The Novels of Toni Morrison: The Search for Self and Place within the Community* (New York: Lang, 1992), p. 1.
6. Henry Louis Gates, Jr., "Criticism in the Jungle," *Black Literature and Literary Theory* (*New* York: Methuen, 1984), p. 7.
7. Toni Morrison, *Beloved* (New York: Knopf, 1987), p. 190.
8. Satya P. Mohanty, "The Epistemic Status of Cultural Identity: On *Beloved* and the Postcolonial Condition," *Cultural Critique*, 24 (Spring 1993), p. 65.
9. *Ibid.*, p. 67.
10. Jean Wyatt, *Reconstructing Desire: The Role of the Unconscious in Women's Reading and* Writing (Chapel Hill: University of North Carolina Press, 1990), p. 4.
11. Qtd. Mervyn Rothstein "Toni Morrison, in Her New Novel, Defends Women," *New York Times*, 26 August 1987, Cl 7.
12. Toni Morrison, "Knitting and Knotting the Narrative Thread: *Beloved* as Postmodern Novel," *Modern Fiction Studies*, 39.3 and 4 (Fall-Winter 1993), pp. 689-707.
13. Timothy Walsh, "The Cognitive and Mimetic Function of Absence in Art, Music, Literature," *Mosaic*, 25.2 (Spring 1992), pp. 69-89.
14. Nellie McKay, "An Interview with Toni Morrison," *Contemporary Literature*, 14 (1983), pp. 413-29.

Collective Class Struggle against Capitalism in *Beloved*

K. SUMANA

K. Sumana gives an account of the original story on which Beloved *is based. Morrison rightly describes Capitalism as the primary enemy of African descent people which she appropriately calls the gentleman's form of slavery. According to Sumana, Morrison's focus in* Beloved *is on the collective struggle of African descent people, through the vicissitudes of the central character Sethe. In* Beloved*, stress is on the shared relationships and African principle of collectivism.*

Editor

A slave is enslaved
Can be enslaved by unwisdom
Can be enslaved by black unwisdom.
Speak the truth to the people
To identify the enemy is to free the mind
Speaks truth.

Mari Evans

The big bee flies high,
The little bee makes the honey;
The black folk makes the cotton,
And the white folk gets the money.

William Wells Brown, *Clotel*

In her four earlier novels, *The Bluest Eye*, *Sula*, *Song of Solomon* and *Tar Baby*, Morrison demonstrates a keen awareness of, concern for, and dedication to African people in America. As Mbalia puts it, almost "like a scientist, she uses each work as a laboratory in which to research a hypothesis as to the nature of oppression experienced by African people and to posit a solution to it"[1] in terms of fictional art. Starting with the issue of race as the primary form of oppression in *The Bluest Eye*, demonstrating that sexism is as oppressive as racism in *Sula*, adding the problem of class exploitation to that of race in *Song of Solomon*, and then recognizing capitalism as the primary target against which the. blacks must struggle in *Tar Baby*, Morrison proposes in *Beloved* (1987) collective class struggle against capitalism as the only viable solution possible for the African people in the white-dominated American society.

To show the historical truth that collective struggle is the only practical solution for African people, Morrison writes a historical novel, *Beloved*, which explores the most oppressed period of slavery in the history of African people. The novel is based on a newspaper clipping about a fugitive slave in Ohio who killed her own infant rather than see her return to bondage in the South. Morrison found the news-clipping in *The Black Book* which chronicles the life of the African people in the United States from slavery through the civil rights movement. Morrison gets the kernel of her novel from the news article entitled "A Visit to the Slave Mother Who Killed Her Child":

> I found her with an infant in her arms only a few months old, and observed that it had a large bunch on its forehead. I inquired the cause of the injury. She then proceeded to give a detailed account of her attempt to kill her children.
>
> She said, that when the officers and slave-hunters came to the house in which they were concealed, she caught a shovel and struck two of her children on the head, and then took a knife and cut the throat of the third, and tried to kill the other,—that if they had given her time, she would have killed them all—that with regard to herself, she cared but little, but she was unwilling to have her children suffer as she had done.
>
> I inquired if she was not excited almost to madness when she committed the act. No, she replied, I was as cool as I am now; and would much rather kill them at once, and thus end their sufferings, than have them taken back to slavery, and be murdered by the piece-meal. She then told the story of her wrongs. She spoke of her days of suffering, of her nights of unmitigated toil, while the bitter tears coursed their way down her cheeks and fell in the face of the

> innocent child as it looked smiling up, little conscious of the danger and probable suffering that awaited it. . . .
>
> The two men and the two other children were in another apartment but her mother-in-law was in the same room. She says she is the mother of eight children, most of whom have been separated from her; that her husband was once separated from her twenty-five years, during which time she did not see him; that could she have prevented it, she would never have permitted him to return, as she did not wish him to witness her sufferings, or be exposed to the brutal treatment that he would receive.
>
> She states that she has been a faithful servant, and in her old age she would not have attempted to obtain her liberty; but as she became feeble, and less capable of performing labor, her master became more and more exacting and brutal in his treatment, until she could stand it no longer; that the effort could result only in death, at most—she therefore made the attempt.
>
> She witnessed the killing of the child, but said she neither encouraged nor discouraged her daughter-in-law,—for under similar circumstances she should probably have done the same. The old woman is from sixty to seventy years of age, has been a professor of religion about twenty years, and speaks with much feeling of the time when she shall be delivered from the power of the oppressor, and dwell with the Savior, "where the wicked cease from troubling, and the weary are at rest."
>
> These slaves (as far as I am informed) have resided all their lives within sixteen miles of Cincinnati. We are frequently told that Kentucky slavery is very innocent. If these are its fruits, where it exists in a mild form, will some one tell as what we may expect from its more objectionable features? But comments are unnecessary.[2]

With the essence of this news-clipping, Morrison concocts the story of *Beloved.* She, however, expands, refines, and shapes it so that *Beloved* picks up where *Tar Baby* leaves off. While mulling over this news article, what evidently clicked in Morrison's mind was the fact that conditions of oppression then and now as well as our reactions to them have not qualitatively changed.

Because Africans are faced with circumstances almost equally oppressive as those in slavery, Morrison shows them the need to unite as one to confront a common enemy—capitalism, the same enemy they struggled against more than one hundred years ago. Certainly Morrison has come to understand that "capitalism is but the gentleman's form of slavery."[3]

Morrison's conscious focus on collective rather than individual struggle is clarified through her repeated assertions that *Beloved* is the story of a people rather than a person. She says: "The book was not about the institution—Slavery with a capital S. It was about those anonymous people called slaves. What they do to keep on, how they make a life, what they are willing to risk, however long it lasts, in order to relate to one another—that was incredible to me."[4]

Although the novel begins as Sethe's story, it evolves into a story about "these people who don't know they are in an era of historical interest. They just know they have to get through the day . . . and they are trying desperately to be parents, husbands and a mother with children."[5] Morrison's conscious focus on the collective rather than Sethe's personal history is further clarified when she says that the novel "has to be the interior life of some people, a small group of people and everything they do is impacted on by the horror of slavery, but they are also people."[6] The impact of slavery on a people, thus, involves the way internalization of oppressors' values can distort all intimate human relationships and even subvert the self.

Beloved deals with not only 'reconstructed memory,' but also deconstructed history. Set in post-civil war Ohio, this haunting narrative of slavery and its aftermath, traces the life of a young woman, Sethe, who has kept a terrible memory at bay only by shutting down part of her mind. The novel deals with Sethe's former life as a slave on Sweet Home Farm, her escape with her children to what seems a safe haven, and the tragic events that follow. Although Sethe physically survives, she remains emotionally subjugated, and her desire to give and receive love becomes a destructive force. Morrison also addresses the difficulties faced by former slaves in keeping the horrors of their pasts submerged within the subconscious. In the words of Ann Snitow, Morrison "twists and tortures and fractures events until they are little slivers that cut. She moves the lurid material of melodrama into the minds of her people, where it gets sifted and sorted, lived and relived, until it acquires the enlarging outlines of myth and trauma, dream and obsession."[7] Thus, Morrison recreates a past, however painful, to undercut the ideological basis upon which it has largely been constructed by whites, employing not only available accounts in slave narratives, but also disengaging the materials from historical documents in order to revitalize them as lived experience.

The novel hinges on the death of Sethe's infant daughter, Beloved, who mysteriously reappears as a sensuous young woman. Beloved's spirit comes back to claim Sethe's love. Sethe struggles to make Beloved gain full possession of her present and throw off the long, dark legacy of her past. Sethe's experience is treated with many ironic overtones that point to certain paradoxes and many fundamental complexities of her quest for freedom.

On a socio-psychological level, *Beloved* is the story of Sethe Suggs' quest for social freedom and psychological wholeness. She struggles with the haunting memory of her slave-past and the retribution of *Beloved*, the ghost of the infant daughter whom she has killed in order to save her from the living death of slavery. On a legendary and mythic level, *Beloved* is a ghost story that frames embedded narratives of the impact of class, race and sex on the capacity for love, faith and community of black families, especially of black women, during the Reconstruction period. Set in post-civil war Cincinnati, *Beloved* is a womanist neo-slave narrative of double consciousness, a post-modern romance that speaks in many compelling voices and on several time levels of the historical rape of black American women and of the resilient spirit of blacks in surviving as a people.

Beloved contains Morrison's most extraordinary and spellbinding womanist remembrances of things past. As Alice Walker's epigraphs to *In Search of Our Mother's Gardens* suggest, womanist connotes a black feminist, "a woman who, among other things, is audaciously committed to [the] survival and wholeness of entire people, male and female."[8] And it is "because of the silences in the slave narratives due to authorial compromises to white audiences and to self-masking from a painful past, Morrison sees her role as a writer as bearing witness to the interior life of people who didn't write their history and to filling in the blanks that the slave narrative left."[9] Unlike James Baldwin, who also defines the role of slave as bearing witness, Morrison privileges the authority and epistemology of black and Third World women in America.

As in her previous novels, the need for women to re-establish connections with one another is powerfully rendered in Morrison's *Beloved.* It was all the more important in that era of slavery because there was a profound and real need for physical as well as psychological survival. Commenting on her effort to explore a relationship between two women, Morrison says: "We read about Ajax and Achilles willing to die for each other but very little about the friendship of women, and them having respect for each other, like it's something new. But black women had always had that, they have always been emotional life supports for each other."[10] When Sethe arrives with her new-born daughter tied to her chest, Baby Suggs welcomes her. Sethe has a powerful culture mentor in Baby Suggs who kindles a desire in her to know her past and to love herself as a person.

Sethe, like Morrison's other female protagonists, is a victim of both sexist and racist oppression. She is a runaway slave woman, a slave mother, who is brutally treated by white men, the schoolteacher and his nephews. Morrison explores a black woman's self-conscious protest to the dual oppression. It is not only the sexual exploitation that Sethe feels most oppressed by, but the humiliation of her nurturing abilities as a mother—the stealing of her milk.

One of the most damaging effects of the dual oppression of black women, against which Morrison writes, is murder of one's own child. Murder becomes Sethe's act of mother love, which she explains saying, "I took and put my babies where they'd be safe."[11] She prefers to murder her daughter, Beloved, rather than see her in bondage. According to Deborah Gray White, infanticide represents one of the avenues of resistance on the part of a slave woman. Although Sethe's murder might be viewed by contemporary standards as limiting the context in which she committed it, it does not diminish her stature, If it was possible for a black slave woman like Sethe to live with her family with dignity and self-respect in the America of the 1850s, she would not have committed this hideous crime which was the mutilation of her vibrant mother love.

Balancing the polemics—racial and sexual—that is at the back of every personal outrage suffered by Sethe, is the brilliant "poetics . . . of the long black song of many thousands gone. Sethe's back is so hardened that she cannot feel Paul D pressing against it, "but could not feel, that his cheek was pressing into the branches of her chokecherry tree." (21) Similarly, through another powerful image, that of the track-less quiet forest abruptly appearing after the first dialogue of Sethe and Paul D the implied author brings out the metaphysical ambivalence of Sethe, the slave mother. As observed by Bernard W. Bell: "This metaphorical silence is an ingenious, ironic use of the technique of call and response that invites the implied reader in Wolfgang Iser's words, that network of response inviting structures, which impel the reader to grasp the text."[13]

By choosing to narrate the real life and actual experiences of a runaway slave woman, Morrison proves the power of art to demolish stereotype. Sethe's experience is treated with many ironic overtones that point to certain paradoxes and many fundamental intricacies of her quest for freedom. Other novels like *Song of Solomon* and *Invisible Man* have done this through numerous adventures of the hero examining the intricate legacy of the past and of history. Yet, *Beloved* strikes a different and perplexing note because it deliberately avoids chronological development of the narrative and linear structure. Beloved's mother, Sethe, is caught in the ambiguities of a quest that presents itself as a succession of rememories. Each recorded incident, act or word further unfolds her story. Sethe's story is presented piece by piece through the act of rememory, a pattern of revelation of her past, of recognition of the history.

Sethe's black awareness and rejection of white perceptions and inscriptions of herself, her children, and other slaves as non-human are synthesized with her black feminist sense of self-sufficiency. Sethe reconciles gender differences first with her husband, Halle Suggs, and later with Paul D, in heterosexual, endogamous relationship. Although by implication the author blends racial and sexual consciousness, the structure and style of the text foregrounds the ambivalence of slave women about motherhood that violates their personal integrity and that of their family.

The feminist qualities that Morrison advocates through Sethe's portrayal are the traditional beauty, strength, resistance and integrity of black women. She is sensitive to feminist concerns and includes all those elements of black female experience in her text which are of compelling significance to a woman. In her interview with Rosemarie K. Lester, Morrison expresses her views on an extremely painful and unattractive history of black women in the States where black women have always been both mother and labourer, mother and waiter, and have worked in the fields along with men: "They were required to do physical labour in competition with them, so that their relations with each other turned out to be more comradeship than male dominance/female subordination. . . . Black women are both ship and safe harbor."[14] Morrison, thus, uses a beautiful metaphor to emphasize that black women are much more suited to aggressiveness in the mode that feminists are recommending.

III

Morrison's thematic astuteness is reflected in her artistic narrative structure, thereby integrating her social and political concerns into the norms of fictional art. In *Beloved*, on the one hand she creates a text unencumbered by symbols indicating divisions and defiant of the linear tradition of the western world in order to create in form what she does in substance—the qualitatively unchanged status of African people. On the other hand, she creates such a text in order to point to a solution which is collectivism.

To crystallize the dire necessity of collective action for the survival of African people, Morrison juxtaposes isolated struggle with collective struggle and selfish individualism with individualism conditioned by social responsibility. In *Beloved* most forms of isolation are genocidal for the race. For instance, when Baby Suggs labours alone to feed the community, she insults it: "Too much, they thought. Where does she get it all. Baby Suggs, holy? . . . And loving everybody like it was her job and hers alone. . . . Loaves of bread and fishes were His powers." (136) Since it is usually best for all that individual needs and desires be conditioned by those of the collective, Baby Suggs' self-oriented behaviour is tantamount to heresy. Indeed, the repercussions of this God-like action—the attempt to do alone which should be done together—is felt for two generations. For the community, in spite, refuses to warn Baby Suggs that slave trappers are approaching, setting in motion the conditions under which Sethe murders Beloved:

> The good news . . . was that Halle got married and had a baby coming [Baby Suggs] fixed on that and her own brand of preaching, having made up her mind about what to do with the heart that started beating the minute she crossed the Ohio River. (147)

Interestingly enough, Beloved becomes the symbol by which African people are to measure the devastating effect of isolation. Isolation literally tears apart the family. The personification of isolation and all things inherent in it, including selfish individualism, greed and destruction, Beloved succeeds in dividing 124 from the rest of the African community. Denver's isolation in life, 124's isolation in the community, and Beloved's isolation in death all serve to further divide the African community and, as a consequence, leave it vulnerable to the oppression and exploitation of the slave society. It is she who drives Howard and Buglar from home and separates Paul D, Sethe, and Denver just when their three shadows hold hands and just when they erect bonds with the African community: "Paul D made a few acquaintances; spoke to them about what work he might find. Sethe returned the smiles she got Denver was swaying with delight. And on the way home, although leading them now, the shadows of three people still held hands." (49)

Not until the cause of the separation is clarified, struggled with and struggled against, can African people come together again. Beloved must materialize into a visible, tangible entity of which the community is aware, instead of an amorphous apparition, an oppression of which the community is unconscious. Paul D gives this apparition substance. He is the son who does not give up but returns to struggle again and again, the Malcolm who teaches his people the value of struggle. His presence sets in motion the necessary purgative confrontation between Sethe, and the Cincinnati African community. Significantly when he comes, things become what they are, not what Sethe and African community has imagined. Once the enemy is identified, the community struggles collectively against that which divides them.

Thus, the stress on shared relationships, community and race responsibility—the traditional African principle of collectivism—is the dominant theme of the novel. As we go through the novel, we find that life is hell, but togetherness, shared experience and brotherly love help the characters to survive, if not to forge better lives for themselves. This emphasis on social responsibility, the unselfish devotion of Africans helping other Africans, makes *Beloved* Morrison's most conscious novel.

IV

In the spirit of the flying African of the Virginia Hamilton myth, Hi Man takes the responsibility for the collective. One, more experienced with the hardships of slave existence, teaches other Africans that a man could risk his own life, but not his brother's. And, most important, he teaches that all must be freed from oppression or none. This lesson, which has its beginning in *Song of Solomon*, is learnt in *Tar Baby* and acted out in *Beloved.* Focusing on the post-slavery convict lease system, Morrison uses the chain as a literal symbol of the spiritual link necessary between African people: "They trusted the rain and the dark, yes, but mostly Hi Man and each other." (110)

Crucial in her exploration of the collective solution to the African's oppression is the slave setting, for it serves to enhance the theme of *Beloved* by painting up the dialectical relationship between problem and solution. The solution to the problem arises from the conditions that create it. Simultaneously, Morrison's setting has to be one in which the strategy for solving the problem is not only clearly evident but also inevitable. For she understands that the solution then is the solution now. The most skilful method of unveiling this truth is by choosing a historical period in which the African's primary enemy, capitalism, is unobscured by its secondary and consequential effects—race and gender oppression.

In *Beloved* gender oppression is not a visible problem that exists between African men and women, but is one that exists within the context of the economic relationship between master and slave and race is only a later justification for the oppression of the African people. Clearly, then, Morrison's choice of setting is germane in crystallizing the nature of the African's oppression, for the economic source of both race and gender oppression is unobscured in slavery.

Refreshingly, the relationship between African men and women is generally positive. Paul D is the Son of *Tar Baby* who returns to the struggle, wiser and more committed. In regard to women, he is characterized as a man who has never mistreated a woman in his life and as a man who is grateful to women for his life. He is described as Christ-like on occasions, at least in his manner toward women: "There was something blessed in his manner. Women saw him and wanted to weep—to tell him that their chest hurt and their knees did too." (17) Not long after he sees Sethe for the first time in many years, "He rubbed his cheek on her back and learned that way her sorrow, the roots of it; its wide trunk and intricate branches." (17) It is his presence at 124 Bluestone that forces the necessary purgative confrontation between Sethe, the community, and Beloved. Paul D is, in fact, the only major male protagonist in the Morrisonian canon who has a positive relationship with a female and, furthermore, who struggles with a female to forge this positive relationship. He believes that "only this woman Sethe could have left him his manhood like that. He wants to put his story next to hers." (213)

It is a mark of Toni Morrison's heightened consciousness that she depicts the life that Paul D struggles to build with Sethe as one based on a common history and a common struggle. It is not based on sex like the Milkman-Sweet affair in *Song of Solomon*, nor on physical appearance like the Son-Jadine affair in *Tar Baby.* Sethe is a typical African woman who is satisfied with the real happiness love brings, not with the artificial contentment bought by status and wealth:

> Perhaps, it was the smile, or may be the ever-ready love she saw in his eyes—easy and upfront, the way colts, evangelists and children look at you; with love you don't have to deserve—that made her go ahead and tell him what she had not told Baby Suggs, the only person she felt obliged to explain anything to. (161)

Unlike Son and Jadine, Paul D and Sethe struggle together to forge a positive life under the most oppressing conditions. Like gender oppression, race oppression is examined as a consequence of the economic exploitation of African people. The thesis of Eric Williams's *Capitalism and Slavery* is threefold. According to him the economic demands of the budding capitalist nations led to the slave trade and slavery. And out of the need to justify the enslavement of human beings, these nations institutionalized racism. He rightly feels: "Slavery was not born of racism: rather, racism was the consequence of slavery."[15] Morrison seems in agreement with Williams's thesis. The very fact that African people today are oppressed equally because of the colour of their skin and their poverty clearly proves that race is a later justification for the enslavement of African people.

To accomplish her goal of clarifying the dialectical relationship between race oppression and class exploitation, Morrison documents history by showing that the European and the Native American Indian were enslaved before the African. The European slave is represented by Miss Amy Denver of Boston. Denver says: "My mama worked for these here people to pay for her passage. But then she had me and since she died right after, well, they said I had to work for 'em to pay it off." (34) The parallels between her experiences and those of Africans are similar. She shared the same work experience and punishment as those of Africans. She too is denied education, making her English vernacular almost indistinguishable from that of the African slave.

Also, the novel precisely speaks of the bond forged between the African and the Indian based on their common oppression. Morrison shows the Indian's willingness to make a home for runaway African slaves, allowing them to become a part of the tribe or to leave as they pleased:

> Buffalo men, they [the Indians] called them [the runaway slaves]. . . . Nobody from a box in Alfred, Georgia, cared about the illness the Cherokee warned them about, so they stayed, all forty-six, resting, planning their next move. Paul D had no idea of what to do and knew less than anybody it seemed. (112)

The primary enemy of all the three groups—the exploited European indentured servant, the Native American Indian, and the African—has been capitalism. First the theft of raw materials for developing industrial countries and then the theft of a labour force to work within these countries have created the notions of inferiority and superiority leading to race and gender oppression. According to Walter Rodney, "The simple fact is that no people can enslave another for centuries without coming out with a notion of superiority, and when the colour and other physical traits of those peoples were quite different it was inevitable that the prejudice should take a racist form."[16]

Morrison seems to be at her best in documenting slavery and its aftermath. The treatment of slaves as beasts of burden and the sexual exploitation of African women by European men are driven home to reader. Perhaps, more important than Morrison's skilful way of bringing to life the facts about slavery is her adeptness at correcting myths about slavery. One such myth is that slave life for some was good. Morrison shows how slavery was slavery, on Sweet Home or any other plantation. The conditions of slavery were qualitatively indistinguishable whether the slave had a 'good' master or a 'bad' master. For instance, Baby

Suggs reveals that life for her has been one continuous cycle of oppression. Her past has been intolerable like her present. Also for a 'free' African living in a slave society, life is not qualitatively different either. Morrison, therefore, demonstrates that the African's plight can be potentially extirpated only through a collective struggle: "Days of company: knowing the names of forty, fifty other Negroes, their views, habits; where they had been and what they had done: of feeling their fun and sorrow along with her own, . . . at 124 and in the Clearing, along with others she [Sethe] had claimed herself." (95)

Unity is the only way by which African people can survive. It is only when the African, through self or forced isolation, exists outside the collective that the struggle appears endless and the burden unbearable. In *Beloved*, Morrison reinforces her theme of one people, one struggle and one solution in several ways. First, she begins each chapter in the novel in the present, and then returns to the past in order to bridge the gap between occurrences of the past and those of the present. Second, the beginnings are often structured in such a way that they seem more like middles thereby emphasizing the fact that oppression for the African exists as one uninterrupted continuum. Another skilful structural device that Morrison uses to reflect the unchanging status of African people is the repetition of key words, phrases or sentences.

Morrison further shows that Africans all over the world are one people having the same history and sharing the same plight since they are seen as one by those outside the African nation, no matter what their class status might be. Clearly she wants African people to see themselves as one people, undivided by their class status. The novel reiterates its theme of solidarity by implicitly reminding the reader chapter after chapter that collective struggle is the only practical way to alleviate the oppression African people have been experiencing.

V

Thus, in *Beloved* Morrison comes to terms with both the dilemma confronting African people and a part of the solution that must be espoused by them. The novel makes it clear that the plight of Africans in America stems from their nation-class oppression, that their primary enemy is capitalism in all its disguises, and that the solution to this problem lies in collective, not individual, class struggle against capitalism. Furthermore, Morrison crystallizes the strategy which ushers in the solution of collective struggle.

Morrison's greatness as a novelist, however, lies in her extraordinary power of achieving a harmonious fusion of her social concerns and the demands of novel as an art form. The ultimate solution of collective struggle to the problem of economic exploitation of the blacks in white America is offered invariably in terms of fictional art. What Morrison has worked out in *Beloved* is an extraordinarily effective Gothic blend of post-modern realism and romance as well as of racial and sexual politics. For the characters of the novel as well as the implied author, the scars of racial, sexual and class oppression are more horrible on the soul than those on the body.

Thus, Morrison has brilliantly succeeded in her attempt to make *Beloved* "unquestionably political and irrevocably beautiful." It is a beautiful narrative about the survival of the heritage of slavery, on the power of rememory, and the collective memories kept alive through oral tradition. It is also a story of the genesis of a culture and of a people who, living on the edge of life and death, have managed to create that culture and to keep their history alive. Morrison's self-conscious interest in the celebration of black women's strength, their values and beliefs, stems from a desire to correct the wrongs that have been historically levelled against black women. She seeks to celebrate the legends of black women like Baby Suggs and Sethe, and weave their dreams into myths that allow us to recover their past.

By using the kind of narrative pattern in which each character becomes part of his or her own history and must be put together in quilt fashion, Morrison reminds us that the oral tradition is so strong in black culture that it is still alive. The stories of different characters bear witness to the past, to the struggle of black slaves to survive and escape to freedom. The reality and fantasy of their lives create history. Thus, in form and content, *Beloved* is about gaps which must be imaginatively filled in and intelligently interpreted by the reader.

Thus, *Beloved* is as artistically appealing as it is socially and politically gratifying. It is full of beautiful prose, dialogue as rhythmically satisfying as music, living characters and scenes so clearly etched. Morrison tries to do what Dickens did—"create wild, flamboyant, abstractly symbolic characters who are, at the same time, not grotesques but sweetly alive, full of deep feeling."[17] Usually in contemporary fiction, the grotesque is mixed with irony, not with passion and romance. Morrison rejects irony, a choice that immediately sets her apart. Instead, like Alice Walker, she wants to tend the imagination, search for an expansion of the possible and nurture a spiritual richness in the black tradition even after three hundred years in the white desert.

NOTES

1. Doreatha Drummond Mbalia, *Toni Morrison's Developing Class-Consciousness* (Selingrove: Susquehanna University Press, 1992), p. 87.
2. P.S. Bassett, Fairmount Theological Seminary, Cincinnati (Ohio), Feb. 12, 1856.
3. Kwane Nkrumah, *Conscienism: Philosophy and Ideology for De-Colonization* (New York: Modern Reader, 1964), p. 72.
4. Angelo Bonnie, "The Pain of Being Black: An Interview," *Time*, 22 May 1989, p. 48.
5. Miriam Horn, "Five Years of Tenor," *US News and World Report*, 19 October 1987, p. 75.
6. "Toni Morrison's *Beloved* Inspired by a slave who chose to kill Her Child," *Atlanta Journal and Constitution* (29 August 1987), p. 33.
7. Ann Snitow, "Death Duties: Toni Morrison Looks Back in Sorrow," VLS, No. 58, September, 25.
8. Alice Walker, *In Search of Our Mother's Gardens* (New York: Harcourt, 1983), p. xi.
9. Wilfred D. Samuels and Clenora Hudson-Weems, *Toni Morrison* (Boston: Twayne, 1990), p. 97.

10. Mary Helen Washington, *Midnight Birds: Stories by Contemporary Black Women Writers* (New York: Anchor Press, 1980), p. xvi.
11. Toni Morrison, *Beloved* (London: Pan, 1987), p. 163.
12. Bernard Bell, "*Beloved:* A Womanist Neo-Slave Narrative, or Multivocal Remembrances of Things Past," *African-American Review*, 26, 1 (1992), p. 11.
13. *Ibid.*, p. 9.
14. Rosemarie Lester, "An Interview with Toni Morrison," Hessian Radio Net Work, West Germany. In McKay, 1988, pp. 48-49.
15. Eric Williams, *Capitalism and Slavery* (New York: G.P. Putnam's, 1944), p. 7.
16. Walter Rodney, *How Europe Underdeveloped Africa* (Dar es Salaam: Tanzania Publishing House, 1972), p. 100.
17. Mbalia, p. 89.

The Saga of Black Suffering: A Study of *Beloved*

ASHOK MAHASHABDE

Beloved *is a novel written with the purpose of destabilizing racism. Ashok Mahashabde draws our attention to the true incidents on which Morrison fleshed out the characters of Sethe and Baby Suggs. The novel is based on the true story of Margaret Garner who killed her child. Garner had a mother-in-law who, like Baby Suggs, was separated from her husband for twenty-five years. She did not wish for her husband's return to witness her suffering. Mahashabde equates the character of Beloved with the ghost and stolen lives and memories of slave past and calls* Beloved *a woeful saga of millions of Black people.*

Toni Morrison (b. 1931), one of the leading African-American writers, has written a number of novels like *The Bluest Eye* (1970), *Sula* (1973), *Song of Solomon* (1977), *Tar Baby* (1980), *Beloved* (1987), *Jazz* (1992) and *Paradise* (1998). Acclaimed as the most powerful black novelist she has bagged several prestigious awards and held important offices. She is the first African-American recipient of the Nobel Prize (1993). She has also won the Modern Language Association of Commonwealth Award in Literature (1989), Sara Lee Corporation Front Runner Award in Arts and the Distinguished writer of 1987 Award of the American Academy and Institute of Arts and Letters.

As a black writer Toni Morrison is fully aware of the wrongs the blacks and particularly the black women had to suffer at the hands of the whites during the days of slavery. It is a past very few African-Americans can ever forget. Toni Morrison's writings centre round the predicament of the blacks in the past and the present, but she scrupulously avoids any direct censure of the whites, because she is least interested in the racial confrontation and wants to write for the readers of her own race in particular. In an interview with Cecil Brown she says:

> There are lots of ways to destabilize racism and protest novels are only one way. Maybe, they're the best way and maybe they aren't. I'm not interested in that. I'm interested in black readers and me.
>
> I think that when you constantly focus on the Nazi, you give him more power than he should have. That's what confrontation in art sometimes does. It's like asking a jazz musician to play his music so white people will like it; and I don't think that's what's going on with black women.[1]

During the days of slavery the blacks were reduced to the status of animals. The dehumanizing phenomenon continued for decades. The blacks were victims of economic slavery with various restrictions imposed upon them. They were forbidden to marry without the consent of their white masters. The black women were whitemen's slaves and mothers of their mulatto children. They were made to breed children so that the owner's stock of slaves could increase. A black woman was thus an easy prey, an object of desire, a creature for the satisfaction of the master's lust. The black husband being economically poor, dependent and not free to move away with his family had no say. The man-woman relationship in the black community was thus seriously impaired. The black woman was subjected to sexual assault without any feeling of guilt because she was considered the Whiteman's personal property. Such treatment had a devastating effect upon the black women. They were prevented from breast-feeding their children so that their work would not suffer. The blacks being illiterate and poor, there was no question of protest; they continued to suffer from ignominy without hope. Such a past is difficult for the blacks to forget even though slavery has been abolished. It has become a part of their racial memory. Such a past is bound to creep into the writings of the black writers time and again.

Toni Morrison's *Beloved* (1987) offers a most realistic picture of the black life portrayed from within. She has done so in her earlier novels also but here she has excelled over them. *Be-*

loved which won Pulitzer Award (1987) is based on an actual incident she came across in a newsclipping she found while compiling a history of the blacks, a project she was associated with. The newsclipping narrated the incident of a slave woman Margaret Garner, a Kentucky slave, who killed her child because she did not want her children to suffer as she had in her life. The article entitled "A Visit to the Slave Mother Who Killed Her Child" ran as under:

> I found her with an infant in her arms only a few months old, and observed that it had a large bunch on its forehead. I enquired the cause of the injury. She then proceeded to give a detailed account of her attempt to kill the children.
>
> She said that, when the officers and slave-hunters came to the house in which they were concealed, she caught a shovel and struck two of her children on the head, and then took a knife and cut the throat of the third, and tried to kill the other—that if they had given her time she would have killed them all—that with regard to herself, she cared but little, but she was unwilling to have her children suffer as she had done.
>
> I inquired if she was not excited almost to madness when she committed the act. "No," she replied, "I was as cool as I am now; and would much rather kill them at once, and thus end their sufferings, than have them taken back to slavery, and be murdered by the piece-meal." She then told the story of her wrongs. She spoke of her days of suffering; her nights of unmitigated toil, while the bitter tears coursed their way down her cheeks and fell in the face of the innocent child as it looked smiling up, little conscious of the danger and probable suffering that awaited it.
>
> The two men and the two other children were in another apartment but her mother-in-law was in the same room. She says she is the mother of eight children, most of whom have been separated from her; that her husband was once separated from her twenty-five years, during which time she did not see him; that could she have prevented it, she would never have permitted him to return, as she did not wish him to witness her sufferings, or be exposed to the brutal treatment that he would receive.
>
> She states that she has been a faithful servant, and in her old age she would not have attempted to obtain her liberty; but as she became feeble and less capable of performing labour, her master

> became more and more exacting and brutal in his treatment, until she could stand no longer; that the effort could result only in death, at most—she therefore made the attempt.
>
> She witnessed the killing of the child, but said she neither encouraged nor discouraged her daughter-in-law, for under similar circumstances, she should probably have done the same. The old woman is from sixty to seventy years of age, has been a professor of religion about twenty years, and speaks with much feeling of the time when she shall be delivered from the power of oppressor and dwell with the Savior, "where the wicked cease from troubling, and the weary are at rest."
>
> These slaves (as far as I am informed) have resided all their lives within sixteen miles of Cincinnati. We are frequently told that Kentucky slavery is very innocent. If these are its fruits, where it exists in a mild form, will some one tell us what we may expect from its more objectionable features? But comments are unnecessary.[2]

The newsclipping is cited here in full because Toni Morrison has followed every detail of it and transposed it into her novel, a work of art, to project the sociological and psychological problems of the blacks. She chose to write on this theme probably because of a feeling that the living conditions were still equally oppressive even at the time of writing the novel. Morrison was deeply impressed and agonized by the account. The mother's act was an act of love and courage though it was criminal in the eye of law. "I took and put my babies where they'd be safe." (164) The novel revolves round this incident and its consequent effect upon the mother whose heart is at times filled with a sense of guilt and remorse. It makes the past unspeakable. The mother who kills the child in the novel is Sethe and her mother-in-law is Baby Suggs. The names of the places have been retained and a few more invented. Sethe is convicted for seven years. Morrison has invested the narrative with something of the folk-lore and Biblical allusions which add layers of meaning to the narrative. Mysteriously enough there is a resurrection of the dead child who comes back to live with Sethe introducing herself as Beloved. All this lends a complexity to the novel. Sethe is unable to forget the incident of killing the child; she cannot even talk about it to anybody. Linden Peach rightly points out:

> Sethe's decision to kill her child rather than have her taken into slavery has to be seen in the context of her past. Only a month previously she had endured an almost fatal whipping and suffered the denigration of being chained while the whitemen sucked her lactating breasts.[3]

She is not only reluctant to narrate it; she is also unable to recall the exact details. The incident of the child killing is repeatedly recalled and narrated by other characters providing additional details but not all at a time. The incident thus remains a mystery and invests the narrative with intricate patterns. Joseph T. Skerritt, Jr. observes: "Story telling is the primary folk process in Toni Morrison's fictional world. In Morrison's novels everybody tells stories for reasons of self-dramatization, self-justification, ego-action, but most significantly and productively for self-understanding and making touch with the spiritual resources of Afro-American folk-traditions."[4]

The novel begins long after the incident of infanticide. The house at 124 Bluestone Road, the place where Sethe now lives with her only daughter Denver, is a spiteful place. Baby Suggs is already dead. Howard and Buglar, the two sons of Sethe, have run away from home out of fear of Baby's ghost.

Paul D, a former slave-fellow at Sweet Home, now homeless and without work, comes to stay with Sethe. His advent is resented by Denver in the beginning as she thinks that it is an intrusion upon their private life. She, however, yields when she finds that his presence in the house has cheered up her mother and might help her overcome her miserable past. Paul D's shouts at the ghost drive it away but very soon the killed infant is resurrected. She walks into their life as a girl (named Beloved) in her early twenties. She is thirsty and weary and later tells that she has nowhere to go. Sethe and Denver take fancy to her, Denver because of her own loneliness and Sethe because of maternal affection. Paul D and Beloved's absorption in the family signifies the hospitality of the blacks despite the poverty and squalor in their life. Paul D is opposed to the idea of Beloved staying in the family. Although himself a hanger on, he tries unsuccessfully to drive away Beloved. Sethe silences him because Beloved reminds her of her lost child. Although Denver finds a companion in Beloved, someone to care for and talk to, she gradually realizes that Beloved is not a natural being but tolerates her because she is not evil. In the beginning her presence means cheerfulness in the family. In her company Sethe becomes more and more talkative as if possessed by a narrative frenzy. Beloved keeps asking her questions about things and events which no outsider would think of. Sethe is surprised but she tries to satisfy Beloved's curiosity by trying to remember the long forgotten things. It is through this kind of conversation that the past of Baby Suggs, Sethe and Paul D is unfolded before the readers embodying the predicaments of all blacks in general. The past and present are thus intermingled in the novel.

The story of growing attachment between Sethe and Beloved and the final departure of the latter forms the main theme of the novel. Although Beloved comes to Sethe's house as a sick, sleepy stranger in need of food and shelter, she gradually becomes very inquisitive, mean and demanding. Sethe tries to make amends for the wrong she has done to her lost child and bestows more and more affection on her. She tries to justify her act of killing the child in its own interest. Beloved somehow grows more vindictive. Seeing that her mother's life is in danger, Denver seeks the help of other women of the community to exorcise revengeful Beloved from the house. The Beloved incident has no place in Margaret Garner's story. It is an invention of Morrison's own, aimed at working out of the mother's grief and forgiveness.

It would be a mistake to think that Beloved is a personal history of Sethe's life. Although it symbolizes Sethe's search for wholeness in life, the novel has greater significance, for it also projects the collective consciousness of a people subjugated to political and economic slavery. According to Morrison:

> The book was not about the institution slavery with a capital S. It was about those anonymous people called slaves, what they do to keep on, how they make a life, what they are willing to risk, however long it lasts, in order to relate to one another—that was incredible to me.[5]

Although *Beloved* is a sad novel, it has a hopeful ending. The ghost of *Beloved* is in a way ghost of slavery which the blacks must forget to make a fresh beginning. As Paul D says to Sethe: "Sethe, me and you, we got more yesterdays than anybody. We need some kind of tomorrow."[6]

At last Beloved is forgotten like a bad dream, "Like an unpleasant dream during a troubling sleep." (275) Sethe was unable to assault the white schoolteacher who with the slave-hunters had come to take away her children. At the end of the novel when the black women come to her house to exorcise Beloved she finds Bodwin approaching her house and she mistakenly tries to murder him although he is a sympathiser of the slaves and stands for abolition of slavery. To quote Andrew Levy: "Bodwin receives in Sethe's attack the same response that Sethe received from Beloved: a paradoxical breakdown in communication (love turned to violence) that drives him further away from the desire to live."[7]

The suffering of the blacks is not merely a back-drop to the unusual story of mother and daughter's love-hate relationship. Beloved narrates the woeful saga of the suffering of millions of black-people. The novel is replete with the description of such wrongs. A few examples should suffice here. Baby Suggs, like the mother-in-law in the newsclipping, has eight children. She says:

> I had eight. Everyone of them gone away from me. Four taken, for chased and all, I expect worrying somebody's house into evil. . . . My first-born. All I can remember her is how she loved the burned bottom of bread. Can you beat that? Eight children and that's all I remember. (5)

Slightly earlier she observes: "Not a house in the country ain't packed to its rafters with same negro's grief." (5) Paul D at one place recollects:

> Eighteen seventy four and whitefolks were still on the loose. Whole towns wiped clean of Negroes, eighty-seven lynchings in one year alone in Kentucky; four coloured schools burned to the ground; grown men whipped like children; children whipped like adults; black women raped by the crew; property taken, necks broken. (180)

Ella another black woman also recalls how "her puberty was spent in a house where she was shared by father and son." (256) Taken together, such incidents form a chronicle of the horrors of slavery. The greatness of Toni Morrison lies in the fact that she does not anywhere directly pass any comment on whites excepting at one or two places. For example, Baby Suggs observes: "There is no bad luck in the world but whitefolk." (180)

Not that all whites are bad people. A few white persons like Amy and Bodwin are remembered for their goodness, but such instances are very rare. The blacks suffer because they are illiterate, poor and unorganized. They can improve their lot through concerted efforts is suggested through the incident where about thirty women join together to drive away Beloved from Sethe's house and liberate it from her influence.

Sethe is the ideal of a black mother. Her character is romanticized, even though her act of infanticide cannot be justified, but her plight symbolizes the plight of the black-women in general—stripped, beaten and often subjected to the onslaughts of racism and sexism. It is surprising why Beloved even after so much maternal affection shown by Sethe, wants to kill her mother. One wonders if it has something to do with Sethe's intimacy with Paul D whom Beloved herself often seeks and compels for coupling to which he unwillingly yields. She probably feels that so long as Sethe is alive, Paul D would never belong to her. For Paul D as the narrator observes: "Coupling with her wasn't even fun. It was more like a brainless urge to stay alive." (265)

Beloved's assumed shape of a pregnant woman remains unexplained in the novel. Nevertheless *Beloved* remains a classic saga of the black suffering and their ethos.

NOTES

1. Cecil Brown, "Interview with Toni Morrison, *The Massachusetts Review*, vol. 36, Issue No. 3, 1995-96, pp. 456-57.
2. P.S. Bassett, Fairmount Theological Seminary, Cincinnati (Ohio), Feb. 12, 1856.
3. Linden Peach, *Modern Novelists: Toni Morrison* (Hampshire, London: Macmillan, 1955), p. 9.
4. Joseph T. Skerritt, Jr., "Recitation to the Griot: Story telling and Learnings in Toni Morrison's *Song of Soloman* in Pryse and Spiller, *Conjuring*, p. 195.
5. Angelo Bonnie, "The Pain of Being Black: An Interview," *Time*, 22 May 1989, p. 48.
6. Toni Morrison, *Beloved* (1987; U.K.: Vintage, 1997), p. 173.
7. Andrew Levy, "Telling Beloved," *Texas Studies in Literature and Language*, Vol. 23, No. 1 (Spring 1991), p. 118.

Voice-less Discourse: Silence as Strategy in *Beloved*

MEENAKSHI PAUL

Meenakshi Paul's use of silence as strategy can also be equated with gaps and spaces. Morrison leaves for the readers to intervene. Silence acts as a means of an alternative discourse. The gaps and silences in black history can be interpreted through the vicissitudes of central character Beloved. In fact, silence was a strategy for black survival as slaves.

Since sound first vibrated, its counterpart, silence, has been concurrently audible. Whether it be the progenetorial brooding before the 'word'; a tongue-less Philomela weaving her outrage; or the voiceless 'scream' of Picasso's Guernica, the reverberating power of silence has been long acknowledged. Silence as narrative has been examined often and necessarily so. Yet, it lends itself more readily, either to romanticisation or to restriction as a 'weapon of the weak.' Further, its resonance being infinitely interpretative, silence becomes a goldfield for theoretical elitism and aesthetic fetishes. It remains to be seen whether silence is also strategy or a part of it, and if so, how effective it is.

Meaningful silence is a cauldron where resilience and rebellion often seethe. Perpetrators of gagging hegemonic structures repudiate this truth to their own peril. Here, it is essential to note that the indicators of silence as inferred in this study are not limited to the absence of words. They include non-verbal communication of gesture, totem, subtle social behaviour, encoded music and metaphor, as also verbal non-communication in which the unheard and unregistered are also effectively defined as silence, encrypted song and genealogy, cultural legend, and words not extended cognizance to, being instances of this articulate silence.

This absence of voice, unsaid or unheard can become a potent means of alternative or alternate discourse. For, codified silence becomes a highly sophisticated and esoteric language engaged to exclude some 'other' from its expression.

The spectrum of silence spreads from meditative stillness to quiet resolve, as the protagonist of Margaret Atwood's *Surfacing* realises in her silence, "This above all, to refuse to be a victim."[1] Refusal to voice, then, is not essentially negation and can well be an expression of affirmation. Silent stemming from non-cognizance of the spoken has led to resistance movements around the world. The tribals in Central India, it has been observed, assiduously kept silence even when beaten. Their voicelessness was not due to an absence of words but because there were too many. They acknowledged the necessity and potency of articulation, but their collective unconscious avoided possible de-culturisation through direct expression. So, they sublimated or voiced their anger, despair, and their hope in encoded song and dance, thus generating silence of the unregistered and, hence, the 'unheard.' The averted eyes of black slaves, therefore, can also possibly be viewed as a deceptively submissive response to the master's presence. Perhaps, it was a willed refusal to make eye contact, and so reveal their feelings, as the force of history and culture behind them. Black music, from pulsating drums and field songs to gospel music and later the blues and jazz and manifests different aspects of slave experience. Ranging from intense, yet, harnessed passion of an individual to the interactive rhythm of the collective, blacks used music competently as an alternate text, of the unvoiced and unvoice-able, to the stated. This complementarity, direct or through inversion, of the said and the unsaid, of the said and the sung, underlines a very important component of the strategy of silence.

The metaphors of their hymns, such as 'steal away, steal away to Jesus' and 'swing low, sweet chariot' were employed by slaves to exchange meaningful discourse, whether it be stealthy flight or silent perseverance for the while. Through all this communication, whites were unaware of the superior encoding abilities of blacks and signified the silence of the unheard or the uncomprehended. The tables were turned somewhat on the oppressor, by blacks abetting this ignorance and closely guarding their skills in silence. Innumerable such manifestations of silence are evident as strategy to sustain survival, dignity, affirmation, and protest. Thus, abject and helpless silence has no role to play in strategy and passive, brutalised, and dumb silence is excluded from the ambit of voice-less discourse. Thoughtful and purposeful silence, on the other hand, is the turning point where the process of meaningfulness and proaction begins. It forms the interface between the heavy and mute silence of the marginalised and its articulation of protest. Thus, silence, words, and actions become strategic extensions and correlatives of each other. While focusing on the articulation, inaudible processes that made it possible, cannot but be considered.

Silence as a language of resistance has two operatives: those of psychology and of praxis. The former is limited to token protest as a feel-good exercise. Mimicry, behind the back spitefulness and disorderliness are some examples of silence that serve only to mitigate absolute helplessness. Strategic silence needs to be praxis-oriented. Often, the two intermingle as in this old, black folk-song:

> Got one mind for white folks to see,
> 'Nother for what I know is me;
> He don't know, he don't know my mind.[2]

The smugness of 'he don't know my mind' can effortlessly be undone by proposing that white folks do not want to know a slave's mind, even if they can bring themselves to admit his having one. Alternatively, the song could be the singer's fierce guarding of his identity, the refusal to be totally enslaved, a precondition to his protest. Roger D. Abrahams pertinently observes that certain black musical expressions represent their "hidden life and its accompanying hidden language . . . [and] is one of those features of the apartness of black-white existence which has proved convenient for blacks and which has therefore been capitalized upon and developed."[3]

Nowhere is the eloquence of such voice-less discourse more pregnant than, perhaps, in Toni Morrison in whose works these submerged voices of race and also of gender become almost deafening. She is acutely aware of evasion and silence through history in literary discourse. These are instrumental in engendering an *alternate* language which is encoded and, therefore, esoteric.[4] Morrison problematises the issue by speaking of words and of their absence in both the oppressed and the oppressors, and between them. Thus, muffled voices of the non-verbal and the uttered but unheard, half-heard, or mis-heard, acquire dimensions of the Tower of Babel, requiring careful unraveling. At the level of narrative, too, ironic inversion of the said reveals the pattern of the unsaid. The following analysis seeks to examine Toni Morrison's *Beloved* through this vital symbiosis of voicelessness and its discourse.

Beloved charts the movement of silences from the weak and the limited to the employment of silence for healing and regeneration. The novel opens with a pall of helpless numbness over house 124 because of the spite of a baby girl's ghost and its wordless, nevertheless, strong expression in overturned, broken and charred things. The family of the spirit, Beloved, can only muster willy-nilly coping tactics: of flight, by her brothers, Howard & Buglar; of fighting, "a perfunctory battle"[5] by her mother, Sethe, and sister, Denver; or of partial amnesia, by her grandmother, Baby Suggs, and Sethe. This helplessness and resignation gradually moves toward praxis where the entire community, in silent solidarity, decides that the phenomenon of Beloved must be "Disremembered and unaccounted for . . . [Since] It was not a story to pass on." (274-75) This resolution is not a relegating of the past to that silence which George Steiner rightly decries, "To unspeak the actual past, to eradicate the names, acts, thoughts of the unwanted dead, is a tyranny of peculiar horror. Pursued rigorously, it cuts off humanity, or certain societies, from the vital responsibilities of mourning and of justice. Man is set back in a landscape without echo."[6] For, in *Beloved*, the past is not eradicated but re-lived. Not only its words but its silences too are explored, claimed, and finally laid to rest.

The mourning is just over and justice even now birthed. The clearest indication of this process is the protagonist being a visitor from a different time and place. Beloved is a complex and inexhaustible metaphor. She is the confluence of slavery, of being denied self-definition, of helplessness, and of despair turned on itself and therefore self-destructive. Yet, she is also the way out. Her tyrannical hold on Sethe exhibits control over feelings, familial ties, and the past; on Paul D over sexuality, dignity, and the present; on Denver over identity self-esteem and the future. So, it is imperative that Beloved be re-experienced to fill out the silent and the unsaid in her story and to rise beyond the death-in-life level of mere survival she forces her people to confront. The long-lasting effects of slavery are given shape to by Beloved, thus, she must be 'disremembered' for free life to blossom. So, the community decides to bring forth a silence in which light, colour, water, and wind are not threatening anymore, for they finally are "Just Weather." (275) The novel completes the journey where the past is present in Beloved's footprints that "are so familiar. Should a child, an adult place his feet in them, they will fit" (275) but the brutality is past menacing and hardly dispiriting in the voice-less reminder. They have all walked that road, but the stage to alter course has been made possible, and here Beloved is a signpost that leads to the crossroads beyond which her people go.

The strategy thus effectuated is realised through a tactical pattern of alternate silence, and voice which it facilitates, throughout the novel. A perusal of the significant incidents in the narrative bears this out. The central image of the novel is that of Sethe standing with her baby she has just killed in her hand and surrounded by the babies she has tried to kill. The description is not verbal but strikingly visual in which Morrison focuses on the eyes of all present, living or dead, "Little nigger-boy eyes open in sawdust; little nigger-girl eyes staring between the wet fingers that held her face so her head wouldn't fall off. . . . But the worst ones were those of the nigger woman who looked like she didn't have any . . . she looked blind." (150) The contrast between the 'staring' eyes of the dead child and the unseeing eyes of her mother-murderer is built-up so, that it makes Beloved's return possible and evokes the inward-turning effects of dehumanisation. What follows is the chilling silence of the neighbourhood, "Sethe walked past them in their silence and hers." (152) It is the silence of mutual withdrawal based on incomprehension and seeming pride which takes a long time and Beloved's extended visit to overcome. So, the songs that would have reached out, "like arms to hold and steady her on the way" (152) are checked to mere, "Humming. No words at all." (152) This alienating and horrified silence draws into itself the dumbstruck response of animalised slavery. But, it also becomes the vortex where a design could be made toward assertion. In stark contrast to the frozen picture of Sethe and her children is the vacuity of the whites, stilled in a tableau of incomprehension. The blood of Beloved screams its answer to the 'skinless' nephew's uninformed, "What she go and do that for?" (150) It defies and reduces whatever the slavemaster had done or could do to utter insignificance and irrelevance. Nevertheless, Sethe's action is a silent scream of mutilated resistance and it draws the past and the future unto itself.

In the past is the slave farm of Kentucky, beautiful and lush, and deceptively named Sweet Home. The subterfuge of the place causes its slaves, Halle, the three Pauls, Sethe, and even Sixo—the relatively experienced, to be doubly victimised in their innocent acceptance of its promise followed by its ugly reneguer. It is only in hindsight that Sethe wonders, "if hell was a pretty place too." (6) Owned by Mr. Garner, whose attempts at 'civilized' slavery are not only ineffectual but dangerous in its contradictions, the Sweet Home 'men' and Sethe allow complacence to blunt their apprehension of the underlying menace. Garner's refusal to whip his slaves and to trust them with guns, does not make them less owned, as is amply proved in his bawdy jokes about his 'men' which highlight his manhood among other slavemasters. His wife, Lillian, who herself is a picture of the absolutely silenced in her tears and the lump in her throat which constricts her voice, is still capable of selling Paul F after Garner's death. Her calling for her brother-in-law schoolteacher, to look after the estate in spite of her able and loyal slaves, breaks any illusions the slaves still had. From mild indicators of bondage, such as no wedding ceremony for Sethe and Halle; Baby Suggs being called by her tag name Jenny; and 'allowing' Halle to 'buy' his mother's freedom by renting himself out during Garner's lifetime, the Sweet Home henceforth bonded, henceforth, feel the keen edge of slavery at the hands of schoolteacher and the nephews. Being stripped of their guns effectively reduces them to hungry, pilfering boys. Locks and bars show them their place and being observed as guinea pigs disconcerts them. Schoolteacher's questioning and recording of their answers alienates and silences all of them, but it tears, "Sixo up . . . for all time" (37) and he gives up speaking English, for a while, as a language with no future in it and begins to use an alternative code. Sixo's refusal to use the oppressor's idiom, makes possible his conversation with the 'Redman's Presence' to seek permission for his rendezvous with the Thirty-Mile Woman, even though it comes to nought since the woman does not reach the appointed spot. Further, all his loquacity dissolves into raucous laughter and song when Paul D and he are caught trying to escape. The song convinces schoolteacher of Sixo's unsuitability, and the breakdown of discourse between the two ends in Sixo being burnt at the stake. His ironic laughter and calling out, "Seven-O! Seven-O!" (226) before he is shot, "to shut him up" (226) are irrelevant to the whites as they themselves are to him. Only Paul D recognizes Sixo's marginal defiance in naming his unborn child as an extension of himself. Sixo's resistance is, thus, personal and his protest is proclaimed in death. However, it fails as a feasible stratagem for other slaves. Therefore, Paul D cannot join in his song, of loathing and defiance, perhaps of warning, because "the words put him off—he didn't understand the words. Although it shouldn't have mattered because he understood the sound." (227) It is this tone of hatred and Sixo's resounding laughter which urge a collared and shackled Paul D to try and kill Brandywine, his new master. The futile attempt sees him a prisoner at Alfred, Georgia. Feeling mocked at even by roosters, the seismic turbulence within him lies unseen, "the boiling blood was shaking him to and fro. But no one could tell" (107) till he is linked in more ways than one with forty-five other men. Far from the embrace of the tree "he called Brother." (21) Paul D joins the brotherhood of fellowmen and the trust common to both which was voiced to Brother is now signalled to the men. Paul D's swerve away from Sixo's private protest to group dynamics begins at a place where all are imprisoned in individual cages but chained together when put to work. The efficiency of non-verbal language is explored fully by the convicts. Sustenance and support are quietly held out, although, "Not one spoke to the other. At least not with words. The eyes had to tell what there was to tell: 'Help me this mornin's bad' 'I'm a make it' 'New man' 'steady now steady.'" (107) The non-words called to begin or end work, 'Hiiii' and 'Hoooo,' become significant with the belief that Hi man "alone knew what was enough, what was too much, when things were over, when the time had come." (108) This trust in a fellow sufferer predicates the collective escape finally actualised. This confidence is further strengthened by their songs at work, encoded so only they understand the import of what they sing, "they sang it out and beat it up, garbling the words so they could not be understood; tricking the words so their syllables yielded up other meanings." (108) Their sledge hammers kept time in beating out all that reduced them to haplessness. United in anguish, Paul D's mouth is open in a scream whereas the sound may have come from "somebody else" (110), they are also banded together in overcoming it. The use of the very shackles that they seek to break away from, in their bid for freedom is the most ironic point in the narrative. The whole process demands transcribing at length: Convinced of certain death, Paul D intuitively throws himself in the envisaged but unvoiced plan of his confederates:

> It happened so quick he had no time to ponder. Somebody yanked the chain—once—He never figured out how he knew—how anybody did—but he did know—he did—and he took both hands and yanked the length of chain at his left, so the next man would know too. . . . They waited—each and every one of the forty-six. Not screaming although some of them must have fought like the devil

> not to. . . . Then it came—another yank—from the left this time. . . . It started like the chain-up but the difference was the power of the chain. One by one, from Hi Man back on down the line, they dove. . . . Some lost direction and their neighbors, feeling the confused pull of the chain, snatched them around. For one lost, all lost. The chain that held them would save all or none, and Hi Man was the Delivery. They talked through that chain like Sam Morse and, Great God, they all came up . . . holding the chains in their hands, they trusted the rain and the dark, yes, but mostly Hi Man and each other. (110)

The escape postulates solidarity and implicit trust in the face of great risk as prerequisites in the silent conceptualisation of escape and its realisation. Still, Paul D lacks the tactically significant third dimension, that of mentally releasing the torture after its physical cessation, as also does Sethe. Paul D's heart closes shut like a rusted tobacco box just as Sethe clamps down on her reasons at being driven to slay her child.

The driving force is hidden in her flight from Sweet Home. Its first unstated existence is represented by Sethe's ritual of taking, "some pretty growing thing" with her to work in Mrs. Garner's kitchen, "to take the ugly out of it." (22) A more assertive avowal of her spirit than mere token aesthetic concessions to make life bearable is her response of quietly putting together a wedding dress after Mrs. Garner's non-response to her need for a wedding ceremony. Shocked by schoolteacher's assignment to his nephews of listing her 'animal characteristics,' Sethe is plunged into bewildered agitation. So, Sethe falls into the plan for escape, brought by the Thirty-Mile Woman through Sixo to Sweet Home. Even as the men, taking her to be a soldier but not a strategist, silence her role in the devising of its details for all her early ignorance of even what a train is, it is only Sethe who successfully makes a getaway. Elaborately designed, the plot is hatched between Sweet Home and the Thirty Mile Woman's place in conspiratorial whispers and initiated through codes. The time appointed was autumn when the almost ripe corn would harbour them in secret and the signal decided upon was a rattle's sound. When the time and sound arrive, Halle proclaims the action by beginning, "to sing to the others: 'Hush, hush. Somebody's calling my name. O my Lord, O my Lord, what shall I do?'" (224) Only Sethe, who is inside the house is removed from his song which is soon silenced and its message lost to her.

Nurtured long and hard, the Sweet Home men's bid to be free fails even though it has qualities of a fair game plan. Detailed planning, mutual trust, brotherhood, provisions, secrecy, and flexibility were all present, but the one thing they ignored was the contingency of failure. Speaking English again, Sixo has underestimated schoolteacher. Once caught, none of them has a plan to fall back on, and fleeing like rabbits, are burnt, hanged or collared and sold. Presence of mind is Sethe's advantage in this exigency and she first sends her three children away to the train before returning in search for Halle in the barn. It is here that the seeds of what happened at the shed of Baby Suggs home are sown. Lactating and pregnant, Sethe suffers the worst a mother can. As she puts it, "those boys came in there and took my milk. . . . Held me down and took it." (16) Her attempt to voice the violation to the almost muted, Mrs. Garner results in her back being opened by the boys' whiplash. What follow are two diverse aspects of silence, given in clear visual images. One, of Halle secreted in the loft seeing his wife being sported with and then sliding into the annihilating silence of the insane with butter smeared all over him. The second, of Sethe's dead back closing to form, "A chokecherry tree. Trunk, branches, and even leaves." (16) The pus blossoms and her torn feet notwithstanding, Sethe makes her way to Cincinnati and freedom. On the way, she learns to count on the generosity and strength of total strangers. Significantly, the first person who props Sethe is a white girl who looks like, "The raggediest-looking trash you ever saw." (31-32) Marginalised herself, Amy Denver is the unlikeliest of all deliverers. Following her own dream of finding beautiful velvet, "Clean and new and so smooth," (33) Amy tarries to help bring just such a baby into the world. Years later, the child, named Denver after her, will unite the yearning for a dream of deliverance, with its fulfilment. Regardless of Amy operating within the language system where the word 'nigger' is available to her for self-definition, and despite Sethe's withholding her name and extending a fictitious one, the women establish a tenuous bond as seen in the one taking upon herself to massage the other's lacerated feet. Therefore, in the narrative's relative silence concerning the whites, where most are uni-dimensional and merely incidental to the stories of Beloved's kin, Amy Denver is the most visible. The points of reference in the novel are re-located from those visibly privileged to the seemingly superfluous. Accordingly, in order of their closeness to the blacks' life the whites are allocated prominence. Amy's foregrounding is underlined by the narrative providing space for her singing her mother's song. All other songs in the novel belong to the blacks who beside using them as signals as Halle did, employ the words and the rhythm for multitudinous expression. Songs are sung to express their suppression (221); to sing of their family—its uniqueness and its legacy (176); encoded expression of suffering for psychological survival (71); re-live the horrors of the past and keep the fire stoked (40); alienate oneself from the community (171); sustain life (89) and to as many more purposes.

After Amy's departure, Sethe relies on Stamp Paid's silent offering of food and covering for the infant. Trusting herself to him when, "Evening came and the man touched her shoulder," Sethe allows Stamp to ferry her across the Ohio, a taste of whose free waters he had already given her. Following an understood code, Stamp signals Sethe's arrival at the hideaway by leaving the sty gate open and tying a white rag to the post to announce Denver's presence. Sethe is soon taken quietly into the care of Ella who had perceived the signs. Ella provides for her and for her passage to Baby Suggs' home. Thus, strangers make it possible for Sethe to have twenty-eight days of freedom and family with her children and Halle's mother.

The astringent fruit of her tree, however, ripens with schoolteacher's arrival and her realisation that places in the memory never go away as she explains to Denver, "Because even though it's all over—over and done with—it's going to always be there waiting for you. That's how come I had to get all my children out. No matter what." (36) Schoolteacher's encroachment onto Baby Suggs' yard is thus countered with the blood of the children in her shed and Sethe's mystifying wordlessness. For "If they didn't get it right off—she could never explain. Because the truth was simple. . . . She just flew. Collected every bit of life she had made . . . out, away, over there where no one could hurt them . . . outside this place, where they would be safe." (163) In her action and her refusal to explain its momentum Sethe defies definition.

The fixity of the dictum, "definitions belonged to the definers—not the defined" (190) is severed in the slit throat of Beloved. Notwithstanding the enormity of Sethe's action, it is an impelled reaction of a desperate victim, a gothic nightmare and, so, severely limiting. It is at once a frustration of schoolteacher's intentions but even more a mark of the extent of Sethe's brutalisation and its inward directed preoccupation.

The only two survivors of Halle's family from Sweet Home, beside Baby Suggs, further need to learn and discover affirmation beyond survival of using their past, silent except in 'rememory,' to live the present and devise a future—a lesson half-learned and half-taught by Baby Suggs in the Clearing. Her silent prayer and her Call to the gathering to laugh, dance, and cry evoked these responses without verbal signifiers dissolving in one message, of love, as a possible beacon in their lives. So, "In the silence that followed, Baby Suggs, holy, offered up to them her great big heart." (88) The Clearing assemblies, a celebration of the here and now, discounted both the terrible past as well as the nebulous promises of the Beatitudes. Outside the woods, however, the silence of the white world to her Call, the oblivion to and the disregard of "The word" (178) she offered, defeats Baby Suggs. She retreats to pondering colour, the harmlessness or perniciousness of pigmentation, and the only words left to her after the 'rout' are her quiet judgement on the whites that, "They don't know when to stop." (104)

The sum of all these silences, of defiance and of submission, of time and of place converges in the person of Denver. Born in untamed country, Denver steps "into the told story" (29) of her family. Yet, its telling and re-telling increases her silence and her withdrawal from the world outside the porch. Her only visits are to a womb-like enclosure of boxwood bushes in the wood behind the house. Armed with cologne, as incense to a shrine, Denver stood tall in its emerald light. The green of Denver's 'room' is in striking contrast to the 'red' light of Beloved's venom before it turns blue and harmless. Denver's loneliness at the leaving of her brothers and grandmother is increased by her awareness, "that her own father's absence was not hers" (13) and by her wariness of the killer mother's presence. Her longing for even the spite of Beloved underlines her silent retreat into the embracing bushes, "First a playroom (where the silence was softer), then a refuge (from her brothers' fright), soon the place became the point." (28) Enwrapped in a world where words fall soundlessly, Denver had shut her ears when a classmate, Nelson, had told her about Sethe and her baby sister. It will take the return of that sister for Denver to build power into her traumatised silence.

So, Denver, Sethe, Paul D, and Beloved congregate to play out their weakness and guilt, to re-define their words and to re-assign their silences. The battle begins with Paul D loudly and violently chasing Beloved's spirit from the house. A day of re-mission is spent by the three at the carnival. Sethe focuses on the significance of their shadows holding hands and the less abrasive resentment of Denver at Paul D's intrusion. The isolation clamped upon them by the haunting past seems to crumble a little with people acknowledging them while passing. Beloved's return, in person, sets the stage for their final confrontation with their own selves. Sethe becomes increasingly subservient to her. Her need to explain her 'too thick' love and have it accepted by Beloved gradually takes her away from Paul D, her work, Denver, and also from herself. The silence of the unvoiced 'Dearly' before beloved on the gravestone of her daughter breaks out resonantly at this juncture. Beloved is loved dearly but the price of that love is too dear both in the past and in the present. A chattel to Beloved, Sethe now realizes that, "Counting on the stillness of her own soul, she had forgotten the other one; the soul of her baby girl." (5)

Beloved's insistence that Paul D call her by her name and her seduction of him underscores his frigid impotence after the shattering of the Edenic illusion of Sweet Home. Yet, their turtle like coupling resuscitates his heart so he can feel again. Her moving him like a rag-doll breaks his judgemental attitude toward Sethe. The conviction and resolve he aspires for come to him with his acceptance of Sethe, her pain, and her "trying to outhurt the hurter." (234) The promise held out to Sethe when he gravitated to her house after eighteen years and "rubbed his cheek on her back and learned that way her sorrow, the roots of it" (17) is finally fulfilled. The pattern of alternate silence and the articulation it has now made possible is most clearly brought out here. By wanting "to put his story next to hers" (273) Paul D also acknowledges the silence which preserves the other's dignity and the quiet knowledge of having a friend of the mind. His assurance to Sethe, "You your best thing," (273) after his prolonged silence would have meant nothing at all but for the silent expression of his touch, "He leans over and takes her hand. With the other he touches her face . . . His holding fingers are holding hers." (273) The entwined fingers speak of a tomorrow free from flight, of possession, or possessing, of claiming and owning, the runaway slaves can finally quit running.

The complex progression of Paul D and Sethe is more clearly visible in Denver's movement from mute silence to an articulate one and then on to visible expression. Part Three of the novel places Denver at the threshold of change with the words, "124 was quiet. Denver who thought she knew all about silence was surprised to learn hunger could do that." (139) This quietness, coupled with the silence of being left out in the 'games' Sethe and Beloved play, since the last time all three skated as though in a ritual dance, and fell holding hands, is enervating and crushing. Denver is somewhat an outsider in the triad because of her non-experience of first-hand-slavery. It is this partial outside view which facilitates her arrival at a silent determination to protect Sethe from Beloved and "to look out for and preserve herself." (252) The resolve to, "go ask somebody for help," (243) thus, makes it possible for Denver to articulate her need and reach out across the alienating silences between her and the community. Beginning with a courteous greeting by two blackmen to which, "Denver believed her eyes spoke gratitude" (245) and a warm acceptance by Lady Jones, her childhood teacher, Denver is quickly embraced by the women of the neighbourhood. Food as metaphor has many aspects in *Beloved*: of a medium of forgetting for Sethe, a celebration of life for Stamp Paid, of generosity for Baby Suggs, of independence for Sixo. It now stands for breaking bread together, for unreserved acceptance. The women leave food quietly for Denver and two words of thanks suffice to complete the bond. The estrangement which had begun as resentment of Baby Suggs' bounty at the blackberry party and sealed by misunderstanding Sethe's silence as one of pride, is now overcome by Denver's proactive silence which made her words spoken and heard.

An ironic inversion of the central incident completes the reparation. Once more, a white man rides toward Sethe's yard but he is the man who had always helped her and even now is her landlord and Denver's employer. Once again, her offspring are out in the yard, and yet again Sethe feels, "Little hummingbirds sticks needle beaks right through her headcloth into her hair and beat their wings." (262) The difference now is that instead of taking the ice pick to Beloved, this time she flies at the intruder. More importantly, the sisterhood of a once indifferent community is present to wordlessly and efficiently help a quietly determined Denver hold Sethe from self-destruction. A final voiceless oneness, willing hands stretched out in solidarity, complete the strategy, "Leaving Beloved behind" (262) and with her, their helplessness and alienation too. George Steiner in his essay "The Distribution of Discourse" states: "there is a history, a morphology, a rhetoric of inner speech as there is of outer. The relationships of internal language to the environment are dialectical, precisely as are those of voiced utterance; they help to create the world of experience and, at the same time, reflect it."[7] This premise of the unvoiced posits dynamics and change, and within the experience of Beloved, conceivable reparation and reclamation are brought about in its three prominent concluding images: that of Sethe and Denver joining a pile of people to make a hill, of Paul D's fingers holding Sethe's and of Beloved disremembered.

Silences, as discovered in *Beloved*, are more than private deviations which are of little significance in themselves. Rather they form a comprehensive system where a part contributes to the overall strategy for effecting a transformation. Thus, *Beloved* reveals layers of silence that accommodate: those words which are spoken, but lost due to mis-communication, or breakdown of communication; words that fail to bear the full weight of what is to be voiced; words and silence that alienate, and those that bond; the language of touch, of the eyes and the face, of gesture and the body; the silence of practised amnesia; the silence of encoded words; and the silence of the unspoken. Yet, it must be conceded that all strategies are finite and cannot exist always by themselves. The strategy of silence also needs to cultivate its familiars. Thus, silence which procreates and crystallises praxis-oriented thought and ultimately makes spaces for deep and forceful articulation is a powerful weapon of change. In tandem, silence, and its discourse—unvoiced before being voiced—provide for a highly complex but effective strategy.

NOTES

1. Margaret Atwood, *Surfacing* (1972; Toronto: McClelland and Stewart, 1994), p. 191.
2. Qtd. Lawrence W. Levine, *Black Culture and Black Consciousness: Afro-American Folk Thought from Slavery to Freedom* (New York: OUP, 1977), p. xi.
3. Roger D. Abrahams, "Rapping and Capping: Black Talk as Art," *Black Americans*, ed. John F. Szwed (Washington D.C.: United States Information Agency, 1969), p. 144.
4. Toni Morrison, *Playing in the Dark* (1992; New York: Vintage, 1993).
5. Toni Morrison, *Beloved* (1987; London: Picador, 1988), p. 4.
6. George Steiner, *Extraterritorial: Papers on Literature and the Language Revolution* (1968; Harmondsworth: Penguin, 1975).
7. Toni Morrison, *On Difficulty and Other Essays* (1972; Oxford: OUP, 1978), p. 91.

Convergence of History and Feminism in *Beloved*

USHA PURI

Usha Puri shows how historical and feminist concerns combine to form Morrison's "genuine black book." The year 1873 and the specificity of the place (Ohio, Cincinnati) ground Beloved *within the political and geographical realities of history. This novel shows the power of art to demolish stereotype. Infanticide was one of the avenues of resistance open to Sethe. Beloved's ghost is the manifestation of Sethe's guilty conscience; it stays with her till women of the neighbourhood come to her rescue and exorcise the ghost.*

Editor

Toni Morrison and other black women writers do not view the present Renaissance as an isolated phenomenon; they see it as a part of a long and continuous literary tradition that has evolved after slavery. Their black female literary tradition is enriched by a wealth and oral tradition that offers verbal forms and skills and their language is both visual and metaphorical. Expressive of a new innovative force, their works are rediscovering history, are obsessed with it and obsessed with rewriting it. They are opening areas of exploration of the lives of slave or free women and of women abolitionists of the post-civil war era. Margaret Walker's *Jubilee,* Ernest J. Gaines' *The Autobiography of Miss Jane Pittman* and now Morrison's *Beloved* share a revisionist view of history.

The early struggle of black women writers to achieve an authorial voice was clearly associated with the quest for freedom. Frances Harper's *Iola Leroy or Shadows Uplifted* (1892) and Pauline Hopkins' *Contending Forces: A Romance Illustrative of Negro Life North and South* (1900) reveal post Reconstructionist's influence. Pivotal to Harper and Hopkins is the quest for freedom for their black heroines and their outrage at women's victimization. Contemporary black women writers are doing today what Hopkins promised to do in 1900, when she published her first novel, *Contending Forces* i.e. preserve the rich Afro-American heritage.

Harper and Hopkins paved way for the contemporary black women writers to set the tone for further development of their tradition. As Morrison says: "their strategies for survival become our maneuvers for power." She believes that this continuity between past and present is very crucial because it creates bonds, mutual obligations and a shared communal history of struggle. Morrison's own articulation of her motives in *rediscovering* history for artistic expression in the article "Rediscovering Black History":

> There is no need to be nostalgic about "the good old days" because they weren't . . . but to recognize and rescue those qualities of resistance, excellence and integrity that were so much a part of our past and so useful to us and to the generations of blacks now growing up.[1]

reveals how deeply she is concerned with celebrating the unique feminine cultural values and "qualities of resistance, excellence and integrity" that were so much part of the black women's past.

The phenomenal success of her fifth novel *Beloved* shows that Morrison has succeeded in plumbing the depth and breadth, the diversity and wonder of the black feminine experience. In *Beloved* historical and feminine concerns combine to produce *what* Morrison has elsewhere called a "genuine Black. . . . Book."[2]

Beloved is a historical novel based on the true story of Margaret Garner, a fugitive from Kentucky who attempted to kill her children rather than have them enslaved when they were all captured in Ohio in 1850. She, like *Beloved's* Sethe, succeeded in killing only one. Morrison's motive in this Pulitzer prize winning novel is not only to unveil that "peculiar phase of slavery" which "has generally been kept veiled"[3] i.e. the tale *of* sexual abuse but also to smolder at the inequities that black women still face.

Morrison explains in her interview "The Pain of Being Black" with Bonnie Angelo that she had "terrible reluctance about dwelling on that era. . . . Suddenly the time—300 years—began to drown me."[4] Set in post Civil War Ohio, this haunting narrative of slavery and its aftermath traces the life of a young woman, Sethe, who has kept a "terrible memory" at bay only by shutting down part of her mind. The novel concerns Sethe's former life as a slave on Sweet Home Farm, her escape with her children to what seems a safe haven, and the tragic events that follow. She lives on the edge of town with her daughter Denver and her mother-in-law Baby Suggs. The novel hinges on the death of Sethe's infant daughter Beloved, who mysteriously reappears as a sensuous young woman. Beloved's spirit comes back to claim Sethe's love. Sethe struggles to keep Beloved gaining full possession of her present and to throw off the long, dark, legacy of her past.

In order to depict the historical reality of the period Morrison focuses on the 1860s and 70s and how an Afro-American heritage was maintained during the period of dramatic social changes before and after the Civil War. Morrison carefully pinpoints temporal and historical markers. In the beginning of Chapter One, the mention of the specific year 1873, and places such as Cincinnati and Ohio, ground Beloved within the political and geographical realities of history. The description of a particular slave family—Baby Suggs' family—takes the story back to the pre-civil war period:

> 124 was spiteful. Full of Baby's venom. The women in the house knew it and so did the children. For years each put up with the spite in his own way, but by 1873 Sethe and her daughter Denver were its only victims. The grandmother, Baby Suggs, was dead, and the sons Howard and Buglar, had run away by the time they were thirteen years old . . . leaving their grandmother, Baby Suggs; Sethe, their mother; and their little sister, Denver, all by themselves in the gray and white house on Bluestone Road. It didn't have a number then because Cincinnati didn't stretch that far. In

> fact Ohio had been calling itself a state only seventy years when first one brother and then the next . . . crept away. (3)[5]

Beloved expands the period of the 1870s by looking back to the mid-nineteenth century when black "men and women were moved around like checkers." (23) They were hanged, rented out, loaned out, bought up, ran off, brought back, stored up, mortgaged, won, stolen or seized. Their life choices were severely limited and freedom was an unimaginable dream for them. The freedom to marry and to have their own family did not exist. Baby Suggs' eight children had six fathers, slave life had "busted her legs, back, head, eyes, hands, kidneys, womb and tongue." (87) She had nothing left to make a living with but her heart. She was able to keep her son, Halle, the longest, for twenty years. It was Halle who gave her freedom when it didn't mean a thing. Baby Suggs straggled to belong to the community of other free Negroes to love and be loved by them.

The author develops the social and psychological aspects which characterize the lived experience of historical transition. Paul D, a sweet Home man, recalls that during and after the war blacks were homeless and without people, moving, walking, running, hiding, stealing and moving on:

> During, before and after the war he had seen Negroes so stunned, or hungry, or tired or bereft it was a wonder they recalled or said anything. Who, like him, had hidden in caves and fought owls for food; who like him, stole from pigs; who like him, slept in trees in the day and walked by night. . . . He saw a witless colored woman jailed and hanged for stealing ducks she believed were her own children. (66)

Sethe moved too, like jaws inside. Hungry and exhausted, she took flight from the white schoolteacher, his nephews, Sweet Home, Slavery and Kentucky: "the bloody side of the Ohio River" after "her husband disappeared; that after her milk had been stolen, her back pulped, her children orphaned, she was not to have an easeful death. No." (31) Then Amy, a white teenaged woman, meets Sethe and restores her to life by massaging her swollen feet "until she cried salt tears." (82) It is Amy's role as midwife who delivers Sethe's daughter, Denver, that bonds the women together. Sethe's womanhood is nurtured by Amy's strength.

Morrison is trying to make Sethe's story "a personal experience." She reveals her intention in an interview: "The book was not about an institution—slavery with a capital S. It was about these anonymous people called slaves. . . . What they are willing to risk, however long it lasts, in order to relate to one another—that was incredible to me."[6] By choosing to narrate the real life and actual experiences of a runaway slave *woman,* Morrison proves the power of art to demolish stereotype. Sethe's experience is treated with many ironic overtones that point to certain paradoxes and many fundamental complexities of her quest to freedom. Other novels have done this—*Song of Solomon* and *Invisible Man* for instance, though numerous adventures of the hero examine the intricate legacy of the past and of history. Yet, *Beloved* strikes a different and perplexing note because it deliberately avoids chronological development of the narrative and linear structure. Beloved's mother, Sethe, is caught in the ambiguities of a quest that presents itself as a succession of rememories; each recorded incident, act or ward further unfolds her story. Sethe's story is presented piece by piece through the act of rememory; a pattern of revelation of her past, of recognition of the history.

The story is narrated through a series of flashbacks. Morrison is not only concerned with what history has recorded in the slave narrative but what it has omitted; the "unspeakable past" (58) of the black slave woman. As Sethe tells her story, her memory is "loaded with the past." (70) Every mention of "the past life hurt. Everything in it was painful or lost." (58) Paul D's visit to Sethe's house 124 initiates Sethe's journey into the past. With his arrival, there was "sweet Home rolling, rolling, rolling out before her eyes." (6) Straining her "terrible memory," Sethe remembers that though now a haunted house, once 124 had been "a cheerful, buzzing house where Baby Suggs, holy, loved, cautioned, fed, chastised and soothed." (86-87) Baby became "an unchurched preacher" who taught black people to love their lives and their flesh because the whites despised it. The moment Sethe came to fall into the wide arms of Baby, she knew that white folks had taken all Sethe had. Baby Suggs' love and care restored Sethe: "Baby Suggs' long distance love was equal to any skin-close love she had known." (95)

As in her previous novels the need for women to re-establish connections with one another is powerfully rendered in Morrison's *Beloved.* It was all the more important in that era of slavery because there was a profound and real need for physical as well as psychological survival. Commenting on her effort to explore a relationship between two women, Morrison says:

> We read about Ajax and Achilles willing to die for each other, but very little about the friendship of women, and them having respect for each other, like it's something new. But black women had always had that, they have always been emotional life supports for each other.[7]

When Sethe arrived with her newborn daughter tied to her chest, Baby Suggs welcomed her. Sethe was too ugly looking to wake her children in the night so Baby Suggs bathed her in sections, cleaned and oiled, warmed and consoled Sethe and cleaned the eyes of the new born with its mother's urine. (92-93) As Sethe learnt female rites from Baby it brought her close to her ancestor. Baby initiated Sethe into the wisdom and beliefs and souls of her people. Symbolically the performance of these rites is for Sethe the threshold, which represents the liminal phase of her rites of passage, the precursor of a real and permanent change that will involve a long and exacting pilgrimage. Sethe has a powerful culture mentor like Baby Suggs who awakens her desire to know her past and to love herself as a person. Thus Baby enhances Sethe's sense of womanhood and their bonds to one another are made stronger.

First twenty eight happy days Sethe spent in the company of Baby Suggs were followed by eighteen years of disapproval and a solitary life because the community that loved and respected Baby Suggs stepped back and held itself at a distance when Sethe killed her own daughter, Beloved.

One of the worst effects of historical transition for used-to-be slave mother was alienation and repression. As the author defines it, Sethe's alienation is not simply the result of a black woman's separation from the family or her cultural centre but also the result of her murdering her own daughter to protect her from living an abject life of a slave. Like Sula, Sethe is an outlaw. Just as Sula is determined to "make" herself even at the risk of distancing herself from other black women and seeks to assert a sense of self, Sethe does not care for the community because she had no choice:

> That she lived with 124 in helpless, apologetic resignation because she had no choice; that minus husband, sons, Mother-in-law, she and her slow-witted daughter had to live there all alone making do. (164)

Sethe bears with the outrageous behaviour of the place to make peace with the fury of the ghost of her two-year-old baby, Beloved. Sethe is marginally incorporated into the black community. After committing this "staggering" (256) crime: Sethe lives in a state of schizophrenia, in which her marginality is constantly confronted with the outside world.

The tragedy of Sethe's alienation is its effect on her role as a mother. Her daughter Denver feels neglected and socially cut off because nobody speaks to them, nobody comes to their house anymore. And Denver is dying to be related to her grandma, Baby Suggs who taught her to listen to and love her own body. Although "Slaves were not supposed to have pleasurable feelings of her own" (209) she taught Denver to feel pleasure deep down. Though scared of Sethe, Denver wants to be loved by her mother. She wants to be related to her sister Beloved whose blood she had swallowed right along with her mother's milk because Sethe had killed her. She is willing to risk anything to be related to her daddy, Halle, who had disappeared. She dreams about him: "My daddy was an angel man. . . . I always knew he was coming. Something was holding him up. The river flooded; the boat sank. . . . My daddy was coming for me." (207) She moves around as a sensual young woman amongst the living members of the family to claim her mother's love.

Morrison seeks to expose a truth about the interior life of people who did not write. She is trying to fill in the blanks that the slave narratives left. And what makes her approach authentic is her "recollection that moves from the image to the text."[8] When Sethe reminisces, her present collides with her past and her family's migration to 124. Eighteen years of her "unlivable life" was interrupted by the arrival of Paul D, who brought her "Short-lived glory." (173) Their past is represented through stories and flashbacks. Paul D. Garner, Paul F. Garner, Halle, Suggs and Sixo, the wild men all worked at Mr. Garner's farm Sweet Home along with Sethe. As Sethe and Paul D exchange their past and want to catch up on eighteen years in a day, Sethe tells Paul D that she had a chokecherry tree on her back. This is the way Sethe remembers her past. The chokecherry tree was the result of cowhide beatings on Sethe's back and it is an image that recreates her painful history.

What distinguishes Morrison's fiction from autobiographical strategies is her "reliance on the image."[9] In addition to "recollection," she relies on "picture" and the feelings that accompany the picture. In her fiction sensuality is embedded in the past and sensual descriptions explode the effects of alienation and repression. Sethe's remembrance of girlhood sensuality at Sweet Home coincides with her Womanhood in Cincinnati. Both are metaphorically condensed with the alienation she experiences as a black emigrant and social outlaw in Ohio. Morrison's metaphorical language "he saw the sculpture her back had become, like the decorative work of an ironsmith too passionate for display,"(17) produces the effect of pain, cruelty and alienation. Indeed, the image of chokecherry tree evokes the poetics of surrealism while the language reveals the historical process through which the image is produced. Sweet Home is the site where images are produced. Paul D's desire to learn Sethe's sorrow, to share it with her, produces a liberating effect: "He rubbed his cheek on her back and teamed that way her sorrow, the roots of it; its wide trunk and intricate branches." (17) And Sethe's back skin which had been dead for years, feels the hurt it ought to. She remembers things with the hope that the last of the Sweet Home men was there to catch her if she sank. As Paul D dropped twenty-five years from his recent memory to share bed life with Sethe, she remembers her first experience with her husband, Halle, in the tiny cornfield of Mr. Garner. Sethe spends a few months of "the sunsplashed life" (173) with Paul D who resented the children she had, the code they used among themselves that he could not break. Paul D knew that "They were a family somehow and he was not the head of it." (132) Finally when Paul D learns about Sethe's past, he sneaks away without saying a "goodbye."

Sethe, like Morrison's other female protagonists, is a victim of both sexist and racist oppression. She is a runaway slave woman, a slave mother, who is brutally treated by white men—the schoolteacher and his nephews. Morrison explores a black woman's self-conscious protest to her dual oppression. It is not only the sexual exploitation that Sethe feels most oppressed by but the humiliation of her nurturing abilities as a mother—the stealing of her milk.

One of the most damaging effects of the dual oppression of black women against which Morrison writes, is murder of one's own child. "Murder becomes Sethe's act of mother love,"[10] which she explains by saying, "I took and put my babies where they'd be safe." (163) She prefers to murder her daughter Beloved rather than see her in bondage. According to Deborah Gray White, infanticide represented one of the avenues of resistance on the part of a slave woman.[11] By killing Beloved, Sethe was showing the degree of the limitations she would be bound with. Although Sethe's murder might be viewed by the contemporary standards as limiting, but the context in which she did it does not diminish her stature.

Through the character of Beloved, whose haunting presence makes the boundaries between myth and reality disappear. Morrison explores the possibility of the existence of various levels of consciousness. At one level Beloved's ghost is a manifestation of Sethe's guilty conscience. In a world where whites wish to see black people dead, it is not surprising that the birth of Sethe's daughter, Denver, looks like a miracle; that murder of her another daughter Beloved is the subject of so much talk and the ghost of Beloved appears and disappears among the living like "the sunlit cracks." (124) And the living can become wholly dedicated to the dead—as Sethe and Denver are to Beloved: "But my love was tough and she came back now." (200) At another level, Sethe's identification with Beloved is very deep: "I am Beloved and she is mine." (214)

As an individual whose cultural and communal exile is the most profound, Sethe is haunted by waking visions born out of guilt and fear. Once again, Morrison explores the psyche of a slave mother who must deal with haunted life on every level from the fires of the flesh to the heart-breaking challenges of the spirit:

> Tell me the truth, Didn't you come from the other side?
> Yes, I was on the other side.
> You come back because of me?
> Yes.
> You rememory me?
> Yes, I remember you.
> You never forgot me?
> Your face is mine.
> Do you forgive me? Will you stay? You safe here now?
> Where are the men without skin?
> Out there. Way off.
> Can they get in here?
> No.

In the final part of the novel, the roles of mother and daughter are reversed. And the job Denver started out with, protecting Beloved from Sethe, changed to protecting her mother from Beloved: "Sethe no longer combed her hair or splashed her face with water. She sat in the chair licking her lips like a chastised child while Beloved ate up her life, took it. Swelled up with it, grew taller on it." (250)

The community watches silently these scenes of madness. And the craziness of the black world is only matched by the white world's devices. When the women of the neighbourhood assemble outside 124 and make the ghost of Beloved disappear, in her final leap, Beloved wheels into her mother's arms and then is left behind alone, she flies freeing herself.

Morrison's portrayal of Beloved as a sensual woman with otherworldly aura provides us an insight into the author's vision. Had it teen possible for black Slave Woman like Sethe to live with her family with dignity and self-respect in the America of 1850s, Sethe wouldn't have committed this hideous crime which was the mutilation of Sethe's vibrant mother love. Morrison's use of supernatural and folk belief in spirit and Living-dead confirms the fact that she draws on traditional African folklore and mysticism has an integral place in her work. Ella tells Stamp Paid: "you knew as well as I do that people who die bad don't stay in the ground." (188) Morrison's interest in mysticism and the supernatural is exhibited in her portrayal of Beloved.

Morrison readily concedes that she is "trying to fill in the blanks that the slave narratives left—to part the veil that was so frequently drawn, to implement the stories that [she] heard."[12] She draws upon the memories within and uses the significant act of "rememory" to make her story acquire the structure of an oral narration. Each story in *Beloved* recreates a particular patch of the past and reveals a new mystery and then calls for another story. In different places, by different characters the same story of Sweet Home is picked up, retold, expanded into further complexity and mystery. The accumulation of the stories of Sethe; Denver, Beloved, Baby Suggs, Paul D, Halle of Sweet Home men, Amy Ella, the call and response pattern, their gradual merging into a single story, Sethe's story, create an interesting structure. Sometimes it is the omniscient narrator, at other times the voices of different characters replace that of the narrator, each offering its own fragmented perception of the truth while the author bridges the gap between the telling and what is being told. Thus Morrison uses a combination of the point of view of various characters but still retains the power to slide in and out.

By using this kind of narrative pattern in which each character becomes part of his or her own history and must be put together in quilt fashion, Morrison reminds us that the oral tradition is so strong in black culture that it is still alive. The stories of different characters bear witness to the past, to the struggle of black slaves to survive and escape to freedom; the reality and fantasy of their lives create history. Thus in form and content *Beloved* is about gaps which must be filled and interpreted by the reader.[13]

The narrative technique and content are complementary in their appreciation of how to create presence out of absence.

The structure of the novel is also interwoven with stories about naming, birth, death and rebirth. Naming was an essential part of black identity, associated with the manhood of a black man. But did a white man ever care? Nothing that was important to black people could become a part of their legacy, could be put down on paper:

> Was that it? Is that where the manhood lay? In the naming done by a Whiteman who was supposed to know? Who gave them the privilege not of working but of deciding how to? (125)

Baby Suggs prefers to hold on to her name, her identity: "Suggs is my name, Sir," she tells Mr. Garner, because "Baby Suggs was all she had left of the 'husband' she claimed." (142)

The feminist qualities that Morrison advocates through Sethe's portrayal are the traditional beauty, strength, resistance and integrity of black women. She is sensitive to feminist concerns and includes all those elements of black female experience in her text which are of compelling significance to a woman. In her interview with Rosemarie K. Lester, Morrison expresses her views on "an extremely painful and unattractive" history of black women in the States where black women have always been both mother and labourer, mother and worker and have worked in the fields along with men:

> They were required to do physical labour in competition with them, so that their relations with each other turned out to be more comradeship than male dominance/female subordination. . . . Black women are both ship and safe harbor.[14]

Morrison uses a beautiful metaphor to emphasize that black women are much more suited to aggressiveness in the mode that feminists are recommending. Sethe is an embodiment of that image. When Paul D, who had earlier deserted Sethe for her "Staggering Crime," returns because "Sweet Home Gal" had made him lose his mind, (263) he admits:

> She is a friend of my mind. She gathers me man. The pieces I am, she gathers them and give them back to me in all the right order.... Only this woman Sethe could have left him his manhood like that. He wants to put his story next to hers. (272-73)

Paul D pays this tribute to Sethe because she has the ability to be "both ship and safe harbor."

Beloved is a beautiful narrative about the survival of the heritage of slavery, on the power of rememory and the collective memories kept alive through oral tradition. It is also the story of the genesis of a culture and of a people who, living on the edge of life and death, have managed to create that culture and to keep their history alive. Morrison's self-conscious interest in the celebration of black women's strength, their values and beliefs stems from a desire to correct the wrongs that have been historically levelled against black women. She seeks to celebrate the legends of black women like Baby Suggs and Sethe and weave their dreams into myths that allow us to recover their past.

In *Beloved,* Morrison's convergence of history and feminism and her application of the sophisticated technique such as "re-memory," flashbacks, dramatic voice in narration, stream-of-consciousness, oral tradition and her magic realism "extend, fill in and complement"[15] the matrix of slave autobiographical narratives.

NOTES

1. Toni Morrison, "Rediscovering Black History," *New York Times Magazine*, 11 August 1974.
2. Toni Morrison, "Behind the Making of The Black Book," *Black World,* February 1974, p. 89.

3. Toni Morrison, "The Site of Memory," *Inventing the Truth, The Art and Craft of Memoir*, ed. William Zinsser (Boston: Houghton Mifflin, 1987), p. 110.
4. Bonnie Angelo, "The Pain of Being Black," Interview, *Time,* May 22, 1989, p. 48.
5. *Beloved* (New York: Plume, 1987).
6. "The Pain of Being Black," p. 48.
7. Mary Helen Washington, ed., *Midnight Birds* (New York: Anchor Press/Doubleday, 1980), p. xvi. Morrison depicts in *Sula* how Sula and Nel are "emotional life supports for each other." At the end of the novel Nel discovered that it was not her husband that she had missed all those years, but her friend Sula.
8. "The Site of Memory," p. 113
9. *Ibid.*, p. 112.
10. Marcia Ann Gillespie, "Toni Morrison," *MS,* 1988, p. 60.
11. Deborah Gray White, *Aren't I a Woman? Female Slaves in the Plantation South* (New York: W.W. Norton, 1985), p. 88.
12. "The Site of Memory," p. 113.
13. Claudia Tate, ed., *Black Women Writers at Work* (New York: Continuum, 1983), p. 125. Oral quality in Morrison's fiction is deliberate and it demands "participatory reading." Her language, she says, "has to have holes and spaces so the reader can come into it" and "feel" the experience with the author.
14. Rosemarie K. Lester, "An Interview with Toni Morrison, Hessian Radio Network, Frankfurt, West Germany," *Critical Essays on Toni Morrison,* Nellie McKay (Boston, Massachusetts: G.K. Hall, 1988), pp. 48-49.
15. "The Site of Memory," p. 120.

Motherhood in *Beloved*

BHARATI A. PARIKH

Bharati Parikh explores the concept of 'motherhood' propounded by Toni Morrison in the backdrop of the life of plantation workers during the plantation and slavery era. Morrison projects the 'mother' as a Negro-archetypal-cum-ancestral concept who slaved with her heart and soul and stood out as an 'unchurched' preacher extolling the pricelessness of the 'heart' and the 'soul' in the mother, which no civilization, however, inhuman, can scrape them out of their bodies. Such was the 'sterner stuff' Sethe was made of! Sethe symbolised the archetypal Negro-woman who suffered for the race and she was 'the race' itself, transcending physical barriers beyond the region of physical pain.

Editor

Toni Morrison's 'narratives' have put forth disturbing questions before the society—readers, scholars, 'community' and critics alike. Being an imaginative writer she is, with firm roots in the Afro-American tradition, intensity of feeling and probing mind to examine socio-economic, political, cultural problems during and after slavery, Morrison disturbs and enhances our understanding of Afro-American life during as well as after the Declaration of Emancipation in *Beloved.*

Her technique to recapture the past, mingle it with the present, not to name or number the chapters of her novels render her work complex. The power to name her people, which will evoke the hardships borne by black in and out of slavery commands our respect and inspires awe of her matchless craft.

Beloved is an adjective, commonly used by one and all. Yet, in the novel *Beloved* (1987), Morrison once again brings out the essence in naming the lost, murdered daughter of Sethe, the slave woman of "iron eyes and backbone to match." The terrible ordeals borne by mothers during slavery come alive through the narrative in *Beloved.* The novel also deals with lives of blacks as was lived during plantation era, hence some call this novel written in the plantation tradition. On one hand, we see how Morrison bestows dignity to blacks who were all called 'men' by the plantation owner Mr. Garner, who prided himself in doing so, when majority of plantation owners considered their slaves as 'property'. All men are named alike, Paul, with the variation of last initial, e.g. Paul D. Garner, Paul A. Garner, Paul F. Garner, Mister, Halle Suggs, and Sixo, the tough man.

Thus, there lies the mockery of the system evolved by the whites for keeping slaves as their property, unmindful of Afro-Americans as persons and their entity as human beings. As Scruggs suggests, naming is "an existential act that manifests a vital community whose space is fluid, protean." (171) Even the laws formulated by whites did not proclaim humanity of the blacks. Compared to Morrison's earlier novels, *Beloved* is a historical novel set in the nineteenth century. Though an imagined narrative, it is based on a particular incident in the past.

As the novel unfolds, the first sentence evokes a sense of mystery: "124 WAS SPITEFUL. Full of baby's venom. The women in the house knew it and so did the children. For years each put up with the spite in his one way, but by 1873 Sethe and her daughter Denver were its only victims." (3)

The sheer helpless condition of blacks during and after Emancipation reveals their strong sense of place. Be it a house as in *Beloved.* The place where Sethe lived, didn't have a number then." (3) It was the gray and white house on Bluestone Road on the outskirts of Cincinnati. During slavery, most black women "were not, by and large, domestics in the house," contrary to popular impression, rather, they were labourers in the fields with the men, it also "meant that the women were deprived of houses, of being householders." (qtd. Scruggs, 172) Naturally, these circumstances led Morrison's women strongly attached to houses, even those that seem cursed. Besides individual well-being and sense of identity, Morrison is concerned with the community, which needs to support the individual in a society where survival of women was so hard, as in *The Bluest Eye* or *Sula*, or even in *Song of Solomon*. Thus, in *Beloved*, Morrison evinces "the redemption of the house, the origins of community, and the integration of the individual within the community's life-sustaining body." (173)

Beloved was awarded the Pulitzer prize. It concerns the "awful, lingering effects of slavery on black mothers." (Payant, 196) The story was stimulated by a contemporary newspaper clipping telling of a Kentucky runaway slave, Margaret Garner, who tried to kill her children at the home of her mother-in-law in Cincinnati, rather than have them go back to slavery as noted in *Newsweek* by Clemmons. The story commands utmost attention by taking into its fold all the issues an Afro-American writer must envisage. As Alice Walker projects: "A womanist writer will recognize that, along with her consciousness of sexual issues, she must incorporate racial, cultural, national, economic and political considerations into her philosophy." (qtd. Payant 166) Morrison's writings lay bare the experiences of black women, who "are the touchstone by which all that is human can be measured." (*Ibid.*)

The two figures of mother in the novel naturally arrest our attention: Baby Suggs who celebrates Sethe's reunion with the family along with her four grandchildren. Morrison is deeply interested in the strength of blacks in not only surviving but in the "wholeness of entire people, male and female." Halle had bought freedom for his mother after five long years of hard work. She lived "sixty years a slave and ten years free." (104) These were her last words before she died. But when she was freed, she reached the outskirts of Cincinnati. Baby Suggs had been a beacon of light to the entire community. At the time 124 had been "a cheerful, buzzing house where Baby Suggs, holy, loved, cautioned, fed, chastised and soothed." (87)

It is ennobling how through her own experience of slave life, she had attained a deep understanding of travels of the blacks. After emancipation, she wanted to build a strong community of blacks. Because slave life had "busted her legs, back, head, eyes, hands, kidneys, womb and tongue, she had nothing left to make a living with but her heart—which she put to work at once." (87) She was the best loved and sought after among her people. She reinvents herself, her being and inspires others to follow suit. Thus, Baby Suggs attains 'becoming' from the state of being. Her largeness of heart is described thus :

> Accepting no title of honor before her name, but allowing a small caress after it, she became an unchurched preacher, one who visited pulpits and opened her great heart to those who could use it. (87)

Thus, the nurturing quality of the mother/ancestor in Baby Suggs is symbolically portrayed. The lesson she learnt and taught to all--men, women and children was "love your heart." (89) The men were asked to 'dance' before their wives and children, women were asked to 'cry' and children were told to 'laugh', so that their mothers hear them laugh.

Ceremoniously, she asked all her people to love their own selves, as the whites don't love them; in parts or as a whole. Hence: "You got to love it. This is the flesh I'm talking about here. Flesh that needs to be loved. Feel that need to rest and dance; backs that need support shoulders that need arms, strong arms I'm telling you. And O my people, out yonder, hear me, they do not love your neck unnoosed, and straight. So love your neck, put a hand on it, grace it, stroke it and hold it up." (88-89)

Baby Suggs advocated loving their heart above all the other parts because "this is the prize." Thus, her plea is replete with compassion for her brethren. Then she danced sunlit dance in the "Clearing—a wide-open place cut deep in the woods nobody knew for what the end of a path known only to deer and whoever cleared the land in the first place." (87)

Later on, when her daughter-in-law, Sethe, joins her, Baby Suggs provides her ample consolation. She tells her to lay all misery, sorrow and shock of losing her husband Halle aside. Before nine years, Baby Suggs soothed her by "pressing fingers and the quiet instructive voice." (86) Thus, a sort of defence mechanism was developed among black women to stand by each other, as white slave catchers perpetually haunted them to catch the runaway slaves.

Exactly twenty-eight days after the arrival of Sethe at 124 Bluestone Road, Baby Suggs' "faith, her love, her imagination and her great big old heart began to collapse." (89) The picture totally changes at 124, after nine years when "Baby Suggs, holy, proved herself a liar, dismissed her great heart and lay in the keeping-room bed roused once in a while by a craving for color and not for another thing." (89) The mystery of this changes lies in a shocking, indescribable agonizing experience, wherein "Those white things have taken all." Baby Suggs had or dreamed and broke her "heartstrings too." As a result of a terrible happening :

> 124 shut down and put up with the venom of its ghost. No more lamps all night long, or neighbors dropping by. No conversations after supper. No watched barefoot children playing in the shoes of strangers. Baby Suggs, holy, believed she had lied. There was no grace—imaginary or real. (89)

Thus, the long coveted dream of a happy reunion comes to a halt. The shock proves too deep for Baby Suggs who lead a life suspended between "the nastiness of life and the meanness of the dead, she couldn't get interested in leaving life or living it." (4) Her past had been 'intolerable' like her present. She had eight children. "Everyone of them gone away from her. Four taken four chased." (4)

It is after eighteen years Paul D. Garner visits Sethe and learns about Baby Suggs' death. She died "soft as cream." For her being "alive was the hard part." The baby ghost of Sethe's daughter, Beloved, haunted the house. After Sweet Home plantation was taken over by schoolteacher and his two nephews, Sethe's life is annihilated: "The one who had nursed her (taken away her milk) while his brother held her down." (150) "She was Halle's girl. Pregnant every year including the year she sat by the fire telling him (Paul D) she was going to run." (9)

Among the six men at the sweet Home, Sethe was the only female. When she sent her three children from Kentucky to

Halle's mother near Cincinnati, Ohio, on a wagon, along with Ella and other women:

> "I had milk" she said, "I was pregnant with Denver but I had milk for my baby girl. (9)

After eighteen years when the last of the Sweet Home man Paul D visits Sethe, she recalls her past. She had planned to join her children soon after they were shot.

> Anybody could smell me long before he saw me. And when he saw me he'd see the drops of it on the front of my dress. Nothing I could do about that. All I knew was I had to get my milk to my baby girl. Nobody was going to nurse her like me. Nobody was going to get it to her fast enough, or take it away when she had enough and didn't know it. Nobody knew that she couldn't pass her air if you held her up on your shoulder, only if she was lying on my knees. Nobody knew that but me and nobody had her milk but me. I told that to the women in the wagon. Told them to pout sugar water in cloth to suck from, so when I got there in a few days she wouldn't have forgot me. The milk would be there and I would be there with it. (9)

The dialogue charged with mother love, frantic eagerness, and expectancy to see and suckle the baby, oozes out of every syllable. As blacks were not allowed to possess anything, neither relationships nor any belongings whatsoever, Baby Suggs does not hurry to thank Lord when three children arrive safe with the wagon, but no sign of Sethe or Halle. This very baby girl, when the schoolteacher with one nephew, one slave catcher and a sheriff arrive on 124, the house seems so quiet that they suspect that they have reached too late. There had been celebration with "steely old black man," Stamp Paid's two buckets full black tasting so good and felt so happy, that to eat them as like being in the church. Just one of the berries and you felt anointed." (136) The idea of bringing just freed blacks together by way of a feast brings out Baby Suggs' qualities of sharing the joy with the community. "124, rocking with laughter, goodwill and food for ninety, made them angry. Too much they thought." (137)

Why none informed Baby Suggs of coming doom, maybe because the colored people disliked the excess. Like in *Sula*, the dead robins' rain and it proclaims something is ominous, similarly the grandmother sniffs the disapproval in the air. Morrison is one of the finest artists who evokes atmosphere, builds up ethos and readers feel it, perceive it and dread it, all at a time. The innermost thoughts unfold before the reader and we peep into Baby Suggs' mind:

> She accustomed to the knowledge that nobody prayed for her—but this free-floating repulsion was new. It wasn't white folks—that much she could tell—so it must be colored ones. And then she knew. Her friends and neighbours were angry at her because she had overstepped, given too much, offended them by excess. (138)

When the schoolteacher arrived, both Baby Suggs and Sethe saw them. The slave enters in the woodshed, Baby Suggs was standing stock-still. Stamp Paid was there in the wood pole with an axe. Sethe's 'thick mother-love' overwhelmed her. She wanted to kill all her children. She did not succeed in killing all but one, her two-year-old daughter, Beloved. Sethe's sheer courage to survive through slavery and getting out of it without Halle, her husband was a feat. How she loved her children, she renders to Paul D after eighteen years:

> We was here. Each and everyone of my labbies and me too. I birthed them and I got me out and it wasn't no accident. I did that. I had help, of course, lots of that, but still it was me doing it; me saying, Go on, and Now. Me having to look out. Me using my own head. But it was more than that. It was a kind of selfishness I never knew nothing about before. It felt god. Good and right. I was big, Paul D, and deep and wide and when I stretched out my arms all my children could get in between. I was that wide. Look like I loved em more after I got here. Or may be couldn't love em proper in Kentucky because they wasn't mine to love. But when I got here, when I jumped down off that wagon—there wasn't nobody in the world I couldn't love if I wanted to. (162)

For Sethe, Paul D is the man "who could walk into a house and the women cry." (17) After talking about her mother love again and again, the subject would remain one. After her agonizing experiences of slavery at Sweet Home, it was:

> Simple: she was squatting in the garden and when she saw them coming and recognized the school teacher's hat, she heard wings. Little hummingbirds stuck their needle beaks right through her headcloth into her hair and beat their wings. And if she thought anything, it was No. No. Nono. Nonono. Simple. She just flew. Collected every bit of life she had made, all the parts of her that were previous and fine and beautiful, and carried, pushed, dragged them through the veil, out, away, over there where no one could hurt them. Over there. Outside this place, where they would be safe. (163)

The white schoolteacher whom Sethe faced, "looked him dead in the eye, she had something in her arms that stopped him in his tracks. He took a backward step with each jump of the baby heart until finally there were none." (164) She relates to Paul D: "I stopped him. . . . I took and put my babies where they'd be safe." (164) After a long time, Paul D realizes that he was wrong in believing Sethe, Halle's girl, as helpless woman. He saw:

> here Sethe was new. The ghost in her house didn't bother her for the very same reason a room-and-board witch with new shoes was welcome. This here Sethe talked about love like any other woman; talked about baby clothes like any other woman, but what she meant could cleave the bone. This here Sethe talked about safety with a handsaw. This here new Sethe didn't know where the world stopped and she began. Suddenly he saw what Stamp Paid wanted him to see: more important than what Sethe had done was what she claimed. It scared him. (164)

Sethe's worldview differs here from Paul D's. When Paul D said: "Your love is too thick," Sethe gave her insight and said "Love is or it ain't. Thin love ain't love at all." (164) In a crisp, short dialogue Sethe tells Paul D, about her thick love and how she strived to be on her guard as far as her mother love was concerned about the safety of her loved ones:

> "Yeah. It didn't work, did it? Did it work?" he asked.
>
> "It worked," she said.

> "How? Your boys gone your don't know where. One girl dead, the other won't leave the yard. How did it work?"
>
> "They ain't at Sweet Home. Schoolteacher ain't got em."
>
> "May be there's worse."
>
> "It ain't my job to know what's worse. It's my job to know that is and to keep them away from what I know is terrible. I did that." (164-65)

The above dialogue represents what Morrison wants—to be able to write highly marked, black language with black characters stepped in black culture." (Verdelle 126)

Thus, what makes Morrison's works her own is the unique way in which she negotiates the constraining of a given critical or authorial power and ensures the participation of the reader in the experience of her novel. For her the "lore. . . . Gossip . . . magic . . . [and] sentiment. . . . Centralize and animate information discredited by the west." (Rao 93)

The novel raises many questions. Denver's loneliness when Paul D enters 124 as well as when Beloved possesses Sethe. Morrison creates a world of bygone era, yet alive in every bit and piece. The image of chokecherry tree on the back of Sethe and the countless such black "song of many thousands gone" keep alive the sufferings of the Afro-American people. Morrison has observed that scholarly studies of slavery have always seemed to her "too big and flat." They were like realistic novels that in trying to include all the facts missed the essence. She also believed that "by working within narrow limits instead of broad ones, she might be able to do "something deep." The depth she is speaking is the depth of the human heart, Sethe's heart, which in its misery contains the misery of the race." (Scruggs 186-87)

Beloved proclaims her passionate belonging to Sethe in surrealistic prose and verse. She also demands the reader's recognition of her presence and role as "too real to be Gothic." In an absorbing passage as Rao observes, "dramatically asserting the reconciliation of Sethe and Beloved, individual past and history, repression and relief, Morrison invents a new voice out of a ghost and a dead past." At the end of this section, in a poetic chant, the memories and minds of Sethe, Denver and Beloved combine to make a mutual song of possession:

> I waited for you
> You are mine
> You are mine
> You are mine. (217)

Yet in the novel there is ultimate voice that is collective. It is that of the woman in the exorcism ritual toward the end of the novel. Its power lies in the sensation of sound and not in the logical meaning of the Logos. The women:

> Stopped praying and took a step back to the beginning. In the beginning there were no words. In the beginning was the sound, they all knew what that sound sounded like. (259)

Among all her works, *Beloved* does stand out as an unforgettable creation, which celebrates life of Afro-Americans through slavery with women at the centre. For long, no reader can forget the haunted house 124 on Bluestone Road with Sethe, Denver, Beloved and Baby Suggs. The charged images, poetic language, interspersed with several narratives to top it with strong bond of mother love leave a deep impression on the reader's mind.

NOTES

Clemmons, Walter. "A Graveyard of Memories." *Newsweek*, 110 (28 Sept.) 1987, 75.

Morrison, Toni. *Beloved.* London: Picador, 1988.

Payant, Katherine B. *Becoming and Bonding: Contemporary Feminism and Popular Fiction by American Women Writers.* Westport: Connecticut, Greenwood Press, 1993.

Rao, Raghavendra R.M.V. "In Search of an Authentic Voice: Toni Morrison's *Beloved*," *Indian Journal of American Studies*, Vil, 23:2 (Summer) 1993, 91-93.

Scruggs, Charles, *Sweet Home: Invisible Cities in the Afro-American Novel.* Baltimore: John Hopkins University Press, 1993.

Verdelle, A.J. "Loose Magic: A.J. Verdelle Interviews Toni Morrison," *Double Take*, 13 (Summer), 1998, 121-28.

The Saga of Black Courage in *Beloved*

PASHUPATI JHA and T. RAVICHANDRAN

Beloved *presents a comprehensive picture of the utter exploitation of the Blacks, especially the women, on various levels—individual, familial, social and psychological. Pashupati Jha and T. Ravichandran describe in detail how Sethe, Baby Suggs, Paul D and Denver survive despite immeasurable physical, mental and emotional trauma they undergo.*

Editor

Dedicated to "sixty million and more" black people who lost their lives during the long period of slavery, *Beloved* (1987), Toni Morrison's fifth novel, won her the Pulitzer Prize, and eventually because of the accumulated acclaim, the Nobel Prize for Literature in 1993. Asked about the validity of the astounding figure quoted, Morrison replied that some of the historians told her the number may be two hundred million also, but she has taken, "the smallest number" she got from anybody and that was sixty million.[1] Admired by Margaret Atwood as "another triumph" for Morrison because of the novelist's "versatility and technical and emotional range appear to know no bounds,"[2] this novel, like her *The Bluest Eye*, works on all the levels of individual, familial, social, and psychic dimensions. Morrison succeeds in presenting a comprehensive picture of reality in the context of the utter exploitation of the Negroes, especially, the females among the lot. Just before and after the Emancipation Act, such was the suppression of Blacks during those years that William Styron wrote, "beat a nigger, starve him, leave him wallowing in his own shit, and he will be yours for life."[3] Blacks were treated not as human beings, not even as animals, but worse than them. In Morrison's words, "men and women were moved around like checkers."[4] Always living on the edge of life, they were beaten, bartered, bruised, raped, hanged, rented out, loaned out, bought up, brought back, stored up, exchanged, mortgaged, won, stolen or seized. Beloved is a fictional record of the saga of black courage shown by those sixty million or more who died and the many more who endured as exemplified through Sethe, the central character, and the rest who revolve around her. The novel is as much a history of the living as of the dead, who haunt the living since not a single house of the Negroes is left uninhabited by a grieved ghost. The focus of this paper is to elaborate how some of the major characters of this drama/melodrama, namely Sethe, Baby Suggs, Paul D, and Denver, survive despite immeasurable physical, mental and emotional trauma they undergo. Their survival strategy, amidst unspeakable torment, agony, and isolation, rests only on an indomitable courage to fight all odds.

Beloved centres on a true but bizarre story of the appalling slaughter of a daughter by her own mother in an act of excessive love and anguish for safety and protection from the hell as suffered by the slaughterer. The mother was, in reality, Margaret Garner, a runaway slave in 1856, who attempted to kill her four children to prevent them from falling back into slavery. In that event, only her three-year-old daughter died. In the novel, the mother is Sethe and her daughter is known to be Beloved. Towards the close of the novel, Morrison throws light on the motive behind this heinous act:

> That anybody white could take your whole self for anything that came to mind. Not just work, kill, or maim you, but dirty you. Dirty you so bad you couldn't like yourself anymore. Dirty so bad you forgot who you were and couldn't think it up. Though she and others lived through and got over it, she could never let it happen to her own. The best thing she was, was her children. Whites might dirty her all right, but not her best thing, her beautiful, magical best thing—the part of her that was clean. (251)

Sethe, though ruined by repeated rapes and untold humiliations by the white masters, considers her children the best and the clean thing of herself, and hence, she would not let any body taint that part of her. That Sethe would go to any extent to dirty herself to retain the purity of her children is sadly evident when she agrees for "rutting among the headstones with the engraver, his young son looking on" for ten minutes as a price to be paid for engraving the word "Beloved" on the tombstone of her dead daughter. (5) And those ten minutes for her were more unbearable than even her killing of the small daughter: "but those ten minutes . . . were longer than life, more alive, more pulsating than the baby blood that soaked her fingers like oil." (5)

The history, or rather her-story, unfolds with her after-prison life but there are pages and pages of flashbacks, stirred initially by the return of Paul D to 124 Bluestone Road outside Cincinnati in Ohio. The year is 1873, years after Emancipation Edict. Technically, blacks are free now, but they have to live with their harrowing past of only few years ago. Sethe is the daughter-in-law of Baby Suggs, the wife of Halle and the mother of Howard, Buglar, Beloved and Denver. She is known as an iron-willed woman from the beginning. However, her new master, to whom she is sold, "punched the glittering iron out of Sethe's eyes." (9) As a result, Sethe and the other slaves of Sweet Home (ironically, the farmhouse where they work day and night) flee during which Halle is dislocated and not found, chances are there that he might have been shot dead. Sethe has to run with her three children and the fourth in the womb. However, when the white masters find her, instead of surrendering, she stops them by hacking the throat of her daughter by handsaw. In this manner, she ruthlessly refuses to send back her daughter to the same terrible world, which has fully sucked her virginity and vitality. Above all, what a black woman considers heinous is a forced sex imposed on her by a white man. In this context, one can note the shattering shock of Kizzy when she is raped for the first time by Tom Lea in Alex Haley's *Roots*: "When the inevitable happens, she feels a deep sense of disgrace and defilement—the bruising of her young black body and proud soul leaves on her mind a permanent scar."[5] It is further noteworthy here that Kizzy's only consolation in that novel was that her proud parents were far away from her; "they weren't there to see—and share—her shame."[6] Kizzy's shame of the present is quite comparable to the fear of Sethe of her daughter's similar plight in future.

In this event, Toni Morrison shows validation for the philosophy behind the act, but not the act per se. The physical act of murdering one's own child needs a lot of moral and emotional courage. It is the outcome of a compelling situational background in which survival is uncertain every moment and dignity is put to acid test every second of survival. Therefore, Sethe concludes that killing is putting her daughter to safety. She says, "I took and put my babies where they'd be safe." (164) This viewpoint of Sethe is supported by Stamp Paid, an ex-slave who had helped Sethe in her escape, when Paul D is horrified at this news and mistakes Sethe as mad. Stamp Paid explains to him in order to clarify Sethe's action: "She ain't crazy. She love those children. She was trying to outhurt the hurter." (234) Remarkably, this primal instinct to "outhurt the hurter" is there in the collective consciousness of the suppressed Negroes throughout history. As far as Sethe is concerned, infanticide is very much in her ancestral blood that, in fact, her own mother had killed all the children born of white men—only Sethe was spared because she was a love-child.

Yet, an act of killing is an act of killing and Sethe has to pay the price, not only by going to prison but also even after that. 124 Bluestone Road house where she is living as a free black woman now, has been a haunted house. Years after her slaughter, Beloved returns to the house as a blooming beauty of twenty to take her own revenge on her murderer-mother. For the outside world, she is a ghost but for Sethe and Denver, she is a living entity full of life and blood. Beloved takes all the love of Sethe which initially irritates Denver, but later on, she becomes emotionally attached to her elder sister. Sethe is haunted by her past guilt and so she loves Beloved with refreshed intensity. At this moment, when her daughter has come from the other world, Sethe is obsessed with giving and receiving love and providing safety: "Do you forgive me? Will you stay? You safe here now." (215)

Toni Morrison has relied on Afro-American folklore in this novel, yet she has handled the element of supernatural in a unique way. Instead of the usual awe-inspiring supernatural, here it is so natural that it is believed to be part of reality. As Margaret Atwood remarks: "Students of the supernatural will admire the way this twist is handled. Ms. Morrison blends a knowledge of folklore—for instance, in many traditions, the dead cannot return from the grave unless called, and it's the passions of the living that keep them alive—with a highly original treatment." (1)

In addition, the family background of Morrison was rich in the knowledge of folklores which has contributed to the novelist's application of those folktales with telling effect in *Beloved.* In Afro-American social background, it is the mother, who is the carrier of the ancestral culture with all courage and conviction. Although this element is found in Baby Suggs in full measure, part of it lies with Sethe too.

Sethe, thus, is the embodiment of black endurance and fortitude. She has been whipped so many times and with so much of ferocity by the whites that her back has been pulped to resemble a chokecherry tree. This has left a permanent pain on her back and she does hardly allow any one to touch it. When a kind white girl, Amy, touches that she screams but Amy who has herself suffered so much as an indentured labourer, tells her: "Good for you. More it hurt more better it is. Can't nothing heal without pain, you know." (78) It is precisely through immense pain that Sethe and her fellow-sufferers are greatly healed in the end.

One saving grace in the unkind past of Sethe is her married life with Halle for a wonderful period of six years. However, even the act of marriage for slaves has no sanctimonious meaning in the eyes of their masters. It implied a superfluous meaning of a woman sleeping with one man for quite some time, until either one or both get sold, or are separated in a misadventure. Sethe differs in her moral courage from others in this regard too. She says:

> How bad I felt when I found that there wasn't going to be no ceremony, no preacher. Nothing. I thought there should be something—something to say it was right and true. . . . I thought there should be some ceremony. Dancing may be. . . . A meal maybe, where me and Halle and all the Sweet Home men sat down and ate something special. . . . But it wasn't going to be nothing. They said it was all right for us to be husband and wife and that was it. All of it. (58-59)

She was the only lucky woman in that slave farm and around who, despite pre- and post-marital rapes, bore all the four children from the same father. But the rest of her life was a succession of suffering. Even eighteen years of freedom has not mitigated the memory of her disturbing past. Thus when Beloved returns, she welcomes her: "When I needed you, you came to be with me." (215) And she finds herself one with Beloved: "You are my face, I am you." (216) In fact, Sethe tells Beloved she wanted to be one with her throughout, but it was for the sake of the other children she had to separate herself.

Sethe is further frustrated to see Buglar and Howard run away from her in search of a better future. What remains for her is the sorry sight of "their backs walking down the railroad tracks" away from her forever (192). So, bereft of her husband, her three children, and finally her caring mother-in-law, Sethe has to endure loneliness for eighteen years before the return of Beloved. Beloved comes back neither sad nor evil but a rebuked ghost. Although people advise Sethe to leave the haunted house, she prefers to live in the company of her ghost daughter and seek her pardon.

There are two other glittering moments for Sethe in her otherwise exhausted life; one is the twenty-eight days she spends in her mother-in-law's company and the care of the surrounding community immediately after her escape, and the other, is those few days spent with Paul D on his return. However, in both the cases, she finds difficulty in laying claim to and fully possess her apparently liberated self. However, as it inevitably happens in the typical destiny of slave-life, happiness was short-lived: "Those twenty-eight happy days were followed by eighteen years of disapproval and a solitary life." (173)

When Paul D comes to her life, in the above situation, there is a fresh stirring of new life. Yet, when Paul D offers new plans, Sethe is scared of the very word 'plans.' For her: "It was a luxury she had not had in eighteen years and only that once. . . . The one set of plans she had made—getting away from Sweet Home—went awry so completely she never dared life by making more." (38) Even then, his company is all right because "To Sethe, the future was a matter of keeping the past at bay." (42) Moreover, Paul's presence is strong enough to keep the painful past, including that of the haunting Beloved, at bay. But Paul D leaves her in the lurch when he happens to see the newspaper cutting related to Sethe's unmerciful killing of the daughter.

Nonetheless, Sethe lives through this separation too. She only despises herself for having been so trusting, so quick to surrender to Paul D's advances. She feels that "She should have known that he would behave like everybody else in town once he knew." (173) And at Paul D's desertion, her secluded and introverted life asserts forcibly than before: "The world is in this room. This here's all there is and all there needs to be." (182-83) Thus without the help of any male member, Sethe has to fight the world single-handedly. It is, nonetheless, the black courage, deeply rooted in her blood, that allows her to carry on.

Another epitome of black courage in the novel is Baby Suggs. She is rather more powerful a presence than Sethe even when it comes to strong nerve. It is Baby Suggs who receives Sethe at

Bluestone when she returns to her after running away from slavery. It is the care and concern of Baby Suggs that puts new life into the worn-out body of Sethe. Sethe, after all, is young in the novel; Baby Suggs has already crossed sixty. Except her brave heart there is nothing left intact in her body because slave life had "busted her legs, back, head, eyes, hands, kidneys, womb and tongue." (87) Baby Suggs has been bought freedom by Halle who wants her mother a few last free years, and for that he has to labour hard even during the holidays at Sweet Home. Even though she wonders initially, "What does a sixty-odd-year-old slavewoman who walks like a three-legged dog need freedom for?" (141), soon she realises the pulsating feeling of breathing free air into her expanded lungs.

The self-respect of Baby Suggs surfaces out for the first time when Mr. Garner, her master, tells the reason why he calls her Jenny, because Jenny Whitlow was the name given to her in sale deed. But, she subtly expresses her uneasiness with this name because it is a blow to her black identity: "Suggs is my name, sir. From my husband. He didn't call me Jenny." (142) Though she has lost her link with her husband, the intense emotional loyalty continues. The two had an earlier agreement that whosoever got a chance to run would take the chance. He got his chance first and Suggs presumes that he would be alive still. And if he were to return in search of her how could he find her if she was calling herself some bill-of-sale name? Hence, after getting freedom, she fully restores her original black identity.

Back home, Baby Suggs tries to think of her scattered children and relatives—Patty, Rosa Lee, Ardelia, Tyre, John, Nancy and others but fails to trace them: "slavery's systematic erasure of identity is too thorough for her to combat alone."[7] She then, rents 124 Bluestone Road and keeps it open for all the blacks of the neighbourhood. Baby Suggs assumes the role of griot, in African sense, the historian of the race. She starts to clear a part of the forest and gathers all the blacks of the locality for preaching to them the value of their race, rituals that would endow them with enough stamina to forget the past humiliations and lead a happy life. "Accepting no title of honour before her name . . . she became an unchurched preacher, one who visited pulpits and opened her great heart to those who could use it. . . . Uncalled, unrobed, un-anointed, she let her great heart beat in their presence." (87) There is such a force of conviction in her talk that the blacks gathered there forgot temporarily their miserable plight, and encouraged by her speech begin to laugh full-heartedly: "'Let your mother hear your laugh,' she told them, and the woods rang." (87) Similarly, she tells them to dance and they dance and the ground under their feet trembles. She tells them to cry out all their griefs, their eyes run loose, and they weep out all their sorrows. She teaches them to love everything of life and love "it hard." As whites have exploited all the parts of blackbody, Baby Suggs invites them to love all their limbs. She encourages the black people not to be ashamed of their blackness, not to be distressed by their past slavery but to take a dignified look on all parts of their body, even on, she says, "your life-holding womb and your life-giving private parts." (89) She tells them to love their neck otherwise it would be rung dead by some white men. She requests them to nourish their body otherwise the food would be snatched away; she pleads with them to love their black skin otherwise it would be flayed by the white hands. In all her speeches, she wants to put enough confidence in the black body and heart and finally she succeeds in it to a large extent. Even to her granddaughter, Denver, she tells she should always listen to her body and love it. She quotes her own example. Her eight children had six fathers, the fact resented both by the blacks as well as the whites. For the whites, enjoying sex is not the rightful thing a black woman is expected to do. As told by her:

> Slaves not supposed to have pleasurable feelings on their own; their bodies not supposed to be like that, but they have to have as many children as they can to please whoever owned them. Still, they were not supposed to have pleasure deep down. (209)

However, all the courageous attempts of Baby Suggs to bring the blacks together breaks down because of the misconception in the community that she is something special, something different from them, "blessed in someway they were not." (157) Furthermore, her non-committal attitude towards her daughter-in-law's shocking murder alienates her from her own community. Even the spirited heart of Baby Suggs cracks at this turn of event. Above all, Baby Suggs cannot reconcile with the fact that white men are still allowed to barge into her yard any time, which violates the sanctity of her privacy and safety of her house and annihilates any faint sense of freedom. She painfully realises at the end that there is nothing left for a Negro to do but only to endure everything the white men do to him. Despite the hard won freedom for her by her son, she dies of heartbreak caused both by the whites and by the blacks. And she is "buried amid a regular dance of pride, fear, condemnation and spite." (171)

Among the men who are very much influenced by Baby Suggs and her fighting spirit is Paul D. In his occasional contacts with Baby Suggs since the days of Sweet Home, he had become her admirer and supporter. When he finally visits 124 Bluestone, it is partly to see Sethe and partly to be near Baby Suggs. He is slightly unnerved at the news of her death. Like Sethe, Paul D's past life is full of unbearable horrors. He could not remember his mother and has never seen his father. He is the youngest of three half-brothers—it means, the same mother but different fathers. When he is only a boy, he is sold to Garner and has to live at Sweet Home for twenty years. After the death of Mr. Garner, the brother-in-law of Mrs. Garner becomes the master. Ironically, he is called "a school-teacher" and he is so odious that the slaves plan to run away from Sweet Home. Unfortunately, Paul D gets caught—as part of the punishment, his tongue is held down by iron, and the hands are chained behind. Thus, when there is a need to spit, it would be so deep down that he has to cry for it. In such condition, Paul D is sold to another master, whom he attempts to murder. Later, he, along with forty-six Negroes, is imprisoned in cages in the ground and made to work in mines. After years of "mule work," there is a flood and all the Negroes escape.

But during the period of enslavement, he puts up with "anything and everything just to stay alive." (221) Gradually, he becomes physically very strong, "taller than tall men, stronger than most" but the whites "clipped him." (220) It is less the physical and more the emotional and moral clipping. He remembers how his body is evaluated in terms of money and not human consideration, the "dollar value of his weight, his strength, his brain, his penis and his future." (226) But he keeps all this "in that tobacco tin buried in his chest where a red heart used to be. Its lid rusted shut." (72-73) Finally, he succeeds in coming to 124 Bluestone and, for a few weeks, spends happy days with Sethe but when he hears of her killing her own baby who now visits 124 as a ghost, he abruptly leaves her with a heavy heart. There is a poignant conversation between him and Stamp Paid in this regard as well as about the unmitigated suffering of the blacks:

> "Tell me something, Stamp." Paul D's eyes were rheumy. "Tell me this one thing. How much is a nigger supposed to take? Tell me. How much?"
>
> "All he can," said Stamp Paid. "All he can."
>
> "Why? Why? Why? Why? Why?" (235)

Nevertheless, he has some of the qualities of Baby Suggs; especially his courage is also infectious. Years of suffering has mellowed Paul D and made him a saintly, forbearing figure for all: "Not even trying, he had become the kind of man who could walk into a house and make the women cry. Because with him, in his presence, they could. There was something blessed in his manner. Women saw him and wanted to weep—to tell him that their chest hurt and their knees did too." (17) Forbearance has given the victims a special power to heal others' sorrows, and so, like Baby Suggs, in Paul D also people find in his presence a blessed manner.

Paul D is poignantly moved by the many geographical shapes on the back of Sethe, the results of whipping by the whites. However, Sethe only laments the forced stealing of her milk by the nephews of her master by hanging her down and squeezing it from her breasts. Initially, the soft touch of Paul D on her back fails to awaken her dead flesh, but gradually life sprouts in her afresh: "Paul D dug it up, gave her back her body, kissed her divided back, stirred her rememory and brought her more news." (189)

Finally, Paul D again returns to Sethe and decides to take her up for all she is. This time he has come to convince Sethe that everything is not lost yet, that let the past be past and live in the present. They are two lost souls, it is the courage and conviction of Paul D to obliterate the past finally that gives meaning to the life of both, and there is no other possibility before Paul D but to reconcile the past with the present:

> "Sethe," he says, "me and you, we got more yesterday than anybody. We need some kind of tomorrow."
>
> He leans over and takes her hand. With the other he touches her face. "You your best thing, Sethe. You are." (273)

This would mean real freedom for both because for Paul D freedom means a place "where you could love anything you choose—not to need permission for desire." (162) Since this is the first time Paul D has come back to a place he fled from, the action indicates a resolution, a culmination to his entire running.

Denver's courage, as exemplified in the novel, is twofold; she has to live with the misapprehension of a terrible mother who might go crazy any time and kill her, and later with a glimpse of her mother's guileless mind; she has to take steps to protect her mother from the ghost of her vengeful sister and save the family from disintegration. Because of the loathing the community has for her mother, Denver suffers isolation for most of her life and lacks mental stability. Nevertheless, Denver once mingled with the society without any inhibition. She used to go to school with other coloured children. However, one day a boy asked her a question: "Didn't your mother get locked away for murder? Wasn't you in there with her when she went?" Unable to answer that question, Denver stops going back to the school and chooses the only company of her mother.

But her entrenched timidity turns into courage towards the end. Her mother is out of employment and broke because of Beloved's greediness to gobble up everything, be it Sethe's love or food stuff. Neither Sethe nor Beloved bother for anything. She also realises that her mother was not at fault the day of the murder and reverse to what she thought initially, it is her mother's life that she needs to protect now: "The job she started out with, protecting Beloved from Sethe, changed to protecting her mother from Beloved. Now it was obvious that her mother could die and leave them both." (243) Hence, Denver takes her first step outside of her house—her first step to maturity—and goes out to knock at the gate of a white for help so that she can sustain her family. As she is still weak within, she prefers to go to Lady Jones first, who had been teaching the poor black. Lady Jones understands her predicament and assures help. From that day, onward items of food are brought to 124 and left at the door as charity. Yet, what Denver's self-pride wants is job, not charity. So, she accepts the offer of employment from Mr. Bodwin even though she has to work during the night and leave her mother under the clutch of Beloved for the whole of darkness. Later, it is on her invitation that Paul D comes back to restore the spirits of her ailing mother.

In this way, *Beloved* is the record of courageous fights of the black people against the white cruelty. The slaves have to live without clear-cut identities, or definitions of their selves, because, "definitions belonged to the definers—not the defined" as one of the slave masters puts it (190). Overall, these black characters, like those of Haley, have "a remarkable capacity for suffering and prevailing."[8] Morrison's major objective in this novel is to highlight the sustaining power of the blacks, "to recognise and rescue those qualities of resistance, excellence and integrity"[9] which had been eclipsed under the white burden. Throughout the novel, Morrison makes it clear that slavery, even devoid of whips and hunger, still denies what is essential to life. Because even years after, enslavement's hangover often turns people crazy: "Like Aunt Phyllis, who slept with her eyes wide open. Like Jackson Till, who slept under the bed." (97) However, the courageous ones like Sethe, Baby Suggs, and Paul D, in order to bury the past, and keep the future at bay, live in 'rememory' with their Beloveds!

NOTES

1. "The Pain of Being Black," an interview of Toni Morrison in *Time* (May 22, 1989), http://www.time.com/time/community/pulitzer interview.html, p. 2.
2. Margaret Atwood, "Jaunted by Their Nightmares," a review of *Beloved*, *The New York Times* (September 13, 1981), p.1.
3. *The Confessions of Nat Turner* (New York: Random House, 1967), p. 70.
4. Toni Morrison, *Beloved* (London: Vintage, 1997), p. 23.
5. Pashupati Jha, "The Route to Freedom: A Reading of Alex Haley's *Roots*," T.S. Anand, ed., *Perspectives on the Afro-American Novel* (Jalandhar: ABS, 1994), p. 90.
6. Alex Haley, *Roots* (New York: Doubleday, 1976), p. 435.
7. Nancy Jesser, "Violence, Home and Community in Toni Morrison's *Beloved*," *African American Review* (Summer 1999), http://www.findarticles.com/cf_0/m2838/2_33/55577123/print.jhtml, pp. 12-13.
8. Nathan A. Scott, Jr., "Black Literature," *Harvard Guide to Contemporary American Writing*, ed. Daniel Hoffman (1979; New Delhi: Oxford University Press, 1981), p. 332.
9. Qtd. Usha Puri, "Convergence of History and Feminism in Toni Morrison's *Beloved*," T.S. Anand, ed., *Perspectives on the Afro-American Novel*, p.170.